HOME DESIGN
AND DECORATING

HOME DESIGN

AND DECORATING

JENNY PLUCKNETT

HAMLYN

This edition published 1988 by
Hamlyn Publishing Group
Michelin House
81 Fulham Road
London SW3 6RB

ISBN 0 600 55896 7

Illustrations: Hayward & Martin Limited
Special photography: Dave King
Stylist: Sue Duffy
Editor: Wendy Lee
Art Editor: Pedro Prá-Lopez
Production controller: Trevor Jones
American consultant: Eleanor Van Zandt

Produced by Mandarin Publishers Limited
22a Westlands Road
Quarry Bay, Hong Kong

Printed in Hong Kong

The publishers wish to thank the following for providing the photographs in this book:
Amtico 101; Blue Hawk Ltd 60 left, right, top centre and top right, 61 top left, 89; Jon Bouchier 116 below left; Linda Burgess 7; Camera Press 14, 23, 24, 25, 29, 30, 31, 32, 33, 34, 36, 37, 39, 42, 43, 44, 45, 50, 52 above and below, 64 centre, 95, 109 left, 116 above right, 118 above; Collier Campbell 20, 46, 113 left; Cristal Tiles Advisory Service 82; Dulux Paints 115; Cover Plus Paints 109 right; Crown Paints 18, 47, 51, 63 top right; The Futon Company 48; Good Housekeeping 6; House of Mayfair Ltd (London) 113 right; International Paints 93 left; Kosset Carpets 108; Marley Floors Ltd 96; Sandersons 77 left, 102 left; Smallbone Kitchens 41; Jessica Strang 86; Syndication International/Options 90, Homes and Gardens 19; Tintawn Carpets 104 top left and right; Warner & Sons Ltd 91 right; Elizabeth Whiting and Associates 11, 13, 17, 22, 27, 28, 38, 49, 60 below right, 63 top left, 64 top left, 69 left, right and centre, 70, 77 right, 91 above and below left, 93 right, 102 right.

The following photographs were taken specially for Octopus Books:

Dave King 1, 2-3, 63 cut out, 64 below left, 72-3, 83, 98-9, 104 below, 112, 118 below.

The publishers are grateful to the following companies for providing props and merchandise for photography:

Allied Carpets, 263 Holloway Road, London N7 for carpets; Crown Decorative Products Ltd, Crown House, Darwen, Lancs BB3 OBG for paints and Anaglypta wallpapers; Dulux, Millbank, London SW1 for stains and varnishes; Fulham Tile Company, 90 Wandsworth Bridge Road, London SW6 for marble wall and floor tiles; International Paint, 24-30 Canute Road, Southampton SO9 3AS for paint, stains and varnishes; Paper Moon, 12 Kingswell, Heath Street, London NW3 for metallic wallpapers; Rustins Ltd, Waterloo Road, London NW2 7TX for stains and varnishes; Turner Wallcoverings, 32 Grosvenor Street, London W1 for vinyl wallpapers; and Worlds End Tiles, British Rail Yard, Silverthorne Road, London SW8 for wall and floor tiles.

The author and publishers would also like to thank Chick and Kate Connelly for typing the manuscript; Peter Brooke-Ball for writing the sections on Decorating in a stairwell, Tiling a wall, Laying a new hardwood floor, Putting up shelves and Door alterations; and Min, Fiver, Jimmy and Rosie for their help and support.

INTRODUCTION 7

Part One CREATING A BEAUTIFUL HOME 9

CHAPTER 1 GUIDELINES FOR GOOD DESIGN 10

Using space wisely 10 • Colour 14 • Texture 18 • Pattern 20 • Furniture 22 • Lighting 24 • Adding character 28

CHAPTER 2 ROOM-BY-ROOM PLANNING 30

Hall, stairs and landing 30 • Living rooms 33 • Kitchens 37 • Bathrooms 43 • Bedrooms 46 • Children's rooms 49 • Teenagers' rooms 51 • An extra room 52

Part Two PRACTICAL KNOW-HOW 53

CHAPTER 3 PAINTING 54

Preparing walls and ceilings 54 • Painting walls and ceilings 58 • Using emulsion (latex) paint 59 • Textured paint effects 60 • Preparing wood surfaces 62 • Paints, varnishes and stains for wood 63 • Using gloss paint 65 • Creating decorative paint finishes 69

CHAPTER 4 COVERINGS FOR WALLS AND CEILINGS 72

Materials for walls and ceilings 72 • Preparing to hang a wall covering 74 • Putting up the wall covering 78 • Decorating in a stairwell 81 • Tiling a wall 82 • Papering a ceiling 86 • Fitting coving (moulding) 88 • Borders 90

CHAPTER 5 FLOORING 92

Preparation of surfaces 92 • Making the most of what you've got 93 • Sheet flooring 96 • Laying sheet vinyl 97 • Floor tiles 99 • Laying vinyl, cork or rubber tiles 99 • Carpet 103 • Laying carpet 106 • Laying a new hardwood floor 109

CHAPTER 6 FINISHING OFF 113

Putting up curtains and blinds 113 • Shelving systems 117 • Planning and choosing shelves 118 • Putting up shelves 119 • Door alterations 122

INDEX 125

It's common knowledge that in the natural world colours never clash. Imagine the wonderful hues in a meadow filled with wild daffodils and primroses in spring, or take a look at the beautiful tones in the still life arrangement opposite. The blues in the hydrangea heads range from warm purple to cool green, and are set off to perfection by the black grapes and the figs. Orange pomegranates with a red blush add contrast from the opposite side of the colour spectrum.

The room below picks up on the colour scheme suggested by the hydrangeas. Furnished predominantly in neutral shades, the whole is prevented from looking too bland by the carefully chosen blue of the coffee tables.

INTRODUCTION

The choices and alternatives which face us when we start to design and decorate a new home or to revamp an old one can be confusing and sometimes even a little daunting. Most of us know the sort of effect that we want to achieve, but will the finished result be anything like the picture we originally had in our heads?

I hope that this book will help you to overcome any preliminary misgivings and give you the confidence and know-how to create an interior where you will enjoy spending time – whether working or relaxing – and look forward to inviting your friends.

There are no right or wrong ways to design and decorate a home, but successful results are most likely to stem from being familiar with a few ground rules – the effect of using a dark colour in preference to a light one, for instance. Having the facts at your fingertips can make all the difference to whether or not you achieve the look you were hoping for when you first planned your new scheme.

This book aims to provide you with all the basic information you will require to plan your surroundings and then to put your schemes into operation. The advice and instructions will enable you to make a success of the jobs you are likely to want to tackle yourself, and to achieve really professional-looking results. And this means you can invest whatever money you have to spend on good-quality materials, as you won't have to budget for a carpenter or decorator. You will also have the satisfaction of seeing your schemes take shape and your dreams, little by little, become a reality, thanks to your own efforts and hard work.

It just remains to say that I hope you enjoy this book and that it inspires you to be more adventurous – designing and decorating your home can be an immensely rewarding and exciting experience.

Jerry Puckett

PART ONE

CREATING A BEAUTIFUL HOME

These first two chapters cover the planning stage of decorating and furnishing your home – the period when you can dream a little about its new look.

Chapter 1 gives suggestions on how to make the most of the space you have at your disposal, how to give a room more character and how to make the vital elements of home design – colours, fabric patterns and textures, furniture and lighting – work for you.

Chapter 2 progresses through the house room by room, explaining how to deal with specific problems. Hints are given for colour schemes, floorings, furniture and its arrangement, lighting needs and for the extra touches which will stamp each room with a special individuality.

CHAPTER 1

Guidelines for good design

USING SPACE WISELY

Most of us at some time or other feel that we suffer from lack of space in our homes, yet there are probably parts of the house or flat that are rarely used at certain times and corners and alcoves that, because they are dark or awkwardly placed, are not fully utilized. Or it may be simply that there seems to be clutter everywhere, that a house, whatever its size, does not create an impression of space. (For some answers to this problem see page 12.)

There are no rules about the way space should be used; our homes should work for us and our lifestyle. So don't be bound by convention; be flexible and re-arrange the rooms to suit the way you yourself live. Don't, for instance, set apart a 'dining room' if you and your family rarely all sit down to a meal together.

KNOCKING DOWN WALLS

Most interior walls are not difficult to remove but make sure you are not about to knock down a load-bearing wall before you start and make proper provision for any extra support required if you do decide to go ahead.

Turning two rooms into one to give you a larger area can make all the difference if you have nothing but tiny rooms. A wall removed between a dining room and tiny kitchen will often enable you to expand the kitchen into the bigger space while still having room for a dining table and chairs to fit in comfortably.

MULTI-PURPOSE ROOMS

In recent years the kitchen has again become popular as a family room, rather like the old farmhouse kitchen. If you like this idea, consider turning the largest downstairs room into a kitchen with a dining area and comfortable sofa and chairs. Go further and put the television in here, then a smaller room can become a second quiet relaxation area where members of the family could go to read, study or listen to music.

Bedrooms are more often than not little used during the day; could one double up as an office or study? Or why not replace the bed with a really comfortable sofa bed, add a chair and a second television and use this as an alternative sitting room in which to relax?

Halls often have an unused alcove that can serve as a dining area if you use a folding table and chairs that are hung on the wall when not wanted.

Could the understairs cupboard (closet) become a shower room or lavatory and so take some of the strain off the main bathroom? If not, maybe a series of doors placed along the side of the understairs cupboard instead of the usual one at the end would enable you to use that space much more satisfactorily.

Loft (attic) space can become an extra room – an area for work or play or an extra bedroom. Check first that there is adequate height to stand up in the centre, that there is space for a staircase to it, that the joists will take the weight and also what size windows you will need to conform with planning regulations (state building code). A loft conversion company will be able to advise you, or you can contact your local planning department.

If there is not enough height overall to make the loft (attic) space suitable for another room, turn it into an efficient storage area. Lay flooring and put up shelving. Floor-grade chipboard and plywood decking comes in sheets of various widths. If this would need a lot of cutting to fit the space, use softwood boards instead and place joins over joists. You will use the space more efficiently if you install either folding stairs or a sliding ladder that can be pulled down from the hatch but planning regulations may not allow this if the loft becomes more than a storage area.

If you have a cellar check if the floor can be dug out and the area damp-proofed to provide an extra room or, again, use this for storage – perfect for the home wine-maker or for anyone with a messy hobby!

MAKING SPACE MORE ACCESSIBLE

You may find that because of the way a door opens you cannot place furniture in the ideal position; perhaps a bed won't fit. Don't let this deter you; it is not difficult to turn a door around so that it opens from the opposite side; see pages 123-4 for how to do this.

Spaciousness is created in a small room by the use of pale colours, together with low furniture placed against the walls which leaves the maximum of floor space free. Even the pictures are positioned low on the wall. By painting the ceiling moulding to match the floor covering and furniture, the owner has cleverly drawn the whole scheme together.

SPODE

SMART STORAGE

- Make use of space under the bed by adding castors to drawers that will fit in neatly.
- Use the backs of doors – hang a pocketed holder in the bathroom to take cosmetics.
- Instead of bedside tables use picnic hampers for extra storage.
- Camouflage untidy shelves or clothes rails with a screen or roller blind.
- Old trunks can store little-used items – cover with cloths to convert into low tables.

Creating an impression of space

Very often it is clutter rather than actual lack of space that our houses suffer from. A feeling of spaciousness is created by the way we decorate a room and the way we arrange the furniture in it as much as anything else. Light colours, low furniture, shiny surfaces, reflective images and well-planned storage all contribute to a feeling of easy spaciousness.

Using colour and texture

An understanding of the basic principles of colour can help solve many design problems.

Light colours appear to recede and therefore a room decorated and furnished in pale tones will appear much larger than the same room decorated in deep hues.

Shiny, reflective surfaces act in a similar way to a mirror, creating a more spacious effect. This means that painting walls and ceiling with gloss paint will add to a room's apparent size whereas matt-finish paint will reduce it.

A low ceiling will appear higher if you paint it white and a high ceiling can be 'lowered' by the use of a deeper tone of the colour used on the walls. A pale carpet will make a room seem larger and more spacious.

In the same way that clothes with vertical lines make you look slimmer and those with horizontal lines make you appear heavier, lines that travel along the length of the room on floor or walls will appear to extend the space while those that travel across its width will shorten but widen the area. Any strong colour used as a border around the room – a skirting (baseboard) painted in a deeper colour for instance – will enclose the space and make it appear smaller.

Choosing furniture

Furniture in the same colour as the flooring or floor covering tends to blend in, becoming visually part of it, and if it is low and light in colour it will be even less obvious. Furniture in strong colours, however, especially when placed randomly in the room, will add to a cluttered effect. So if you want your living space to appear streamlined, store everything away in cupboards built along one wall and paint the cupboard doors to match the rest of the room. Minimalism, popular at present, aims for this sort of clutter-free space where everything is stored away out of sight, thus heightening the effect made by the few beautiful items left on show.

Glass-topped tables will give an illusion of space because you can see through them and furniture that looks light, such as cane, adds to the general impression of light and space.

Light

A light house appears much bigger than a dark one. If areas such as the hall, stairs and landing are very dark consider replacing panels in some room doors with glass to let in the light. Where there are children be sure to use unbreakable glass for safety.

Mirrors

Mirrors are wonderful visual space-makers; a wall of mirror will make a room look twice its size. This can be very expensive, but there are cheaper ways of using mirror to create an impression of space. Use it on the back wall of two fireside alcoves so that it looks as if the room extends through archways, or frame a large sheet of mirror so that it looks like a doorway with space beyond.

Tiles or fabric-backed mirror pieces can be used on doors to great effect but check that the door hinges will take the weight as mirror is heavy. In a small bedroom, you will find that cupboard (closet) doors that are covered with mirror will serve a useful dual purpose.

Position mirror carefully so that it reflects light and interest; trained on a plain wall it will simply reflect that wall and lose a lot of its impact. Place it opposite or at right angles to a window to reflect the maximum amount of light; and at night, for the best effect, train a light not on the mirror itself but on to the area it reflects.

Before you put up any mirror tiles or sheets

Mirror can double the apparent size of a narrow room if it is used along the length of one wall. Here it also highlights an unusually decorative wood floor. Together with the light walls and ceiling, this arrangement serves to heighten the effect of the owner's beautiful antique furniture.

move a small mirror about in the area you want to cover to establish the best spot.

Large areas of mirror can be confusing, so position a plant or a piece of furniture in front to make sure no one walks into it.

One mirror placed on a wall opposite another creates exciting multi-images. I noticed this effect when visiting a house in France then owned by Laura Ashley. Two huge mirrors were positioned at each end of the drawing room and when you stood in front of one you saw continuing reflections of reflections of reflections. I have used this reflective trick ever since.

Apart from unframed mirrors in standard sizes and mirrors in frames you can also buy sheets of mirror; these are cut to the size you require and the edges can be bevelled and polished. They are expensive and also very heavy. Check before you buy that you can easily manoeuvre large pieces to the spot where you intend to use them.

Mirror tiles are usually square or rectangular and come with self-adhesive pads. Make sure that the wall you put them on is absolutely flat or you will end up with misshapen images. My favourites are tiny mirror tiles which come on a fabric backing. They do not give a clear image but sparkle in the light and can easily be cut around the tiny tile edges to fit the space available, then glued to the base surface. They come in ½in (1.3cm), 1in (2.5cm) or 2in (5cm) squares and 1 × ½in (2.5 × 1.3cm), 2 × 1in (5 × 2.5cm) and 2 × ½in (5 × 1.3cm) rectangles on sheets 24 × 18in (61 × 46cm) and 12 × 9in (30 × 23cm).

Mirror is heavy and must be fixed securely. On mirrors with pre-drilled holes use special screws with a domed cover which hides the head and a rubber sleeve that prevents contact with the glass. Do not screw in too tightly, as you can easily shatter the glass doing so. Brackets to hold mirrors are also available.

The safest method of attaching mirrors is to use an adhesive. Mastic adhesive has the added advantage of filling out irregularities in the base surface, but it does take about two days to harden, so the mirror will need supporting in the meantime. (Some heavy antique mirrors may need permanent additional support from a batten fixed securely to the wall beneath them.) Impact adhesive can be used on a flat surface and this hardens instantly so be careful how you use it.

COLOUR

Choosing colours for walls, ceiling and floors, and balancing them with those of the furniture, furnishings and accessories can seem daunting but it is also exciting. Don't allow the fear of making a mistake to lead you to give up in despair and paint throughout your house or apartment in white or magnolia (although both of these can look stunning with the right accent colours).

To make these important choices simpler this section is divided into two parts. The first is about making colour work for you by using the right shade for warmth or the right tone to create a feeling of space, and showing how a colour can help to disguise faults. The second part is on how to pick a base for your colour scheme, a point from which to start, whether you are having to integrate someone else's choice of colours (in a fitted carpet bought with the house, for instance) or whether you are starting from scratch.

MAKING COLOUR WORK FOR YOU

The most important points to bear in mind when working with colour concern the power it has to create a mood and to affect the apparent size and shape of a room. Use these basic principles to your advantage; they are easily learnt, but never underestimate their importance.

Always check any colour you are thinking of using in both natural and electric light. Red and yellow tend to appear brighter in electric light, blues darker and more dominant. Fluorescent light will add blue to all colours and the more commonly used tungsten or incandescent light bulbs will bring out warmer, yellow tones.

Colours can also change radically when put next to one another. White, for instance, makes colours seem clearer and paler. This often leads people to choose a paint from a paint chart, where the colour is surrounded by white, in a much deeper tone than they really wanted. Usually it is best to go for the same colour in a tone slightly lighter than your first choice. This way you are more likely to end up with the colour you originally had in mind.

Black makes colours appear darker and stronger and if a dark colour is put next to a different pale colour the light one will appear lighter and the dark one appear darker. This is due to the contrast in tone. In the same way red put near blue appears yellower, but the same red put next to yellow will appear bluer. Next to green it will seem purer and brighter and next to grey it will

White paint on walls, floor and ceiling creates a shiny, reflective background that makes the most of the available space. It is also a perfect setting for the primary colours used for fabrics and furniture, emphasizing their clarity.

appear to lose its brightness somewhat.

Texture also has an effect on colour. Shiny, gloss surfaces appear much brighter than matt ones in identical shades.

Changing atmosphere with colour

There is no doubt that different colours create quite different atmospheres. Some stimulate us and make us feel warm and cosy while others are soothing, and can produce a cool, peaceful background which is very calming. This knowledge can be put to good use to counteract the cold feel of a north-facing room or to aid us in picking a restful colour for a room where we want to relax.

Red actually raises the body temperature. By prompting the heart rate to speed up, red releases adrenalin into the bloodstream and the body temperature rises. Used as the main colour in a room, red can be rather overpowering, for this reason. (In fact the story goes that a canteen painted red in one factory produced such an angry and argumentative workforce that the room had to be repainted green!)

Use red, rather, as an accent colour for cushions, flowers, a rug or in pictures. It can look stunning used with a little black in a room decorated and furnished all in white.

Red is very popular in restaurants, as it is seen as stimulating both appetite and conversation. Use it in your dining area for the table cloth, chair seats or lighting if you feel that either appetites or conversation need encouraging in your home!

Yellow and orange are both warm, happy colours, the colour of the sun, dancing flames in a fireplace and spring flowers that herald the warmer weather. Like red, strong, bright yellows and oranges are probably best used for accent. For larger areas use softer tones of these warm colours – coral, apricot, primrose or jasmine. They are particularly effective used in entrance halls, where they create an attractive and instant feeling of welcome.

Blue, particularly its paler tones, is credited with a calming effect so decorate in blue where you want a restful atmosphere. Use the more intense shades, such as royal blue, and the dark blues, such as navy, mainly as accents. Pale blues are wonderful when highlighted by touches of the warmer colours – golden yellow or coral – which take away some of the 'cold' feel that this colour is accused of having.

Green, the colour of the countryside, is the most restful colour to the eye. (This is because the lens of the eye focuses green almost exactly on the retina.) It is cool and fresh. The colour of the leaves which provide the background to most flowers, green can be safely mixed with pink, orange, red, blue or yellow.

The restful quality of green makes it suitable for almost any room but it is probably most fun in a bathroom with lots of hanging plants (they love the damp atmosphere) and perhaps a parrot or two! Add red towels for warmth. In the kitchen, use green with bright yellow accessories for a sunny and cheerful look.

These three pictures show clearly how colour can be used to influence the apparent shape of a room. In the first, a deep red ceiling and alcoves make the ceiling appear lower and the fireplace wall narrower. When a dado is added in the centre picture the visual height of the wall is reduced. Floorboards and a carpet square elongate the room, whereas in the bottom picture the dado, colour scheme and wall-to-wall flooring all add to the generally spacious effect.

Beige and grey are the neutrals (together with white and black). Beige is warmer than grey but both have the advantage to the home decorator of being both restful and very versatile, since they mix well with most colours. The mood of a room decorated and furnished in neutrals can be quickly and easily changed with accessories. Even a sunny, south-facing room can look cold in winter when daylight and sunshine are scarce if it is decorated in grey or beige but it is easy to add winter warmth with a coral rug, vases of rust-coloured chrysanthemums or dried flowers in golden tones, peachy lampshades and cushion covers. In spring, you can happily revert to your cooler, sharper accessories – mint green or aqua, for instance.

The effect of colour on dimensions

In the same way that some colours are warm and others cold, certain colours will appear to advance while others recede. By using the right colour, or rather depth of colour, you can make a room seem more open, 'bring down' an over-high ceiling or make a room smaller and more friendly.

The colours of the spectrum – red, orange, yellow, green, blue and violet – form a colour wheel. They are divided by the colour that is a mixture of the two on either side of it. Harmonious colours are adjacent; contrasting ones (properly called complementary) are opposite to each other.

THE COLOUR WHEEL

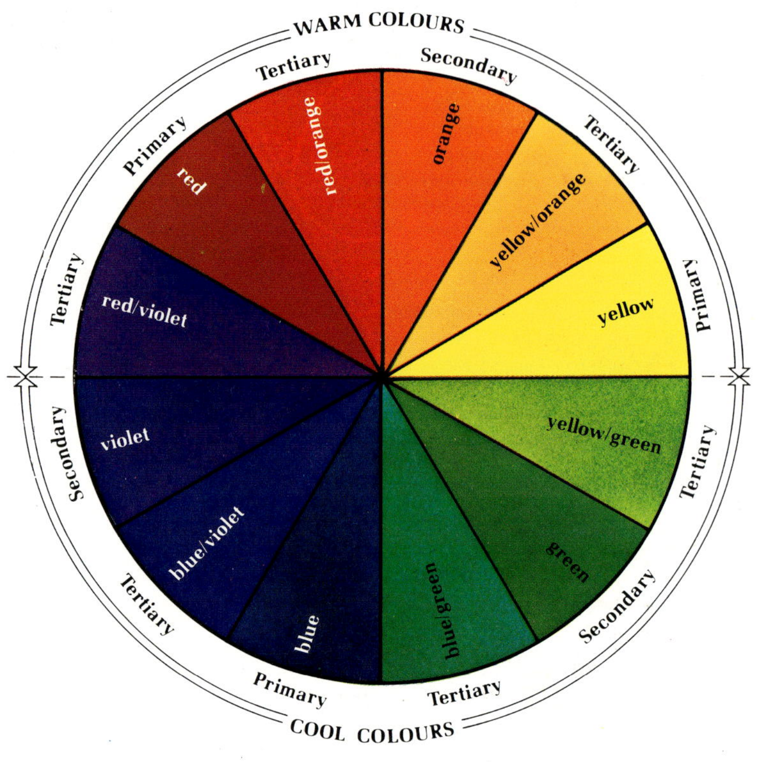

WARM COLOURS
Tertiary
Secondary
Primary
red
red/orange
orange
Tertiary
yellow/orange
Primary
yellow
Tertiary
red/violet
Secondary
violet
yellow/green
Tertiary
blue/violet
green
Secondary
Tertiary
blue
blue/green
Primary
Tertiary
COOL COLOURS

Just as light colours distance walls and ceiling, a light floor covering will make a room appear larger. And if you use the same pale floor covering throughout a house or throughout one level, the whole house or flat will seem more roomy. A pale colour used throughout, however, would look very bland, so add strong colour as accent in lampshades, cushion covers, pictures, blinds, pottery or flowers to make your colour scheme come to life.

If you are thinking of using dark or bright shades for their advancing effect on walls or ceilings, don't go over the top. A very dark ceiling can be disturbing, so if you want to draw it down, just paint it a slightly deeper tone of the wall colour. In the same way, a continuous band or stripe of colour used around a room, or a picture rail painted in a dark colour will diminish the sense of space in a room without giving you claustrophobia. A carpet with a pattern on a dark background will have the same effect.

Make a long, narrow hall appear wider and shorter by painting the end walls and any doors on them in a deep tone and using a lighter tone of the same colour on side walls and doors.

Choosing colour schemes

The colours of the spectrum, those you see in a rainbow, always follow the same order – red, orange, yellow, green, blue, indigo, violet – and there are many shades and tones between each of these colours. Blue, for instance, ranges from aquamarine greeny blues to blues with some pink in them, such as the blue of cornflowers or sweet-peas. You can use the various tones of one colour very effectively as a basis for a colour scheme (called monochromatic). A decor all in yellows, for example, could incorporate primrose, all the tones of daffodils, forsythia, sunflowers and mimosa. Colours close to each other on the spectrum also work very well together – pinky blues mixed with bluey pinks, for example. Look at a mixture of sweet peas to see how wonderfully they complement each other. This way of using colour is called a toning scheme.

When you form a wheel of the spectrum with red and violet merging into each other you can clearly see the colours that are opposite each other: these are contrasts, or complementaries. They enliven a scheme and form the accent. For instance, if you have used blues for a bathroom, add bright red towels and accessories.

Living with someone else's choice

If you can change a colour you hate, then do so. However, if you cannot remove the offending colour – in a carpet you bought with the house, perhaps – try to reduce its prominence by surrounding it with other shades of the same colour. Integrate a brown carpet with seating in softer tones of brown and choose fabrics in the natural tones of stone, clay or peat and furniture in pine, walnut or beech. Paint the walls in cream to lighten the effect and add dash with spice tones of saffron, chilli or ginger.

In another case you might be better off using a contrasting scheme.

Starting from scratch

There are no right or wrong colours, so choose colours to live with because you like them.

Using a coordinated range makes putting a colour scheme together very simple and there are so many ranges available that it should not be difficult to find one you like. For small rooms it is usually best to mix bold patterns with smaller pattern wallpapers or paint walls plain and use pattern for furnishings. Many ranges now include coordinating lighting, bedding and even china.

Using neutrals, such as beige or grey, is a good basis for decorating schemes. Beige is easier to use than grey. From palest cream to soft nut brown it goes with most woods and many other natural materials such as cork and cane. Grey is a more difficult colour to cope with, as it can range widely in tone from blue greys to pink greys or yellow greys. You need to use tones that are close to each other to be effective. Some paint charts show colours in families so if you look at pinks you should find a range of grey pinks there. These will be warmer than yellow or blue greys.

The neutrals need sharp accent colours to make them come alive: best are golden yellow, rich apricot or bright green for beige, and acid yellow, brilliant red or turquoise for grey.

A monochromatic scheme can be stunningly effective. Tones of one colour can look wonderful together but need to be chosen with care. A yellow green, for instance, will not look good if you place it with a blue green, so choose tones that are on the same side of the true colour (the one which has no tones mixed with it): all blue greens or all yellow greens, for example.

Texture adds interest to a monochromatic scheme; the shiny surfaces of gloss paint or chintz will add clear, bright colour whereas matt surfaces, such as carpet or walls painted in a matt finish, will soften and deaden the colour.

In the same way as for neutrals, pick an accent colour from the opposite side of the colour wheel.

Using more than one colour may seem tricky, but is not too difficult. An easy way to work out a colour scheme based on more than one colour is first to pick a fabric for curtains or blinds then base the scheme on the colours found in the fabric. Take the softer shades from the fabric for the main expanse of walls and ceiling, perhaps using a slightly darker tone for the carpet. For soft furnishings choose a small-patterned fabric that amalgamates two of the colours; with furniture go for woods, metal or paint finishes that blend with the colours used; and finally use the bright contrast colour in the fabric for your accessories.

For instance, if the fabric has apricot and aquamarine flowers against green leaves on a cream background you could paint the walls cream and the ceiling white and use a deep beige for the carpet. A striped cream and green fabric would look smart on seating. Furniture in light woods, such as pine or beech, would blend well. Then in winter you could add flowers, cushion covers and lampshades in apricot, changing to accessories in the cooler aquamarine in summer.

In the same way you can base the colour scheme for a room on a favourite picture.

Colours mix wonderfully well if the same depth of tone is used throughout, as this bedroom illustrates. Subtly striped green walls and soft wood hues are echoed by the fabric used for the curtains, and that used for quilt and pillow. Even the sweet-smelling, full-blown garden roses blend beautifully.

Tones of caramel and cream here show off a blend of textures which would not have been so obvious in a mixed colour scheme. A shiny dado rail divides a matt-finish paint on the top section of the wall from a silk finish used to highlight the wallpaper pattern below. Reflection is added by the shiny painted door and the glazed pictures.

TEXTURE

Texture is tactile; it appeals to our sense of touch as much as to our visual sense. Some materials will strike you as cold, others warm; some, such as lace, have a gentle appearance where as others, such as PVC or vinyl, are harsher. Hard, rather austere surfaces – marble and mirror – contrast with the soft, luxurious feel of angora yarn or the homely roughness of hessian (burlap). Think of glass, corduroy, cork, brass, cane, tweed, velvet, wood, felt, wool, paper, satin, leather – each material produces a reaction in us that shows how instrumental texture can be in setting the mood of a room.

PUTTING TEXTURES TOGETHER

Textures really bring a monochromatic scheme to life. They are especially significant here because the eye is not distracted by different colours. Next time you go into a room decorated in neutrals or all in one colour study the textures used and notice what works well with what. Often opposites make the strongest impact – a matt surface leading the eye to a shiny surface next to it and vice versa. In the same way a rough surface will highlight a smooth one.

Textures can be subtle so train yourself to notice the effects of surfaces and materials placed next to one another. The texture of a half-made sweater lying on a sofa might lead you to use the same yarns for a cushion cover. Some freshly picked flowers left in a basket on the floor could display a wonderful balance of shiny and matt textures and a beautiful colour harmony that you could use for an arrangement of flowers in the same basket.

Place the fabric, paint and flooring or floor covering samples you intend to use in a room together on a large card and study not only the colours but also how well the textures work. Remember that the way the light falls on a material will affect tone and texture so choose flooring by looking down on your sample, since this is the way you will see it in the room.

The way style and texture are combined is important too. A country scheme could include a natural wood floor with a rag rug or coir matting on it, cane or polished wood furniture, curtains in a natural fabric such as an open-weave wool, a brick fireplace, baskets of dried flowers and brass light fittings. On the other hand, a modern room would be more likely to use synthetic materials – chrome and plastic. However a traditional room can appear too contrived if it is all perfectly in style and the addition of one or two very modern items, some pictures perhaps, will add an exciting contrast. In the same way, an old chair or a carved chest could add interest to an otherwise purely modern interior.

Flooring and floor coverings

A long-haired flokati rug, a colourful rag rug, or matting all look wonderful on a polished wood or stone floor, the smooth, shiny texture of the floor highlighting the rougher rug finishes. Put a long-haired rug over a smooth fitted carpet for a similar effect. Most floorings and floor coverings have interesting textures that can be balanced against smooth, shiny painted walls or closely woven furnishing fabrics.

Walls

Many textured finishes are available for walls. Textured paint or painted Anaglypta (embossed wallpaper) make a strong impact. Cork will give a matt, coarse-grained finish; ceramic tiles produce a hard, smooth effect. Fabric wall coverings such as hessian (burlap), silk, wood, suede, linen and velvet are available on a paper backing.

Many ordinary fabrics can also be used as wall covering, either flat, pleated or gathered. Special track is available for fixing fabric flat on the wall. The track is attached to the top, bottom and sides of the wall, then the fabric is stretched over its adhesive surface and the raw edges tucked into a channel.

For pleated fabric, put up wood battens along the top of the wall and at the skirting (baseboard), leaving a ¼in (5mm) gap above if you are working at ceiling level or below if at skirting level. Staple the fabric in pleats to the battens and then, using a screwdriver, push the raw edges into the gap. Cover the staples with a border of braid.

A gathered covering can be formed by making a flat curtain with casings at top and bottom and threading over ordinary curtain rods. In Britain you can buy a gathering heading tape for the top and hook this on to a curtain (drapery) track. Curtain wire is threaded through the bottom hem and held on the wall with hooks.

Fabric used on walls creates an impression of comfort and luxury and helps to retain warmth.

Accessories

Consider the juxtaposition of textures when arranging accessories also. Use a leafy plant to break up the solid impact of a large lamp base, or place one or two beautiful lilies with an arrangement of glass to highlight its reflective quality.

Texture is most readily perceived in neutral rooms. Here the white walls and sofa emphasize the rough texture of the coir matting and the rope log baskets, which have been used as plant containers. These in turn highlight the smoothness of the leather chairs, shiny glass table, marble fireplace and black side table.

PATTERN

Pattern creates an illusion of depth and adds character and life to a room. The recent craze for tiny patterns on wallpaper and fabrics has now to some extent been replaced by larger designs and washed-out pastels and, very lately, by bold designs in strong colours and deep rich patterns. Stripes are very popular too and so are the softer paint-finish effects.

CHOOSING PATTERNS

The choice in fabric design and colour is enormous. Patterns range from huge flowers in rich hydrangea blue and pink, plus purples, mauves and apricots, to paisley patterns in dark blue, deep magenta and burnt orange, and colourful spots and stripes.

Fabric

If you are buying a fabric that is going to be pleated or gathered as draperies or curtains, pleated as a Roman blind (shade), or ruched as a festoon or Austrian blind (shade), check how the pattern will look pulled together in this way. Some, more subtle, designs come to life when used like this, while other patterns lose their impact. It is a good idea to squeeze any fabric you are considering for loose covers (slipcovers) in your hand to see if it is crease-resistant.

Patterned fabric gains textural interest when it is quilted. Quilted fabrics look sumptuous as curtains (draperies) and serve as excellent insulators, and they add comfort when used for covers on foam-filled sofas and chairs. If you cannot find a quilted fabric you like, have a go at doing the quilting yourself.

Baste wadding (batting) behind the main fabric, starting from the centre and stitching outwards to form a star shape. This helps to prevent the fabric from moving on the wadding. Then, using small running stitches or machine stitches, quilt around the pattern. (Quilting will shrink the width and depth of the fabric slightly.)

This range of co-ordinated fabrics shows how patterns can blend beautifully if the colours used are matched and of equal strength – as in the three fabrics hanging at the back of this room. The fabric draped over the sofa also works well with its neighbours on the cushions.

Mixing patterns can produce a very subtle effect, too. In this room, a large, random-patterned wall covering forms the background for an interesting combination. The formal geometric pattern of the curtains (draperies) is echoed by the sculptured quality of the carpet and the flame-stitch effect of the sofa. The smooth polished wood of the lamp bases adds textural interest.

Walls

Unless you want to turn a room into a secret garden of strong, bright flowers (which can, of course, be very effective), it is probably safer to use one of the more subtle wallpapers to act as a foil for a bold fabric design.

Walls can tend to 'run away', so use a border paper to contain them. Alternatively, trace off the fabric pattern to make a painted border.

Furniture

Painted furniture makes it very easy to harmonize schemes: simply pick out colours from your fabric and use in the appropriate paint finish (see pages 63-4).

For upholstered furniture the range of choice is again very wide. Stripes are very smart and hardwearing ticking in traditional black and white or softer brown and cream is back in vogue.

Flooring

There are many small-patterned carpets available; choose one of these rather than a strong, bold design if a feeling of spaciousness is important to you. Use a rug on a plain carpet to add pattern to a too-plain room.

Accessories

Books, pictures, flowers and plants and your personal treasures all naturally produce pattern in a room, so don't forget to take them into account when planning your use of pattern.

Mixing patterns

The idea of mixing patterns is not new; it has been used as a decorative effect for centuries throughout the world. We have been overwhelmed in the last ten to fifteen years, however, by matched and coordinated ranges. This has made the putting together of patterns very simple. You need only pick all items from one range and everything – wallpaper, fabric, bedding, paint, even carpets, tiles and lighting – is bound to blend. Unfortunately, this can often lead to a rather bland and boring result.

Coordination has now become much looser, however, with ranges picking up on the same colour but using it for geometrics, stripes and textures as well as bold floral designs. If you want to put patterns together from different ranges, study the use and balance of colour in each to help you pick an effective mix and live with samples for a while to make sure they're what you want.

Indian cottons look wonderful used together. Study the designs to see why they work so well. Although the colours differ, the depth of tone is usually the same because of the natural dyes used, and the designs are meticulously worked out to be in proportion to one another.

Seating is best positioned so that wherever anyone sits, they can easily join in a conversation. In this room the fireplace forms the focus but the furniture could be repositioned easily during the summer months to take advantage of the view through the window.

FURNITURE

Whether you are buying new items or rearranging old familiar pieces, the same rules apply when it comes to deciding how to use the furniture to best advantage and how to arrange it in the room so that you make the most of the space available.

Choosing new items

Before buying furniture measure the area in which you plan to position it and take the measurements and a tape with you to the store to make sure the new item will fit the space available in your home.

Make a scale plan of each room and then cut out pattern pieces – to the same scale – of all your furniture and move them around until you come up with a satisfactory arrangement. Allow about 18in (45cm) leg room between a sofa or chair and a coffee table, 20in (50cm) for getting up from a desk, the same for moving between pieces of furniture and 2ft (60cm) to move between a wall and furniture.

When buying, old or new, check for faults: look at the back, under cushions and at the underside to see if the finish is good or if there is splitting or any other damage. Check that the item is firm and stable. All new upholstery should carry a label that states its composition, how you should clean it and if the interior and covering are fireproof. If you cannot find such a label, ask the store or manufacturer for this essential information.

Children's furniture needs to be robust, easy to clean and safe. Look out for sharp corners or rough edges, and if it is painted make sure that the paint used is non-toxic.

Arranging living-room furniture

Arrange your seating to suit the shape of your living room. Here are some alternatives you might care to consider.

A long room with a fireplace at one end can be arranged to make a focal point of the fireplace. Place two sofas opposite each other (rather as in an old-fashioned railway carriage) and one chair at the end facing the fire. Place a long narrow coffee table in the middle. Depending on space, two- or three-seater sofas are equally suitable, or you could use two chairs opposite a sofa in the same layout.

A good-sized square room with a view is used most effectively by an L-shaped arrangement of two sofas, or two chairs and a sofa, with the window and the view being the focal point. Stand a large, square coffee table between the two sofas for books and drinks.

A small square room need not be restrictive. Arrange unit seating so that it forms a U shape and leaves an empty wall opposite for shelving or a storage system. Unit seating is very versatile, as it can so easily be rearranged to suit circumstances. In this seating plan, place coffee tables within the line of the seating.

Short of space?

Pare down to essential items of furniture only, and where possible select items that serve more than one purpose – a chest of drawers by the bed rather than a table, for example.

Areas of empty floor create a feeling of space, so position large items of furniture around the walls and use seating units pushed together or sofas rather than lots of individual chairs. Provide plenty of storage space to avoid clutter. Fold-up furniture, with chairs and tables that can be hung from hooks on the wall when not in use, is a great boon where space is very limited. Trolleys (carts) that can be wheeled away and stored elsewhere are useful too.

Transparent furniture, glass or perspex (Lucite) or mirrored surfaces all help to make a room seem larger as well as lighter. Bulky pieces of furniture which loom large in a small room can sometimes be a problem. Try painting the wall behind to match or tone with them so that they disappear into the wall; or paint the furniture to match the wall – this has the same effect.

Too much space to play with?

In this case, spread your furniture around: angle large pieces such as a bed or sofa across a corner and have free-standing chairs and tables within the room space rather than round the sides. Make a feature of a cluster of house plants – some tall and narrow, others short and wide – with different leaf shapes and colours to fill empty space decoratively.

Balancing furniture

Large pieces of furniture, such as well-stuffed sofas or old chests of drawers, should really be balanced by smaller, lighter items such as a desk or side table. A wall of storage looks best if it is balanced by a group of pictures on the opposite wall. Think carefully about getting the balance of the room right: one small picture or mirror alone on a wall will look insignificant; a large picture or mirror placed above a small object will look awkwardly top-heavy. In the same way colours in one piece of furniture should be echoed in an accessory somewhere else in the room rather than left in isolation, for good balance.

Low seating, table and storage system add emphasis to the stunning shape of this attic room. A system of sliding screens divides off the less usable area underneath the sloping wall, where plants delight in the abundance of light.

LIGHTING

Lighting performs a very practical function, allowing us to move about safely and to see clearly when we perform tasks at night. But lighting can also make all the difference to the look of a room. Hard, flat lighting makes even a well-furnished room look dull and without character, whereas good lighting will enhance the colours and add interest to the shape of the room and of its contents.

Different types of lighting perform different functions and we usually need more than one type in each room.

It is easy to be confused by lighting terms and information because similar light sources can be used for different types of lighting. The shape of the fitting, the shade and the type of bulb used will all affect the amount of light produced and the effect it creates. Think of lighting as falling into the following categories: general, task, background and accent lighting.

GENERAL LIGHTING

This is lighting that provides clear, overall light. It is usually bright, stimulating us into activity. In some areas – the hall, stairs and landing for example – it may be the only form of lighting used. General lighting is usually provided by ceiling or hanging lights.

Ceiling lights can be found in various shapes and sizes. The most common are fitted flush to the ceiling with a glass or clear plastic cover. They can create a rather flat and monotonous light but are often chosen for bathrooms and confined spaces where a pendant fitting perhaps would get in the way.

Pendant fittings are the most common form of lighting. They come in a wide range from chandeliers to globe-shaped paper lanterns. In fact, almost any shape of shade can be put on a pendant fitting but its size, colour, material and shape will all affect the light given off. A globe shape reflecting light equally all round will be much more restful than one that directs all the light

For cooking and preparing food you need a clear light that shines directly on your task. This is best provided by strip lights hidden underneath wall cupboards. Background light is also necessary to prevent any areas from falling in deep shadow. Here, soft overall lighting is provided by recessed floodlights.

A pendant fitting hung low above a table emphasizes the dining area. Placed at the right height – around 22 to 26in (56 to 66cm), this type of light will allow diners to see each other clearly without shining uncomfortably into their faces.

downward, making the person underneath it feel as if they are being picked out by a spotlight! The bigger the shade on a pendant fitting, the softer the light cast will be.

Shades in dark colours, narrow shapes and opaque materials such as metal will substantially reduce the light output.

A disadvantage of pendant lighting is that it is often obtrusive, taking the eye away from the surroundings. It should be supplemented by a softer form of lighting.

Some forms of hanging lighting, such as the lamp hung low over a dining table, really fall into the category of task lighting as well, since the lamp, by its position, throws concentrated light down on to a specific area.

Task lighting

This should provide a clear light shining directly on your task or activity, be it reading, sewing, cooking, eating or writing. If you are sitting on a comfortable chair or at a desk the light should be positioned so that the base of the shade is level with your eyes. The fitting should be placed about 15in (40cm) to the left of a right-handed person or to the right of a left-handed person. Hand sewing and similar close work need approximately twice as much light as casual reading because of the detailed work involved.

Task lighting can be provided by floor or desk lights, spots or fluorescent strips. Even a classic table lamp, if it is positioned correctly for the job in hand, can act as a task light.

Floor lamps are a very popular form of lighting. The most versatile are pole lamps with two or three spots that are adjustable up and down the stem and that also swivel. If you cannot position the light at eye level, place the lamp behind you so that the light shines over your shoulder on to the work not in your eyes.

Desk lamps are extremely important for those who work at home regularly. If there is no room on the desk for a standing lamp use either a spot clipped to a shelf above or a fluorescent strip attached underneath a shelf above. Don't sit in your own shadow; this will lead to eye strain.

Fluorescent strips can be rather harsh, but when used properly are probably the best working light in a kitchen. Mount fluorescent strips under wall cupboards or shelves so that they are in front of you as you work. Position them at the front edge and hide fittings by a slim batten or baffle if you like. Warm-coloured de luxe strips will produce a more natural colour than the hard blue light of most fluorescents. Fluorescent strips can also be classed as accent lights.

Spotlights used as a pair on a wall track can produce good light for reading in bed. They should be independently switched and positioned so that one reader will not disturb a sleeping partner. A dimmer switch might also be useful.

Spots on a track can also be used to advantage to highlight a picture or group of pictures, or placed to bounce the light off walls or ceilings to act as background light.

Background lighting

This differs from general lighting only in its intensity. The light source used for general lighting can also be used for background light if it is controlled by a dimmer switch. Both general and background light provide overall illumination but background light is designed to be soft and restful. The eye does not adjust easily between brightly lit and dark areas, so background light should be used in conjunction with task lighting. For instance, in a dining area we want good light to shine down on the table and food (task lighting) but also some background light to define the rest of the room. This could be provided by wall lights.

Apart from the above, background light can also be provided by downlights and by pelmet (valance) or cornice lights.

Downlighters (downlights) can be recessed, semi-recessed or mounted on the ceiling and are designed to give downward light. Before buying a recessed fitting check that you have the necessary space above your ceiling in which to fit it. Choose a bulb that gives a wide, soft beam for background light and a soft effect. If you want to use downlighting for accenting an object, however, pick a narrow beam.

Valance, pelmet or cornice lights can be used to great effect in living rooms. A fluorescent strip hidden from view behind a valance or pelmet will flood curtains or draperies with a soft overall light. Make sure the light is positioned at least 3in (8cm) away from the fabric. A strip can be used at cornice level in the same way.

Accent lighting

Use accent lighting to create highlights and to show off pictures, plants, indeed any objects you want to emphasize. Suitable sources of accent lighting are spotlights, downlighters, uplighters, fluorescent strips, even candles, which give a lovely, soft, flickering light.

Where you put a light – in front, behind or at the side of an object – will dramatically alter the effect you create. Placed directly in front, the light will act as a highlight; placed at the side it will emphasize shape and texture; and placed at the back it will act as a halo around a darkened object. Experiment with portable table or floor lamps to see what effects you can create by using a number of lights in different positions trained on one object at the same time.

Spotlights have a narrow beam that throws light on to an object. (Don't confuse spotlights with floodlights, which throw out a wide arc of light.) Pin spots have a very narrow beam and are particularly suitable for lighting small objects.

If you want to use a spot to show off a picture, position it on the ceiling about 3ft (1m) from the wall edge. The light should hit the centre of the picture at 30 degrees from the vertical. Before you position the spot, experiment with a portable desk light trained from the ceiling on to the picture to get the angle right.

A spot cannot be trained with absolute accuracy and it will probably also highlight the wall around the picture. For greater accuracy, buy one of the more expensive shuttered spots which have flaps that can be opened and shut to direct the beam more exactly.

To highlight a plant, you can also fit a spot bulb in a downlighter in the right position.

Uplighters are simple lights that can be plugged into an electric point and placed on the floor so that they throw light upwards. These are best hidden, perhaps behind a sofa or a foliage plant. If you want to highlight a group of pictures on a wall, position the uplights about 3ft (90cm) away from the wall for a really dramatic effect.

Uplighters can also be used to highlight items on glass shelves or on a glass coffee table.

Fluorescent strips can be used to draw the eye to an alcove where you display attractive ornaments, a collection of china or perhaps a flower arrangement.

To light a picture, position a fluorescent picture light just above it. The strip should be about one-third to one-half of the width of the picture. If you choose the wrong size you will get a brighter light at the top of the picture than at the bottom. Likewise, make sure that you pick the correct colour bulb to suit the colours in the painting. Fluorescent strips can also be used as task lighting, but their effect should be softened.

An uplighter placed beneath this glass table accentuates a collection of glass and picks out its beautiful colour, shape and pattern. To highlight a wall of paintings in a similar way position the uplight about 3ft (1 metre) away from the wall and conceal it behind a piece of furniture or a plant.

LIGHT BULBS

The type of bulb you use will affect the strength and shape of the beam, so it is important to choose the right bulb for the job. In Britain some fittings take a bayonet bulb (BC) which hooks into place; in the US Edison screw (ES) is the norm. Both come in a range of sizes so check the fitment (socket) carefully before you buy the bulb.

- **Standard pearl bulbs** – and, in the US, 'soft white' bulbs – give a soft overall light.
- **A clear bulb** gives a brighter, harsher light. Use with glass fittings if you want them to sparkle.
- **A mushroom bulb** (UK only) is designed for use in shallow fittings.
- **A large round bulb** is for display and should be used in situations where you want the bulb to be clearly seen.
- **Crown silvered bulbs** are designed to be used with a parabolic reflector to give a glare-free well-defined spot.
- **A PAR 38 spot** (parabolic aluminized reflector) (UK only) produces a punchy dramatic concentrated circle of light. Use it on a small object or arrangement.
- **A PAR 38 flood** (UK only) should be used on a larger arrangement, as it produces a wide cone-shaped beam.

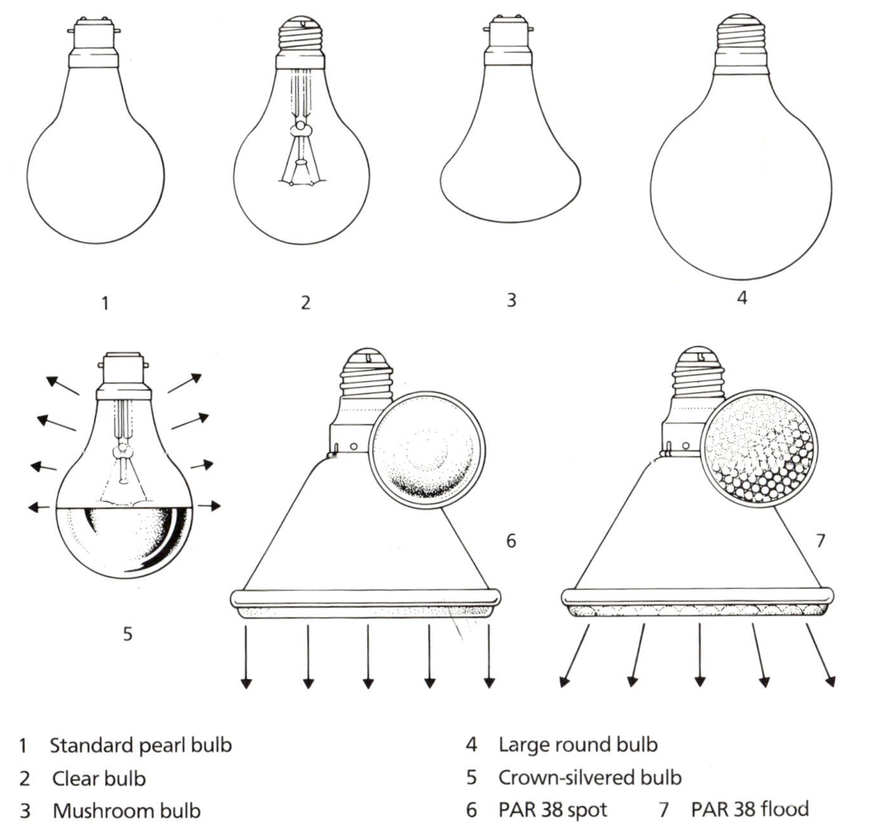

1 Standard pearl bulb
2 Clear bulb
3 Mushroom bulb
4 Large round bulb
5 Crown-silvered bulb
6 PAR 38 spot
7 PAR 38 flood

Plants which love the steamy atmosphere of a bathroom will add instant life and colour to a cold room. Use them to hide an unattractive view by placing them on glass shelves across the window. Here, a large mirror set at right angles to the window extracts double value from daylight and plant life to great effect.

ADDING CHARACTER

Most modern homes contain plain box-shaped rooms that we grumble have no character. Yet this is really an advantage as they provide a plain 'canvas' on which we can 'paint in' whatever exciting detail we like. This is much more difficult to accomplish in the ornate interior of an older house, where the decoration tends to limit our choice of style.

Here are a few suggestions for creating a more individual interior which I hope will spark off some ideas of your own.

CEILINGS

If you want to give a room an 'old world' look remove the ceiling to expose the joists and underside of the floor above. This can then be painted or stained. (Because ceilings act as insulation you should think twice before you go ahead and do this if the room above contains bouncy youngsters or music-mad teenagers.)

Coving (moulding) frames a ceiling neatly and the newer plaster or polystyrene covings are easy to cut to length and glue in place (see pages 88-9). More ornate mouldings are also available, as are central ceiling fittings if you want to give your room real country-house style.

For a sumptuous decorative effect, transform your ceiling with a tent of fabric. This can be gathered tightly at the centre and draped to form soft folds around the edge at picture rail height. Choose inexpensive fabric in a small pattern or plain muslin, sheer curtain or taffeta lining, since you will require a lot of fabric. This is a good way to disguise a bad ceiling or lower a high ceiling in a small room.

A similar but cheaper alternative is to use a large bedspread caught up in each corner of the room to form a canopy. In a large room you may need to sew several together so that they balloon out in the centre of the ceiling. Don't use a central light with a canopied ceiling.

WALLS

If you love the rustic effect of natural materials, remove the plaster from a brick wall to reveal the natural brick. Seal the surface of the bricks and leave them unadorned, or paint them to suit the rest of your decor.

You can also create an old wall effect by using textured paint. Use a stippling brush to give it a rough finish or copy the effect of old, uneven plaster with a palette knife (see pages 60-1).

A painted or papered border will make an undistinguished room more interesting. This can be positioned next to the skirting (baseboard) or flush with the ceiling in a small, low-ceilinged room, or it can help to bring the ceiling down if you place it at picture rail height and paint the wall above to match the ceiling. For more ideas turn to pages 90-1.

Use decorative skirting (baseboard) moulding to form a dado to break up a plain wall surface. This is particularly effective in a hall and up the stairs but can also be a useful technique in a bathroom with strong coloured fixtures. Paint the wall below the dado to match the fixtures so that they 'disappear' into it, then use a lighter tone above the rail and sponge or rag finish it (see pages 69-71). This would be particularly effective if you used a shiny gloss-finish paint throughout the room you are decorating.

Make a focal point of a plain wall by painting it a strong colour and putting up shelves along its length (see pages 117-21), thus forming a bold background for a display. Use a reflective metallic paper behind a display of glass.

Cover characterless walls with fabric for a very special, luxurious effect. For hints on how to put it up see pages 18-19.

Windows

Give a small window a grand treatment and you will forget how insignificant it is. Hang curtains (draperies) from ceiling to floor along the complete length of the window wall, then pull the curtains only partway back during the day.

If the window has a radiator beneath it, fix a pole above the window so that it extends about 2ft (60cm) to each side. Hang a length of fabric so that it drapes over the pole and falls to the floor on either side of the window, thus forming a frame for a softly pleated Roman blind hung at the window itself.

Doors

A flush door is a perfect surface for a simple mural. Transform it into a *trompe l'oeil* window with a beautiful scene beyond and paint in curtains (draperies) to match the real ones in the room. Alternatively, hide the door by papering it to match the surrounding walls. (Visitors may find this confusing!)

One decorative technique used in Britain is to remove the top panels of a panelled door and replace them with decorative painted glass. Paint the design on first. Stick the design you want to copy, wrong side outside, on the glass, then paint from the other side using special glass paint, which comes in glowing colours and lets the light through.

If you prefer, spray on a geometric pattern using masking tape and enamel paint. Thin coats give a more even finish than one thick one.

A small window can achieve grand proportions if you use the window treatment to cover the whole wall. Here, vertical blinds in complementary pastel stripes add seaside colour to a simple bedroom.

CHAPTER 2

Room-by-room planning

HALL, STAIRS AND LANDING

This is the area that friends and strangers see first and yet it is often the area we put least thought into when decorating.

This part of the house presents a great challenge, as it can be full of problems – dark, awkwardly shaped, often little more than a series of passages and possibly housing ugly meters, although the latter are often sited outside these days. It also gets the most wear and tear.

Style and colour

Unless it is divided in some way, treat the hall, stairway and landing as one area, using the same scheme for walls, ceiling and floors throughout. You will find the result most satisfactory if you also bear in mind the colours used in any adjacent rooms. If the differences in colour and tone are too strong it will be like walking into a series of different brightly coloured boxes, making the house seem much smaller than it really is.

Even if the area is dark you should avoid using very pale colours. Decorating hall, stairs and landing is costly and awkward to do (see page 81 for some safety tips) and pale colours will soon show wear. Brighter colours create a welcoming warmth and since this is an area where people are constantly on the move and won't therefore be exposed to a strong colour or colours for too long, it gives you the opportunity to try some more unusual decorating schemes. For instance, fix a dado rail along the hall wall and up the stairs and paint or paper above and below the dado in different colours or tones of the same colour. This also gives you the chance to paint the wall below the dado rail a darker, more practical colour which will wear better.

If you paint below the rail, damage from the moving of bulky items such as furniture, appliances and suitcases, plus wear and tear from small children or animals can easily be repaired and decorated over. Use a paler version of the lower colour on the wall and ceiling above, palest peach with a deep apricot for instance, or tones of yellow, green or blue. Alternatively, paper the area above the rail in a design that picks out the paint colour, or sponge the wall using the pale tone over the dark on the lower part of the wall and reverse this for the top half (see pages 69-71 for decorative paint finishes).

A cheap alternative to wallpaper is to use a border at skirting (baseboard), dado or ceiling height over a plain or sponged wall; this will accentuate the interesting wall angles.

Mirror can be used to great advantage in a hall but its positioning needs to be carefully worked out. Experiment with a mirror you already have to find the right position, bearing in mind that it should reflect light and interest. Tiny mirror tiles on a flexible backing can be glued to a door. If this door is opposite the front door it will mirror light and reflect images when the front door is opened.

Clever use of mirror in a hall or landing can add light and sparkle to a potentially dark, uninteresting area. In this case, mirror tiles have been used to frame the doors and to cover the narrow hall table. Wall and ceiling lights add to the attractive 1930s Art Deco style.

Furniture

There is usually a minimum of space available for furniture so it is best to keep this to a few essential items. A narrow table, or a shelf on the wall if there is no room for a table, will provide a place to put letters, parcels, newspapers, magazines and messages. Put a wall telephone above this if you want to keep call times down to a minimum! If there is no cupboard (closet), you will need to provide a coat rack, or perhaps some hooks on the wall. Site these in an alcove if there is one, and if possible away from the main thoroughfare but not so far away that they never get used. A container of some sort for wet umbrellas is also a good idea.

If you are lucky enough to have a more spacious hall, put part of it to good use as a dining or work area. There may even be enough room in an understairs cupboard (closet) to turn it into a small lavatory. Space on a landing can sometimes accommodate a desk for occasional study or letter-writing and bill-paying, or be partitioned off and turned into a shower room. At the very least, consider utilizing this area to the full by putting up shelving for extra storage.

Flooring

As this area gets more wear than any other part of the house, the flooring needs to be exceptionally hardwearing. It also needs to be practical, safe and easy to clean.

Carpet will help to keep down the noise level. It

Bright colours extend a warm welcome to visitors when they arrive. Yellow is added to a simple black and white colour scheme and a strip of canvas forms an eye-catching band wound around the stair rail. A practical vinyl floor covering has been used on hall and stairs.

SAFETY AND SECURITY

- Never leave things lying around on stairways and landings, especially at the top of flights of stairs.
- Floorcoverings in halls and stairways should be short-pile, non-slip and firmly anchored.
- Lighting should be clear and bright, highlighting any changes in level.
- Decorating in a stairwell can be tricky and special safety precautions should be taken (see page 81).
- If you have children, use a gate by stairways to prevent falls. Make sure that children cannot reach handles on front doors.
- Fit locks on all external doors and windows. Consult a professional to find out the most suitable types for your particular home.
- A variety of security devices, from conventional alarm bells to beams which trigger floodlights when broken, is available for exterior use. A specialist will advise which is best for you.

Halls rarely allow much scope for furniture. The wall space between two doorways has been used to great advantage in this hallway with a colourful floor-to-ceiling shelving system which provides extra storage.

is also warm and non-slip. Buy the best quality you can afford: underlay and laying costs make it impractical to replace carpet too often. Avoid using sculptured, loose weave or shag pile on stairs, all of which could cause accidents.

Mid-tone colours are the most practical for a hall and stairs. Alternatively, choose a small pattern that will pick up the colour of the wall or that used in adjoining rooms.

There are other practical floorings too. Sand and seal a wood floor to provide an attractive natural background, or use sheet flooring, which is hardwearing and easy to clean. Avoid the use of rugs on a slippery floor – these can easily slide under running feet and cause an accident – and never polish the wood on stairs.

Lighting

It has to be safety first when planning lighting. Stairs must be clearly lit, as must any other changes in level – say a small step between landing areas. Avoid lighting which creates pools of light, as this will also produce dark patches. Light switches should be easy to find and it should be possible to switch hall, stairs and landing lights on and off from both hall and landing. Place a light on the landing with a low wattage bulb that can be left on all night for young children or visitors who may need to get up.

Extras

The hall and stairway is the perfect place to hang a collection of pictures. Old prints or maps of the town or village where you live are very attractive and interesting – or frame a montage of holiday snaps including place and date, then add a new set after each holiday. A family tree shown in pictures of as many generations as you can find photographs of would be fun for visiting members of the family. Don't hang large pictures in a confined space; you can't get far enough away to view them properly and their overall effect will be quite wasted.

Add glass shelves across the width of a landing window to display a mixture of flowering and leafy house plants or to show off a collection of old glass, which should sparkle attractively in the light from the window.

Build a shallow cupboard to hold and camouflage any unsightly gas or electricity meters and then decorate this cupboard in colours or patterns to match the rest of the hall.

LIVING ROOMS

Whether moving from one house to another or furnishing a first home, few of us are able to start from scratch; the chances are that we have accumulated some items of furniture and other belongings and these will have to be taken into account when planning a new scheme.

Careful thought will help you to avoid mistakes in choosing furniture that does not fit or a scheme that you won't be happy with. Draw your room shape accurately on graph paper (the larger the better), then cut out paper shapes, also to scale, of any furniture you need to fit in. If you are buying new seating, calculate your needs. How many people do you want to be able to seat? Can you bring chairs from elsewhere in the house when you have extra visitors? Consider the shape of the room and how best the seating can be arranged; this will help you decide just what sort of seating will be best. (See page 22 for some suggestions for seating plans.)

Work out your storage needs in the same way, calculating shelf space for books, records, cassettes, television, audio equipment and computer and disks if you intend to use them in this room. Over- rather than under-estimate space required, as you will almost certainly add to your collection. In a small room, storage all along one wall will give more floor space.

In the same way that a professional designer would, make yourself a samples board and pin to

All the space in this small living room is fully utilized and yet it still appears light and airy. Sewing equipment is stored away neatly in a shutter-fronted unit and just a few decorative items are displayed on a separate low-level shelf. Colours have been kept deliberately pale. Soft yellow and palest turquoise give the room a sunny yet restful air.

A large picture was the inspiration for this colour scheme which incorporates restful aquamarine and accents of terracotta. Unlined white curtains (draperies) with a subtle check allow a maximum of light to filter into a room where modern and traditional furniture have been mixed successfully.

it any paint charts, fabric, wallpaper and carpet samples, and catalogue pictures of new furniture that you are thinking of buying. Include alternative choices and pin your board to the wall of the room so that you can view all the possible ingredients together and at different times of the day. Gradually remove any that you feel won't be suitable until you have only your final choice left.

Colour scheme and furniture choice will probably, to some extent, be affected by the period and style of the house, although it will depend on your own preference too. If you want to accentuate period detail such as decorative plasterwork or arched alcoves paint them to contrast with the surroundings. Use a deeper tone of the wall colour, for instance, in alcoves, or draw attention to the plasterwork mouldings by using a decorative paper rather than paint on the ceiling.

If you have a house or flat composed of plain box-shaped rooms with no interesting detail, let this be your excuse to try something dramatic; see pages 28-9 for some ideas.

Style and Colour

Study the room in daylight and at night, bearing in mind which direction it faces. Its size, lightness and orientation should all be taken into account in your choice of decoration; see pages 14-17 for colour information.

On the whole it is easier, unless you are very confident, to stick to one style for your scheme. But don't be too rigid. One or two items that are totally out of style with the rest of the room will create extra interest – a modern chair in a traditional room, perhaps. If you have an old Victorian rocking chair, don't feel obliged to stick to a traditional or country style for the room. In the same way a collection of modern glass need not restrict you to a modern scheme.

The following is a breakdown of some styles you might like to consider:

Traditional rooms might include flowery prints, papers and fabrics; tables hidden by layers of cloth, old polished or painted furniture; long draped curtains; old photographs.

Country looks mean stripped floors and furniture; plain white natural fabrics; the use of green; lots of plants; rag rugs.
Ethnic styles involve exotic, spicy colours and lots of mixed patterns; Oriental, African or Indian furniture and accessories; brass; wickerwork.
High-tech makes use of immensely practical factory and office furniture and materials – rubber bubble flooring, 'supermarket' shelving, old office or dentist's chairs; strong colours.
Soft modern is produced by the use of subtly pale pastels; textured patterns; paint finishes such as sponging, graining, rag rolling and marbling; soft but simple-shaped furniture; light woods; crazed pottery; fitted carpets in soft colours or pale rag rugs over carpet or floorboards.
Minimal means plain light colours; double-duty furniture (a futon, for example, which serves as a bed at night, seating during the day); only the best-looking objects on show.

Furniture

This will depend on how you want to use the room. If the room is small and you can eat in the kitchen, you will want to keep this room for relaxing, talking, watching television, reading and listening to music. In this case your main requirements will be comfortable seating, good storage and some small tables or one larger coffee table for drinks, books, magazines and so on. Make sure, however you arrange the seating, that a table surface is within reach of each chair; this will prevent stains on your carpet!

Seating should be arranged so that people are close enough to each other wherever they sit to talk comfortably without raising their voices.

Storage

Here, as in any other room, storage needs to be well organized. You can choose from a huge range of storage systems in materials and shapes to suit any style of furnishing. These might be shelves of different widths, with the lower shelves wide enough to take television and audio equipment. Modular systems are also available; these include cupboards, drawer storage and shelves all made to the same dimensions so that a system can be built up from the ingredients you want to include, as and when you can afford it.

Alternatively, use alcoves, fitting in shelves of exactly the height and width to suit your specific needs (see pages 117-21).

Dining area

Your choice of table will be affected by the shape of the space you have. A round table is more sociable than a rectangular one, and you can fit more people around it, but you will need a square area for this. Allow a 3ft (90cm) space for each chair to be pulled back. A long table fits better into a narrow space and you can use a bench against the wall if space is really tight. Drop-leaf or extending tables will give versatility, or you can make a larger table top from chipboard (particle board), store it elsewhere and bring it out to use (covered with a disguising cloth) on the top of the table when you have visitors. A small side table is useful for holding extra china or food from the main table. This can be very narrow and still serve the purpose; even a shelf on the wall will do. If you have enough space to allow for them, comfortable chairs will provide more relaxed mealtimes and china can be stored in the kitchen or dining area, wherever there is space available.

Study area

The living room is not the best place in which to study, as there are likely to be too many distractions from conversations, television and so on. A desk in a quiet bedroom or even in an alcove in a hall or on a landing (provided there is not too much traffic) is preferable. If there really is nowhere else, buy a dining table that will satisfactorily double as a desk and provide for any filing and shelving space necessary in the room's storage system.

Flooring

Fitted carpet is likely to be most people's choice for a living room for reasons of warmth and comfort as well as appearance. It is also easier and quicker to clean on a day-to-day basis than a hard floor and rugs.

A carpet with a large pattern will tend to dominate a room, in which case keep other decoration and furnishing plain or in a small, simple design. A carpet with a small pattern is usually better for a small room. Whatever carpet you pick it should be of the best quality you can afford (see pages 103-5).

As far as plain coloured carpets are concerned, dark colours show up fluff and threads but not stains. They make a small room seem smaller, whereas a light carpet, which *will* show up stains, will also create a sense of space. A

A large, light room has been decorated very simply and furnished in cream and white with natural wood furniture and floor. This allows a jungle of plants to become the focus of the room, their flowers and leaves providing colour and interesting texture.

mid-tone, especially a fleck, is least likely to show marks and bits. The same carpet used throughout the ground floor will also make it appear much more roomy and open.

If you have a wood floor in good condition sand and seal it (pages 94-5 show how) or you can cover a concrete floor with hardwood mosaic panels or strips (see pages 109-12). Cover the wood with a rich-coloured Turkish or Persian rug, a subtly patterned dhurrie or a washable cotton rag or flokati rug.

Lighting

In a living room you are likely to need good background light, some working light for reading, sewing or working and some lighting to show off favourite objects or paintings. If you use it as a dining room, a light above the table will be necessary too.

Background light

Lights which cast areas of intense light and dark shadows can be disconcerting. Background light should softly outline the shape and bring out the colour of the room (see page 26). If you have one central light fitting, a track with a number of spots positioned to shine high on walls and ceiling will create this effect. Use flood rather than spot bulbs, as these provide a wider, softer beam. They can also be used with a dimmer.

Working light

This can be provided by table or floor lamps but positioning of the light is all-important if you are going to see clearly without strain. The bulb should be at eye height when you are sitting down. If you work at a dining table, then a central fixture hung low above the table will serve equally well for mealtimes and for working. A rise and fall fitting will allow you to adjust the height accurately. This light should highlight what is on the table without obliterating the diners' view or shining into their faces – 22 to 26in (56-66cm) above the table top is a good average height.

Highlighting

You may have certain items in the room you want to accentuate. For more information on accent lighting see pages 26-7. Use uplighters to shine through a huge basket of dried flowers, spot lights directed at a favourite print or a collection of china, or wall lights to show off a decorative cornice to best effect.

Extras

Any window treatment is suitable for a living room. Floor-length wall-to-wall curtains (draperies) will add interest to a featureless room, but blinds and shades in all their different guises, or sheer fabrics draped to frame a window with a good outlook can be just as effective. Pictures, books, plants, pottery, glass and cushions collected over the years give a room individuality. For immediate impact in a large, sparsely furnished room, stand a group of plants in one corner. Balance leaf colour and shape so that each shows off the other. Fresh flowers always bring a room to life. Rather than arranging them formally, make a collection of different-sized containers holding natural bunches or just one or two beautiful blooms.

Dual-purpose living rooms

- Divide seating and dining/work areas with a screen or open shelves filled with plants, or pottery or a collection of your favourite ornaments.
- Use lighting to accentuate the different functions of each area.
- Link the two separate sections of the room visually with a border or soft furnishings to provide continuity.

KITCHENS

A kitchen should be designed around the people who use it, complementing their tastes in cooking, their mealtime habits and the way they like to work, and providing planned working space for more than one of the family's cooks to be busy at the same time. Many of us, however, move into a kitchen designed by someone else for someone else and we have to adjust to the kitchen rather than the other way around. However, there are some simple changes you can make to improve a kitchen's efficiency by adding hanging racks, shelves, new interior fittings and simply by planning very carefully where you store food and equipment rather than putting everything away in the first space you come to. In the same way, style and colour can be subtly altered using paint and paper, ceramic tiles, new flooring or a new work surface.

Finally, it is well worth while checking that your lighting and safety provisions are adequate and that the room is well ventilated. Later, if you get the chance to plan a kitchen from scratch, you will have benefited by learning through someone else's mistakes!

A relaxing yet workmanlike kitchen is created by ultra-practical stainless steel work tops and blue-green units, but the effect would be lifeless without the contrast provided by the yellow accessories. The positioning of the table makes an island unit and the kitchen becomes a more practical shape in which to work.

Lines of tidy wall and floor cupboards prevent the most accessible space between hip and shoulder from being used. Manufacturers are now producing ranges of shelves and racks which help you to utilize this space. Practical drawer systems for storage of dry goods, pans and casseroles are also available.

Style and colour

You can change the visual impact of a kitchen without removing all the units. The style of the units – natural wood, shiny white plastic, brightly coloured laminate, or a pastel textured finish – will to some extent set the mood but white units in a white painted room with white tiled floor and no obvious accessories will look totally different from white units in a room painted sunny yellow with cork floor tiles and wooden accessories. Change the decoration to green trellis wallpaper and add lots of plants, or use a sharp pink and decorate with flower-sprigged pottery. Each scheme will create a very different style.

Natural wood units can be brought bang up to date by painting and then sponging or ragging the finish (see pages 69-71) and finally sealing the surface with matt or satin-finish polyurethane varnish. Sand smooth-finish laminate to provide a key, then paint and finish as you like. Shiny, hard plastics and textured finishes are difficult to cover up, however, and alternative measures may be necessary in these cases.

If floor, units and worktop are areas of plain colour, add pattern in the wall covering or tiles. In a small kitchen use a small design and match it with coordinating fabric for blinds (shades) and tablecloth or mats. Sheet flooring comes in a wide range of colours and designs. Replace too bold a pattern with a simple marble or mosaic floor design. Replace an overbearing wallpaper with plain painted walls and match up with smart tiles between worktop and wall units.

Furniture

Apart from table, chairs and – where there is room – a sofa to transform the kitchen into a comfortable family room, the major items of furniture are the fitted units. Even if the kitchen you inherit is already fully equipped it is worthwhile considering the advantages of different types of storage, as extra shelves or interior fittings may make all the difference between an efficient and an inefficient working environment.

Choosing a storage system

Most kitchen storage is made up of cupboards, shelves and drawers but the size, shape and use of these three storage systems has changed radically in recent years. Pull-out storage provides a number of gadgets to help us use space more efficiently.

Cupboards, or cabinets, should be chosen carefully. Low, deep ones are extremely inefficient; you have to kneel on the floor and drag all the front items out to get at those at the back. These are now being replaced by taller, narrow cupboards in which, with the door open, you can see everything at a glance and the most accessible space, between hip and shoulder, can be used. In Britain, the larder is coming back into fashion. This does not mean you must have a separate room – a tall, ventilated cupboard will serve the purpose. Double doors open onto narrow, U-shaped shelves, and racks on the back of the door hold smaller items.

If you have some spare wall space in your kitchen, fix adjustable shelving along one wall and add a series of tall, narrow doors from floor to ceiling to hide their contents; or better still hang roller blinds (shades) that disappear up to the ceiling when the shelves are in use and can simply be rolled down when cooking is finished.

Shelves are improving all the time. Most manufacturers are now providing narrow shelving systems, racks and rails to fit on the wall between worktop and wall cupboards to provide handy storage just where you need it. Racks and rails are available at most hardware shops and are easy to put up. If you need to drill into a tile to do this, break the glaze with a nail head first or stick adhesive (Scotch) tape over the tile to prevent the drill slipping and the tile cracking.

Add sturdy 12in (30cm) wide shelves to a plain wall and display your tableware and glasses. If the kitchen is adequately ventilated they should not become dusty and greasy.

Drawers, when pulled out, ideally show you their contents instantly. A friend of mine uses old, painted filing cabinets to store pots and pans; for years I have used an old chest of drawers. Now manufacturers have taken up this idea with wide pan drawers designed to fit underneath the hob (burners). Pick drawers the height of the equipment you want to keep in them; too-deep drawers will result in internal stacking and defeat the object. In a deep cutlery drawer stack two cutlery containers, one on top of the other, or make your own divisions to suit the contents; alternatively, fit it with a number of different-sized rectangular baskets. Small box drawers, such as old chemist shops (pharmacies) used, can store dried foods.

Pull-out storage is worth investigating. A carousel (rotating shelves) fitted into a corner cupboard will swing round to reveal its contents, and a shelf that rises to working height for use means that heavy equipment, such as food mixers and processors, can be stored out of sight. Plinth drawers will hold kitchen steps, tools or other items. One manufacturer even makes a table that unrolls from the space above and behind a cupboard! There are rack shelves that can be clipped on to a shelf and racks that hold plates in the vertical position.

Shelves are a practical form of kitchen storage: everything can be seen at a glance and, provided the room is well ventilated, there is no reason why containers should become greasy.

Planning layout

If your storage is planned well you will find it much more enjoyable to cook. It is important to keep things where you use them and to place the most often-used items in the most accessible positions. In a professional kitchen areas are divided into work stations – washing and washing up (dish washing), food preparation, food storage, cooking, and serving. This idea can be copied to advantage in a domestic kitchen.

A washing and washing up area covers the sink and ideally a minimum of 2ft (60cm) on either side. Here you will be preparing vegetables and anything else that first needs washing. You will be draining foods and washing dishes and utensils. Therefore, store the following items in this area: peelers, colanders, strainers, saucepans that you first fill with water, washing up and cleaning materials, waste bin and, if you have the space, vegetables.

A food preparation area is best positioned between sink and cooker (oven) and needs a working space of 3 to 4ft (90 to 120cm). It is where foods are chopped and prepared ready for cooking, so you will need to store the following here: knives, chopping boards, weighing scales, mixers, grinders, graters, pastry boards and baking equipment (or if you have room you could have a separate cake- and pastry-making area), mixing bowls, plus, if there is room, food storage for flour, dried herbs, tins, dried fruit and spices.

A food storage area includes refrigerator, freezer and one or more cupboards for dry or tinned foods. Food storage should be within a convenient distance of the place where the food will be prepared. Apart from food you will also need freezer bags, cling film (plastic wrap) and food storage containers.

A cooking area needs hob (burners) and oven, if integral, or you may prefer a combination of hob and microwave. The oven can make up a secondary cooking area by the serving space.

It is important to have working space on each side of the hob of about 2ft (60cm). Store in this area all the items first used on the stove: cooking utensils, saucepans, lids, frying pans, roasting tins, cooling racks, trivets. If the oven is sited separately it should have enough space beside it to put down hot dishes.

A serving area should be near where you are going to eat and could include a tea- and coffee-making area with all the necessary ingredients and equipment stored here. Use this space also for cutlery, tableware and foods that go straight to the table such as cereals, jams, sugar, salt and pepper and other condiments.

Worktops

If you cannot change the units, a new worktop can enhance the surroundings considerably and make a more efficient kitchen in general.

Laminated plastic is the most widely used material for worktops and it comes in a huge range of colours, textures and patterns. Its disadvantage is that it can become damaged and cannot be repaired, so it is wise to keep chopping boards and pan trivets to hand where they will be needed to avoid the temptation of chopping or placing hot pans directly on its surface.

Tiles, either quarry or ceramic, can be used but be wary of using shiny tiles, as the glaze may contain poisonous metals. Tiles can be laid on top of laminate if you sand the surface first to provide a key but if you do the tiling yourself, make sure that you use a heavy, non-porous tile grout. The disadvantage of tiles is that grout is not easy to clean and can become stained in time, as well as being rather unhygienic.

Wood is one of the most attractive materials for a worktop, but a hard wood is essential: maple and beech, teak, iroko, elm and oak are suitable. All the wood will need is a periodic oiling with corn or groundnut (peanut) oil. Apart from its warm look the great advantage of wood is that, if anything, it is likely to improve in looks with age.

Stone covers a multitude of choices, of which granite and marble are most suited to kitchens. Granite makes a beautiful work surface that is easy to maintain but must be carefully selected. Some granites are porous and not suitable; others have natural faults which can crack.

Marble unfortunately stains if it comes into contact with some fairly common cooking ingredients – lemon or fish, for example. It does, however, make an excellent cold, smooth surface for rolling out pastry and may be best reserved for this and in larders.

Stainless steel is nearly always used in professional kitchens because it is the ultimate hygienic work surface.

Corian is a very expensive solid plastic that can be moulded, with sink and work surface made in one continuous piece. It looks a little like marble and comes in a limited range of colours.

Kitchen furniture needn't be bland – in this room it has been given a glossy and striking paint treatment in a deep terracotta. Concealed strip lighting and recessed spotlights add drama.

Lighting

Kitchen lighting enables us to work safely and needs to illuminate the room as a whole. A central fluorescent strip is certainly not the way to deal with these two separate needs. Wherever possible it is much better to make the light source invisible. This is because the eye responds to a bright light source so that other areas will appear dark in comparison.

Working areas

Use small fluorescent strips positioned under wall cupboards (rather than a central fluorescent strip on the ceiling). These will shine light down on to what you are doing. Use the warm light strips rather than white light, as they produce a much softer and more natural image. An alternative to this is spot lights positioned on the wall and trained down on to the worktop at strategic points but this is bound to create pools of light instead of even lighting. Unless they are very carefully positioned you may find that your body creates a shadow over what you are doing.

Background light

The ideal place for this is above the wall cupboards, so that a soft light is reflected on to the ceiling. Spots trained on to the ceiling give a similar effect.

Eating area

A pendant light hung low above the table to illuminate food and diners will provide the best light (see page 26). For special occasions, don't neglect candles – nothing beats their warm, flattering glow.

Ventilation

The smell of yesterday's food may have been mouthwatering yesterday but it is very offputting today. A well-ventilated kitchen will quickly lose smells and, because dirt and grease are expelled along with cooking odours, the room will remain clean, allowing you to keep equipment exposed on shelves, easy to see and easy to reach.

An extractor fan either above the cooker (range) or on an adjacent outside wall will provide the most efficient method of extracting odours. However, for this to work efficiently air must be able to flow into the room to replace that which is removed. There are various ways of achieving this. In some systems an airbrick is placed in the wall; this should be positioned so that the air will flow across the hob (burners) before it is expelled. In open-plan homes, adequate ventilation occurs naturally. In any satisfactory system the air should be replaced at least three times an hour.

A cooker hood is in the ideal position to remove smells. There are two types of hood, extracting and recycling. A recycling hood takes the stale air through filters, which clean it, and then releases the air back into the room. It is very important with this system that filters be cleaned regularly, as a fat-clogged filter can almost instantly turn a pan fire into a raging house fire. A hood with fan that extracts air to the outside is obviously the better choice. This does not have to be positioned on an outside wall, as ducting along the top of the wall can take the stale air along the wall to the outside, but this obviously costs more.

A small kitchen has little space for relaxed eating. It needs ingenuity to turn the confined area to advantage. In this narrow blue and white kitchen shallow shelves have been built along one wall and cleverly incorporate a semi-circular drop-leaf table.

Extras

Adding brightly coloured containers and equipment to a plain kitchen can change the whole look of the room. Use grids on walls or rails on ceilings to hang collections of baskets or old kitchen equipment. Display decorative plates on a plain wall. Plants, which will love the steamy atmosphere of a kitchen window sill, transform a room. Hang baskets in front of the window and use them to hold containers for growing herbs. Sprout seeds on the window sill beneath and use them to add taste and nutrition to winter salads.

If you have the space turn a small area into an office where cookery books can be kept, meals planned and bills paid.

SAFETY

In spite of all the modern labour-saving equipment accidents in the kitchen are increasing. Of these, the most common are cuts caused mainly by knives and tin openers. A sharp knife is much safer than a blunt one, which is more likely to slip and cut you, so sharpen knives regularly and store them in a rack or in a block. Buy a good wall tin opener – much safer than a hand-operated one.

When items are stored at an inconvenient height there is a great temptation to clamber on to the nearest stool or chair instead of getting a stepladder. Not a wise thing to do, as the number of reported falls in the kitchen show. Store often-used items in the area between hip and shoulder height and make sure a pair of steps is close to hand, so that you reach for these before anything else if you have to get to the top of a cupboard. It's worth taking extra care where heavy objects, such as cast-iron saucepans, are concerned.

A kitchen floor should be non-slip. Shiny tiles or an over-polished floor are not a good idea. Remove spills, particularly of grease, the moment they happen.

Safety first also means having a fire blanket near the hob (burners) so that pan fires can be smothered instantly. Keep an all-purpose household fire extinguisher handy.

A bathroom is in great demand for relatively short periods every day. If there is space, incorporating two basins rather than one could help to alleviate the problem. A streamlined unit built along one wall provides plenty of storage as well and does away with the need for a space-hogging dressing table in the bedroom.

BATHROOMS

Even if you intend to change the bathroom when you move into a new home it is a good idea to live with the old one long enough to find out the advantages and disadvantages of its layout. It is cheaper when renewing a bathroom simply to replace the old fixtures with new ones in the same position but if the layout is inefficient it is worth while changing the plumbing to improve it.

For a relatively short period each day the bathroom is in great demand, and the more people there are in the family the worse the bathroom bottleneck becomes. It is well worth while considering some improvements.

If there is room in the bathroom, replacing a large basin with two slightly smaller ones, both fitted into a worktop with a big mirror behind, could be one answer. Another solution might be to replace a conventional bathtub with a short sit-up style one and then you could use the extra space released for a shower cubicle.

Look at space outside the bathroom too. Providing a basin in the room of a 'bathroom hog' could relieve the strain considerably. Is there any unused space on the landing or under the stairs where you could fit a shower? If the understairs space is too small for a shower could you squeeze in a toilet and a tiny corner basin?

Style and colour

It is fairly simple, and not expensive, to transform an inherited bathroom. The simplest option is to add bright-coloured towels, a matching shower curtain and colourful pottery mugs, soap holders and containers. Decorating such a small room is neither costly nor too time-consuming. Here's how to deal with some of the most common bathroom fixture colours.

White fixtures give you an almost unlimited

choice of alternatives. If the room is at present too cold and clinical, paint it a bright pink, add lots of plants and rich royal blue towels and accessories. Alternatively you could introduce some sunshine with a bright yellow paint, a mix of rainbow-coloured towels and cork tiles on the floor and the side of the bath. Display a collection of shells on plain wooden shelves and add a folding deckchair.

Pastel fixtures benefit from the use of a deeper tone of the same colour used on walls and ceiling, perhaps with a bright mid-tone for towels and accessories. Avocado green, a very subdued colour, can be enlivened with a bright red or sunny yellow, and a dark brown would look considerably more interesting if highlighted by sunny spice colours – saffron, chilli or ginger.

Shiny, reflective metallic papers look particularly good in a bathroom and are waterproof. Bathroom wallpaper has to be washable, so for preference choose one of the vinyl types. Gloss paint used on walls and ceiling can be very effective too, with its shiny surface, and it can also be used over ceramic tiles.

The bathroom is also a wonderful place to try your hand at painting a mural – a romantic garden or a seascape perhaps!

Furniture

You don't need much furniture in a bathroom; there is rarely enough space for it anyhow. Building a vanity unit around the basin can provide a useful worktop and good storage under-

It's simple to change the look of an inherited bathroom with an injection of strong colour. Here yellow 'bubble' flooring continues up the wall, extending the space visually. Clever use of clear ridged-plastic sheeting for the shelving system provides unobtrusive and imaginative storage, and a foil effect shower curtain adds a certain glamour.

neath. I built the basin in my old house into an old mahogany sideboard with a damaged top. I replaced the top with a curve-edged marble-look laminate and this unit provided masses of storage and a large make-up area. If you want a bit of a barrier between toilet or bath and the rest of the room, build a shelved room divider, which will also give you some storage space and a display area, perhaps for steam-loving plants.

Cane looks good in a bathroom, as its delicacy offsets the hard shapes of the fixtures, so if you have room add a cane chair and soft cushions.

Flooring

A water-tolerant flooring is a must; sheet vinyl or cork tiles are quite suitable, with a washable cotton rug on top to provide some comfort. If you are like me and walk around barefoot most of the time, then you will opt for a carpet. This should be a man-made fibre: polypropylene is the best, but you can also use polyester, nylon or acrylic. Carpeting designed for bathrooms is available.

Lighting

There are strict safety rules governing electricity in the bathroom. A light switch should be outside the room or should be activated by a pull cord inside it. Light fittings should not have a bare bulb that could be touched by a damp hand but be covered by a glass or plastic cover.

Most bathrooms are adequately lit by a central ceiling light plus a mirror light. Position a mirror light carefully so that shadows are not thrown onto the face. Light should be directed at the face, not at the mirror, and light fittings are best placed down the sides or at the bottom of the mirror rather than at the top.

Extras

You will find a blind (shade) – roller, Roman or festoon – the most practical, decorative window treatment for a bathroom.

Plants love the damp atmosphere and if there is no shelf space available for them, hang them instead in baskets from the ceiling.

Light, amusing books and puzzles are often appreciated. Or you can provide alternative diversion by covering a wall or walls with a multitude of images – holiday snaps, magazine cut-outs, a collection of postcards, just about anything! Protect them from damp with polyurethane varnish.

Modern bathrooms are being given the fully fitted treatment. A square room allows space for an opulent corner bath. Mirror adds decoration and increases the space visually. White, beige or grey fittings mean that you can vary the effect with accessories, as almost all colours will be compatible. Warm colours in winter and cold ones in summer add to a bathroom's comfort and co-ordination.

Rich colours are particularly suited to bedrooms which are viewed mainly at night. A random geometric pattern contrasts beautifully in this exotic bedroom with a traditional floral fabric that uses deep but harmonizing colour tones.

BEDROOMS

Bedrooms are fun to furnish and decorate. There are no essential rules to follow; the style you choose will depend on your personal preference. Most modern bedrooms are small, allowing space for only the basics – a bed, clothes storage, a couple of small bedside tables and perhaps a small, comfortable chair. If, however, the bedroom is relatively large and you are short of space in the house as a whole, think about using it as a second living room.

Style and colour

Collect magazine pictures of rooms that appeal to you and then decide which of these can most effectively be adapted to your room. Here are some styles you might care to consider.

Good old nostalgia is for romantics everywhere. If the floor is wood and in good condition strip and seal the boards (see pages 94-5), lay a pastel patterned dhurrie or rag rug and decorate the room all in white, using white bedding, curtains and light wood or cane furniture with a cane or brass headboard. If you want to add pretty touches, use lace-decorated cloths on furniture and lace cushions.

A richly exotic look is particularly suitable for bedrooms, as many are seen almost always in artificial light, which is perfect for richly patterned fabrics in warm colours, so long as the light is soft. Choose a simple low bed, dark wood furniture and a mid-tone plain carpet.

Pretty pastels mean coordinating fabrics and wallpapers used to give an attractive overall effect. Paper the cupboard (closet) doors to match the walls and paint, then sponge or rag the furniture (see pages 69-71). Fit carpet of the same tone or paint the floorboards and top with a pastel-coloured carpet square. For a luxurious feel add a soft sink-in sofa.

Modern simplicity follows the Japanese minimalist style. Sleep on a futon, which can be rolled up or folded to form seating during the day. Hide shelving behind Oriental screens or bamboo or paper blinds (shades) which can also be used at the window. Keep everything very low and light with paper lanterns hung over low lacquered tables to either side of the futon. On the opposite side of the room, if it is big enough, place low tables or shelving to accommodate stereo, speakers and a small television to turn the room into an area which is suitable for daytime relaxation as well as night-time rest.

FURNITURE

Apart from a storage system to house clothes, shoes and accessories, the one essential item of furniture is, of course, the bed.

Beds

Because you spend about one-third of your life in bed, it is sensible to get the best you can afford. Don't economize by putting a new mattress on an old base; the mattress will just wear out more quickly. Some alternative suggestions are:

A wood base and sprung mattress makes a good bed for back sufferers, who benefit from a firm base. You can make your own very simply by screwing eight 6ft (2m) planks 6in (15cm) wide and 1in (2.5cm) deep across two supports 5ft (1.5m) by 6in (15cm) deep. Space them out so that there is about a 1in (2.5cm) space in between each of the planks.

A curtained bed can be improvised with a standard divan (Hollywood bed). When you have decided where it is to go, screw curtain track to the ceiling about 2in (5cm) outside the perimeter of the bed, curving the track at the corners. Hang eight floor-to-ceiling curtains, two along each side, and tie them back with bows at the corners.

Sofa beds are invaluable if you are short of space. It is well worth while buying a good-quality sofa bed on which some bedding can be left when it is closed for day-time use. Choose one with a proper sprung mattress if it is going to be used regularly and store duvet or quilt and pillows in a chest. The room can then double as a sitting room during the day.

If you are a romantic at heart, pastel colours, traditional lace, a wrought iron bed and cane furniture will probably be your choice. Character is added to this room by the trompe l'oeil *ribbons that 'hold' the pictures in place. The ribbon motif is repeated on the sheer curtain and on the attractive and richly embroidered lace bed cover.*

Futons mean that rooms can do double duty; they roll up in the daytime to create informal seating. Black lacquer, low-level tables and Japanese screens create an atmosphere of sparse Oriental elegance.

Storage

Built-in storage will appear to take up the least space in a small room. Use the whole length of one wall and fit a mixture of shelves and rails along its length. Sliding cupboard (closet) doors are particularly good in a small room and you can paper or paint these to match the scheme. Alternatively, use a series of narrow panelled doors with mirror panels glued and screwed to them. (Check hinges can take extra weight.)

If the room has a chimney breast with alcoves to either side, build two cupboards, one in each alcove, deep enough to take clothes hanging sideways. Then place the bed in the new 'alcove' produced by the extended cupboards. You can add high shelves or cupboards across the top of the chimney breast to provide extra storage.

Small bedside tables – or shelves on the wall if there is no room for tables – will provide space for clock, radio, books and other objects.

Flooring

Most people will go for the comfort of carpet in a bedroom, and here you can use less hardwearing, longer-pile carpet (see pages 103-4). Alternatively, strip the boards and use rugs.

Lighting

A bedroom is the room you relax in, so you'll need overall soft background lighting, which can be supplied by wall lights or by strategically positioned lamps with shades. Good reading light to either side of the bed can be provided by independently switched wall spots (see pages 25-6).

If you have a dressing-table area here, rather than in the bathroom, you will need a good light for this also. Plug-in strip lights fixed to either side of the mirror give the best light for making up or you can use small round bulbs placed on battens all around the mirror.

Extras

If you are troubled by noise from outside the house it may be worth while installing special wide double glazing. To deaden noise, panes of glass should be at least 4in (10cm) apart.

Putting a television or radio in the bedroom will increase the amount of use you get from the room. Decoration can be added by an assortment of coordinating cushions and this is the perfect place to display your most treasured personal possessions and pictures. In this of all rooms, you should suit yourself!

CHILDREN'S ROOMS

It is a shame to impose your own taste on your child's room – far better to provide a colourful plain, tough background so his or her own personality and changing preferences can create the style. Many children will have strong ideas about the decoration they want but as they develop different requirements, likes and dislikes will probably change faster than your wish (or ability) to redecorate.

Plain, brightly coloured walls which can be used as a background for alphabet friezes, animal cut-outs, posters and sports programmes in sequence therefore provide a practical option. Stick up posters and pictures with one of the flexible adhesive 'clays' which can be gently rolled off the wall when it's time for a change. Alternatively, make a large pinboard area from thick wall cork and use colourful drawing pins (thumbtacks) to hold items in place. The cork will also provide some insulation, helping to keep heat and sound in, to the benefit of all concerned!

Style and colour

Small children almost universally prefer primary and secondary colours and research has shown that these, especially red and yellow, stimulate them. Silk-finish emulsion (semi-gloss latex), tough and easy to wipe down, is practical.

A sheet of hardboard painted with three coats of special blackboard paint makes a wonderful problem-free chalking area.

Furniture

This also needs to be practical and adaptable so that it sees a child through more than one stage of development. Secondhand chests and cupboards painted with lead-free paint supply cheap, accessible storage. An old kitchen cupboard with a shelf taken out and replaced by a rail will provide child-size hanging storage. Place this cupboard and a chest of drawers against one wall, then run a table top between them, fixing it firmly in place, to act as a surface for dressing your baby, changing nappies (diapers) and so on, then adapt it as the child grows to make a desk for painting, jigsaws, model-making and, eventually, study.

Colourful and hardwearing metal shelving placed against the whole length of one wall can house brightly coloured plastic boxes, perhaps in different colours, containing different types of toys or clothes. Later the shelves will provide valuable storage for books, records, tapes, stereo and hobby equipment. Make sure the shelving is screwed securely to the wall.

A bed needs to be strong to withstand the leaping and bouncing it will probably suffer. Metal or wood bunk beds are obvious space-savers for two children sharing a room but make sure that the safety rail on the top bunk is positioned so that a child cannot get stuck while trying to slide underneath it – fatal accidents have occurred this way. Or choose a bed with a second foldaway bed that slides underneath for a single child who enjoys having friends to stay. Platform beds or beds on frames built over storage also leave floor space free, vital for play.

Blinds (shades), which roll or pleat up, are the most practical window covering. Pivoting or casement windows should be temporarily covered with vertical bars if you have an athletic child. (Avoid horizontal bars, which just provide a dangerous climbing frame.)

Finally, a few floor cushions will be perfectly adequate for lolling and reading, together with an upright chair for working at the desk top.

Children like rooms that are colourful and fun with plenty of play space and easy-to-reach storage. Here a wide shelf provides a surface for drawing and painting; as the child grows this can become a desk for study.

In this cheerful bedroom a bookcase provides a simple but effective room divider between a child's bed and desk areas and allows items to be removed easily from whichever side they are needed. Thoughtful lighting has been provided in both study and sleeping areas.

Flooring

The floor is the best play area, so leave as much of it as possible free of furniture. Cushioned vinyl or cork will provide the best surface for model cars, building blocks and balancing games, and will also be hardwearing, relatively comfortable and easy to clean. Add a rug by the bed if the surface seems too cold and clinical, but fit non-slip backing to the rug and do not polish the floor.

If you prefer to fit carpet you will find a flecked pattern will not show up threads, fluff or stains as much as either a dark or a light colour. Buy a carpet of medium to heavyweight quality with a short-cut or looped pile. A tough, rough cord or hardwearing jute is not a good choice, as it will be too hard on the knees.

Lighting

For small children, light switches need to be within reach, while light fittings should be inaccessible to adventurous explorers. Fit safety shields to electrical points (sockets) to keep out prying fingers. A low-level nightlight by the bed or a dimmer switch for controlling bedside lighting will make a child who is frightened of the dark feel much safer at night.

Good working light will be needed above a work surface, for reading, writing and playing. This can be provided by clip-on shelf spots, or a well-positioned ceiling track system.

Extras

Some extra fun storage containers may encourage tidying-up. Furry animal wastepaper bins are popular, as are pocketed holders in large animal shapes to hold soft toys. Paint simple silhouette shapes on containers to remind the owner what goes – or should go! – in each one.

Paint a tree shape on the back of the bedroom door and add branches and flowers or fruit at child height each measuring day, plus date and measurement.

The owner of the room will soon imprint his or her character on it with drawings, paintings and other home-made objects; no further effort is needed on your part.

TEENAGERS' ROOMS

A teenager will be happiest in a room that mirrors his or her interests – that is a lively background for studying, pursuing hobbies, listening to music and entertaining friends.

Allowing a teenager to help design and decorate his or her own room will have the advantage for parents that room and contents are much more likely to be well cared for, so don't force your tastes too much. There are a number of unusual ways to decorate a room that are fun to do, and inexpensive; all provide a strong, individual effect which may well appeal to all of you.

It is worthwhile bearing sound insulation in mind: fitted carpet, cork noticeboards and well-positioned loudspeakers can all help.

Night-time sky

Paint the ceiling dark blue. Cut different-sized star shapes and a moon from cardboard. Then, using silver spray paint and the cut-outs as stencils, spray a moon and stars on the ceiling.

Spattered walls

Clear the room before you start and paint the walls in a light base colour. When dry, mask off all surfaces where the spattering isn't wanted. Three colours give the best result: one dark, one bright and white for contrast. Start with the dark colour and mix with water until the paint has the consistency of thick cream. Stand about 5ft (150cm) away from the wall and swing your arm in circular movements, flicking the paint as you do so. If you make any mistakes simply paint them out with the base colour. Use slightly less of your second colour and just enough to highlight in white or a pale colour. Allow the paint to dry out thoroughly between coats.

Silhouette

Add a silhouette to one wall – the teenager, the whole family, pets or friends. The person strikes a pose while someone else holds a light to throw a shadow. A third person draws around the shadow on the wall. Fill in with flat black paint or with clothes and features.

When planning a teenager's room, it is vital to consult the room's occupant! Their emerging personality needs to be reflected in the final result. In this efficient, high-tech bedroom provision has been made for study, sleep and relaxation.

Above: With careful planning a spare bedroom can provide a work or leisure area and also accommodate a visitor when necessary. In this sewing room a convertible chair could open up into a single bed; hanging space is provided by the cupboard on the right; and the desk can easily become a dressing table.

AN EXTRA ROOM

If you are lucky enough to have a spare room, don't just keep this for an occasional guest but put it to daily use too. Extra space is far too valuable to be used only from time to time. This room could double up as a study or office, a place for the computer, a hobby or sewing room, a music room, dining room, children's playroom, or a quiet reading room.

Making sure that the room works satisfactorily in both its guises needs some planning. Make two lists of all the items that will be required for each role, listing them as if you were planning two separate rooms. Then look at the two lists together. The items that overlap – flooring, decoration and so on – will have to be chosen so that they suit either use. Some items of furniture will probably be able to vary in function. For instance, a study, office or computer room will need a desk, storage space for files, books, papers, cassettes or disks. This desk top, with the addition of a mirror on a stand, can become a dressing table when the room becomes a guest room. Lighting for both roles will be similar.

A guest will also require space to hang clothes. This could be allowed for in a storage system, or you could use a temporary fitting, such as a specially designed bracket that fits over the top of the door allowing space for six coathangers and garments to be hung from it. A bedside table for clock, light and books is important – you could make do with a simple fold-up garden table.

If there is room, a divan (Hollywood) bed can double up as a sofa with lots of cushions on it. If space is at a premium use a metal fold-up bed and hide it away behind a curtain or in a cupboard when not in use. A more comfortable alternative is a bed that pivots up against the wall and can be put away with all the bedding strapped in place on it. This could be built into a cupboard that has shelving for office use at the other end. A sliding door would hide the bed when the room is used as an office and slide back, hiding the office storage, when it becomes a bedroom.

If you want a large desk, make it from a strong flush door placed on top of low cupboards or two two-drawer filing cabinets. Simply add a mattress on top of this to turn it into a spare bed, making absolutely certain that it is firmly anchored in place first, of course – unless you are trying to persuade unwanted guests to leave!

Right: A sofa bed allows a spare room to double as a guest bedroom and a quiet retreat. A trolley (tea cart) can become a bedside table when the sofa is opened up. The floor lamp provides good bedside or reading light, whichever is needed.

PART TWO

PRACTICAL KNOW-HOW

Now that all the preliminary planning is done, it's time to put the theory into practice. This part of the book shows you how to proceed. Chapter 3 explains how to use paint creatively, not only emulsions (latex paints) and glosses on walls, ceiling and woodwork, but special finishes and textures too. Or if you opt for a different treatment – wallpaper, fabric, vinyl or tiles – Chapter 4 explains the techniques. Our flooring chapter shows you how to make the most of your existing surface and how to lay a new covering – wooden boards, sheet vinyl, carpet or tiles. And finally, Chapter 6 shows you how to complete your decorating, with tips on choosing the right curtains, draperies and blinds, putting up shelving and making door alterations.

CHAPTER 3

Painting

Paint is one of the most versatile and useful materials available to the home decorator. Not only is it available in an ever-increasing range of shades and finishes, it is relatively inexpensive and is guaranteed to work an instant transformation in any room. The mixing systems now offered by many do-it-yourself outlets mean that you can match your paint exactly to the colour of the wallpaper, floor covering, soft furnishings and furniture, although you'll have to pay a little more for the privilege.

And if plain painted walls, ceilings and woodwork are not for you, textured paints, wall coverings intended for painting over and the special decorative techniques that are currently so popular all mean added interest for painted surfaces. Given the right equipment and a little basic know-how, anyone can achieve a really interesting and professional result.

PREPARING WALLS AND CEILINGS

Pattern, plain or texture; paper, paint or tiles; mirror, fabric or cork; today the choice of how to decorate your home is immense. Whatever you choose you will almost certainly need to put in some time preparing the surface before you even start to apply the new finish – cleaning or possibly removing the existing treatment, for example. It is very tempting to cut corners on preparation and go for a quick result but in the long run it is simply not worth it. Lack of proper preparation will show in the finished product, which means time and money wasted and the irritation of being faced daily by your mistakes! Wallpapers, tiles and other coverings will generally conceal more evils than paint does but, whatever decoration you're planning, all surfaces need to be clean, dry and smooth.

Make sure that you have plenty of liquids to drink and don't try to do too much at once – decorating can be exhausting and if you work when you're tired, it always shows in the final result.

CLEAR THE ROOM FIRST

It is much easier to work in an empty room, so begin by clearing out as much furniture as you can. Take down pictures, lampshades and wall fittings such as shelves. Roll up and remove floor coverings wherever possible. If not, cover carefully with plastic sheeting or old bed sheets, secured to the skirting (baseboard) in places with masking tape to stop them moving about.

Move any big items left into the middle of the room and cover these also with dust sheets for protection.

PREPARATION OF SURFACES

Your preparatory work will vary depending on how the wall or ceiling is decorated at present, what condition it is in and how you want to decorate it yourself.

Emulsion (latex) and gloss paint

First vacuum down the area, particularly the junction between walls and ceiling. Then wash down all the surfaces with a sponge squeezed out in a solution of washing-up (dishwashing) liquid and warm water. If the surface is greasy or exceptionally dirty use sugar soap (de-greaser) instead (**A**), using this according to the manufacturer's instructions. Sugar soap is a mild abrasive which is available in Britain from most ironmongers and decorating shops.

If you are redecorating the ceiling only be careful not to use the sponge too wet or you will splash dirty water all over the walls.

If gloss paint has been used, lightly sand the surface after washing down; this will provide a key for the new finish to adhere to (**B**). Cover nicotine stains on walls or ceilings with a coat of aluminium sealer (**C**).

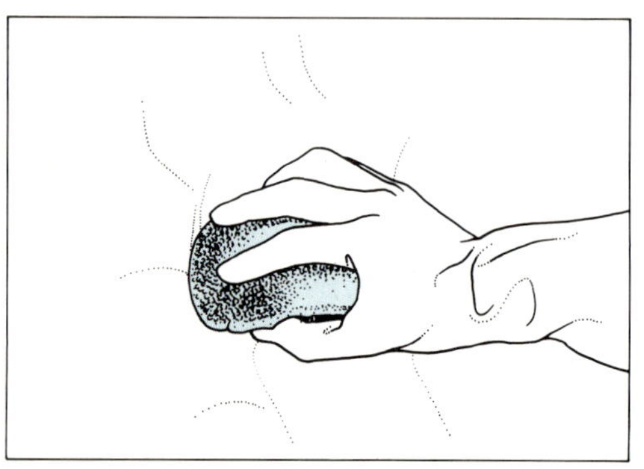

A

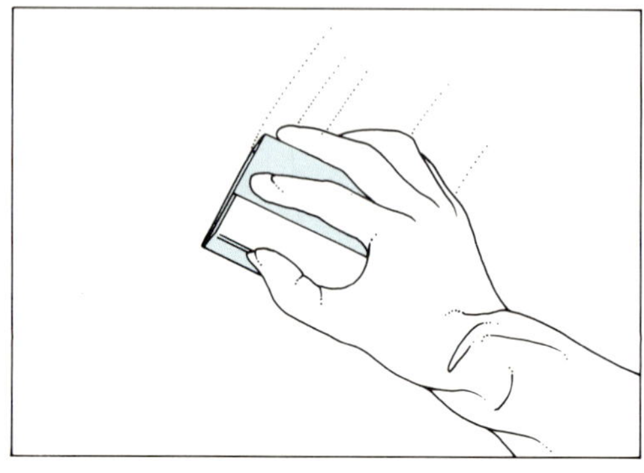

B

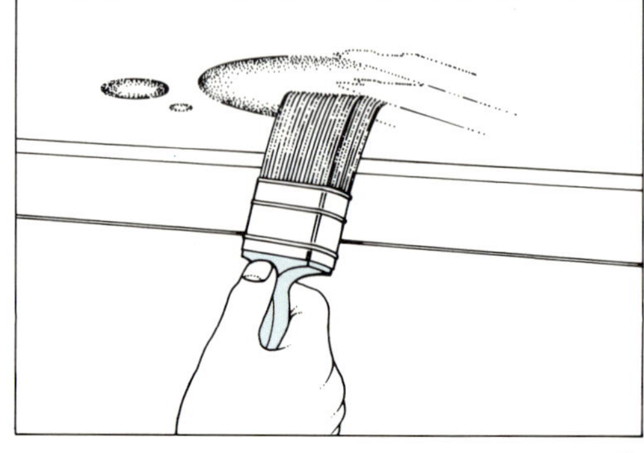

C

Textured paint

If the surface is rough because textured paint has been used (not painted woodchip paper, which also gives a rough finish) treat it as for emulsion (latex) paint if you simply wish to repaint. If you want to paper this area then you will need to remove the rough surface first. This is a laborious job and, be warned, a texture may well have been used in the first place because the plaster underneath was not in good condition – you may be letting yourself in for trouble.

To remove the surface you can buy a chemical stripper specially designed for the job. These strippers are toxic and must be handled with great care: always wear protective gloves and clothing. Protect your eyes with glasses or goggles and work in a well-ventilated room. Apply the stripper with a brush (**A**), leave for the stipulated time and when the paint begins to soften strip it off with a wide scraper, being careful not to damage the wall or ceiling underneath (**B**). Work on a small area at a time. When the finish is removed wash down the surface with cold water and leave to dry. The strippings are highly combustible so collect them together in a bag, store outside and give to the rubbish collectors.

A

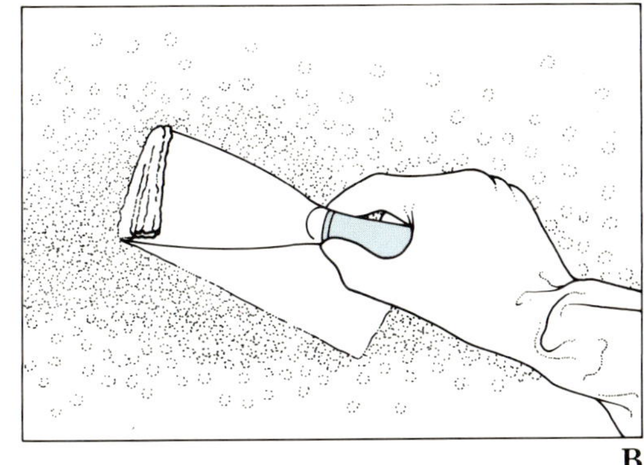

B

Wallpaper

If wallpaper is in good condition and stuck firmly to the wall you can paint over it – just vacuum well first; otherwise it should be stripped off. A lightweight, recently hung wallpaper should strip easily. First try pulling it away from the wall by finding a seam edge, pushing a scraper under it and pulling gently but firmly. If this is not successful then use a sponge or large brush and thoroughly soak the surface with warm water. Allow plenty of time for the water to soak through to the paste before you start stripping – about half an hour is probably long enough. The paper should then lift away easily in wide strips. Score any small areas left with a wire brush or serrated scraper, soak again and scrape off (**A**). Finally wash the walls down.

Vinyl, water-resistant and glazed papers, and some coverings such as hessian often have a paper backing designed to stay in place when the top layer is stripped off. Pull the top layer outwards to prevent the backing from ripping. If the backing is in good condition you can use it as a lining, but make sure that the seams of old and new coverings don't fall on top of each other.

Stubborn papers

Some older papers and any paper that has been painted over already will probably not respond to this treatment. In this case treat the surface with a proprietary wallpaper stripper (following the manufacturer's instructions). Alternatively – or if the proprietary stripper does not do the trick – hire a steam stripper from a reliable local hire company. (A steam stripper is not suitable for use on ceilings.)

A

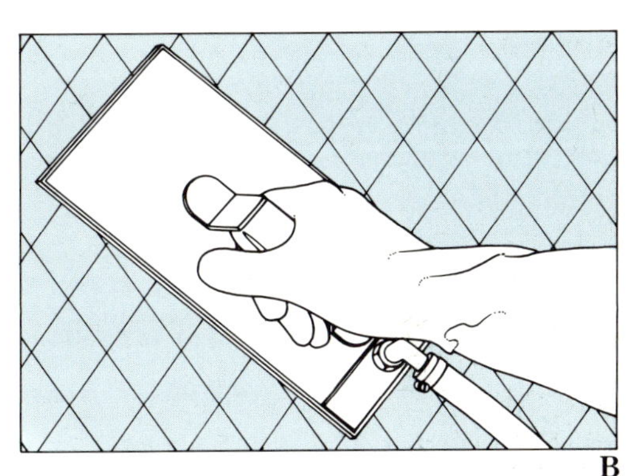

B

Using a steam stripper

Follow the instructions supplied with the stripper carefully: usually you have to allow time for the steam to build up, then you hold the pad to the wall for between 15 seconds and 1 minute (**B**) before using a scraper to remove the damp paper. Do not hold the pad in one position for longer than this as you could damage the plaster underneath. Place the stripper on its side on a protective sheet when you put it down and keep an eye on the water level so that you don't omit to refill it when necessary.

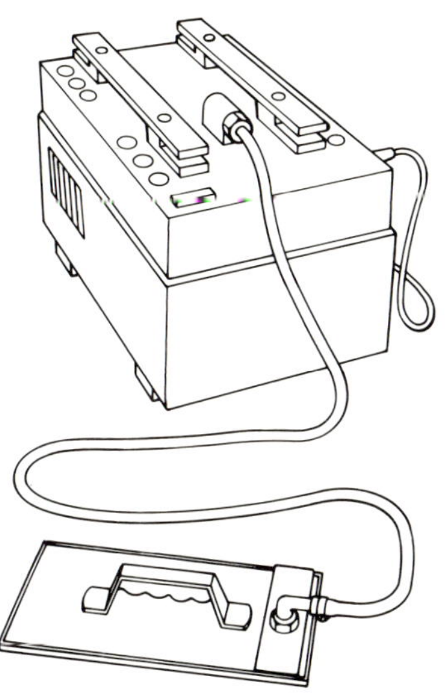

Vinyl

Vinyl should strip easily; some types leave a lining paper behind on the wall. Locate a seam edge, at the top of a wall, and ease this away, then pull the whole length downwards (**A**). If the lining left behind is in good condition it can be used as a base for new wallpaper but make sure that the seams of the new paper do not lie directly over those of the lining. Before repapering, vacuum the lining paper, stick down any loose seams with a latex adhesive and lightly sand any nicks in the surface.

If you intend to paint the wall you should remove the lining just as you would ordinary wallpaper (see page 55).

New or porous walls

New plaster should be sealed with a coat of thinned emulsion (latex) paint, or with an alkaline-resistant primer, and then painted with emulsion (latex). It is better not to wallpaper or use vinyl or gloss paint on a newly plastered wall or ceiling until the plaster has completely dried out – this will usually take around six months.

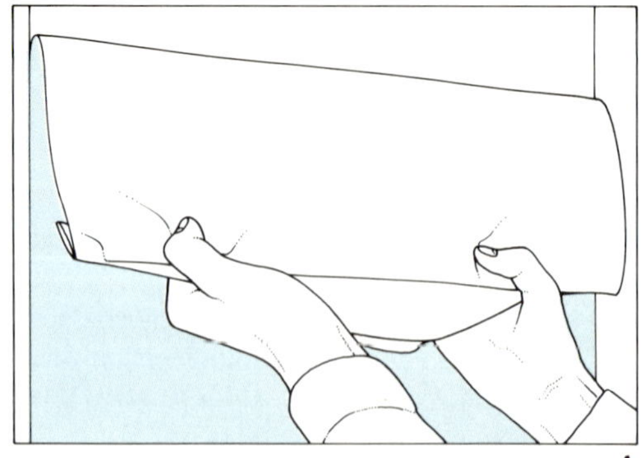

A

MAKING GOOD

Now that you've stripped off the old wall or ceiling covering, step back and consider if remedial work may be required.

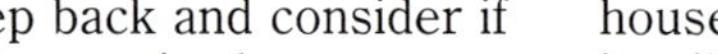

Cracks and holes

Fill all small cracks and holes: it is well worth the time it takes. Clean out the crevices with a knife (**A**), then a wire brush, and fill with a fine interior filler. Fill slightly proud of the surrounding surface and sand back when dry (**B**) – filler tends to shrink as it dries.

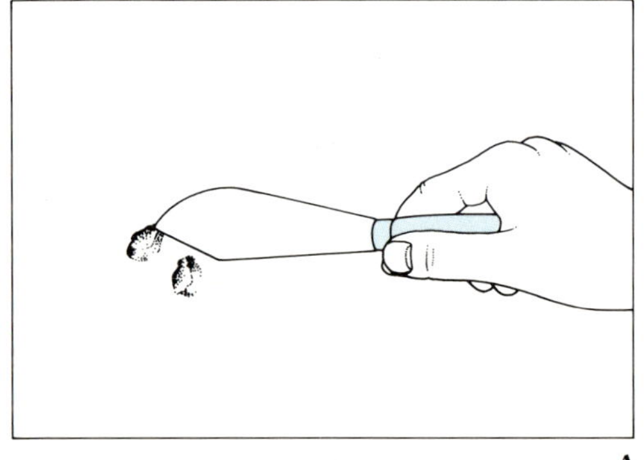

A

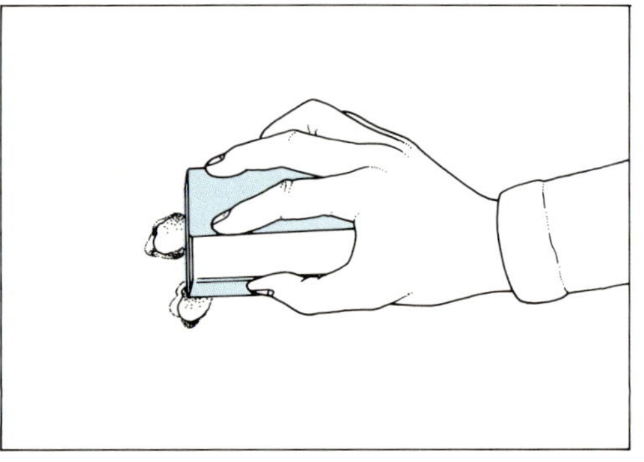

B

Crumbling plaster

This is unfortunately often found in old houses and is usually due to damp. If the area is still damp, deal with this problem first, or your new finish will soon become stained and damaged as well as crumbling. A damp-proof sealer will only mask the damp temporarily.

When the source of the damp has been found and treated let the plaster dry out completely, then remove any loose plaster with a wire brush (**A**) and fill in the same way as for cracks (see left).

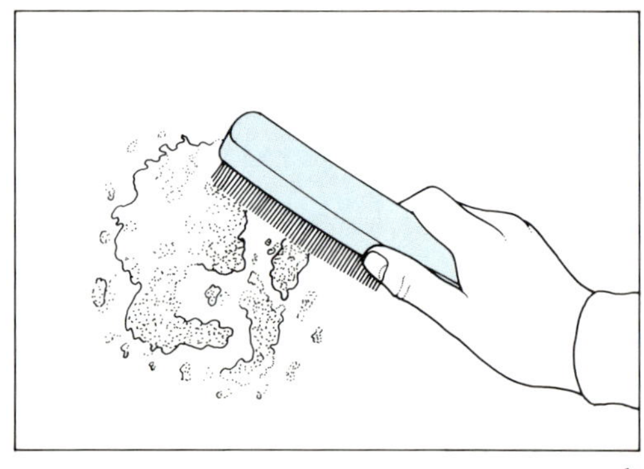

A

Mould

Patches of black spotting on the surface are usually mould caused by damp or condensation. Mould can be killed off with a proprietary mould remover or you can use 1 part household bleach to 16 parts water. Brush this well over the area (**A**) and leave for about four hours, then wash off the mould with a solution of washing-up (dishwashing) liquid and warm water (**B**). Rinse down and then apply a second coating of bleach solution and leave to dry for three days. If you think the mould was caused by condensation use a fungicidal treatment on the surface before applying the new finish. Special fungicidal paint is also available. In any case, you would be well advised to sort out what caused the mould in the first place.

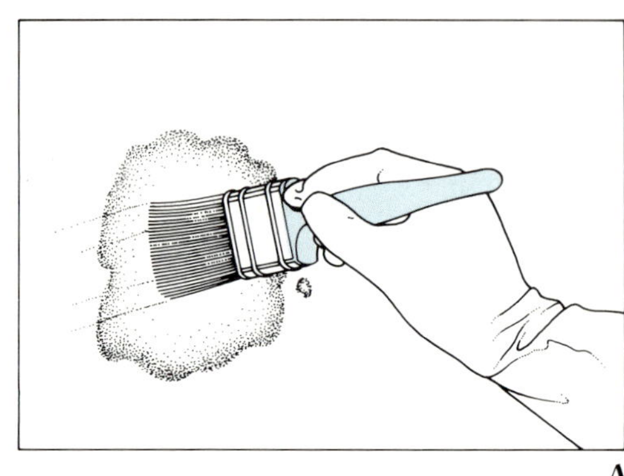

A

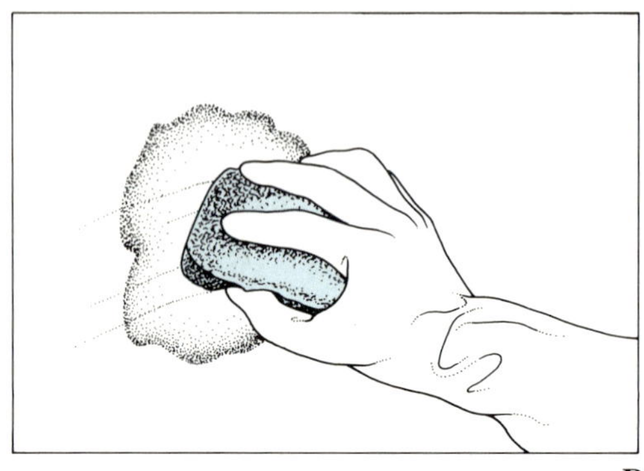

B

LADDERS AND WORK STATIONS

Whichever room you are decorating, it is essential to set up a safe work station. Halls and stairways present a particular set of problems and tips for working in these areas are covered on page 81.

There is a wide variety of convertible step ladders on the market, all designed to make decorating a much safer proposition. Some are even available which will stand on two levels at once – look for ones with suction pads on their feet for extra security. When using a ladder, never climb up too high or lean over too far.

If you are decorating walls or ceilings set up a platform with two stepladders, or one ladder and a stout trestle or tea chest, along with a strong plank. If spanning more than 5 ft (1.5 m) use a tea chest for extra support. Check the platform for stability each time you move it.

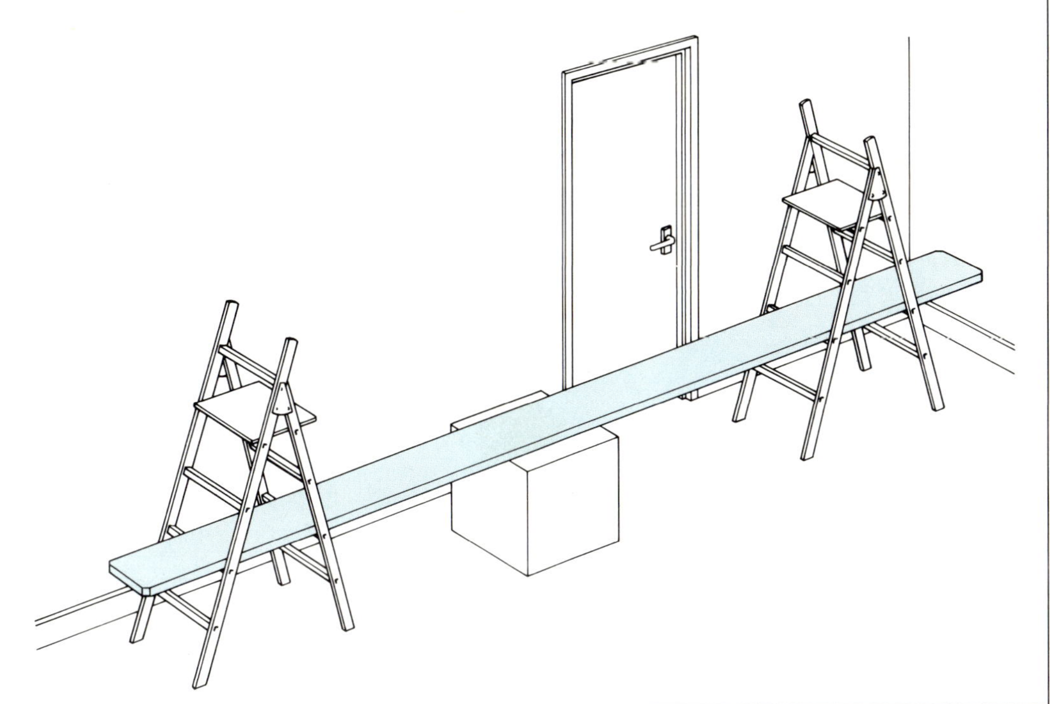

Distemper

Distemper is practically never used now but you may come across it in an old house. If you paint on top of the distemper the surface will simply flake away so it is important to recognize it and deal with it appropriately. Place a length of sticky (Scotch) tape on a surface you suspect may be distempered, press down well, then pull away: if the 'paint' has come away with the tape it probably is distemper. In this case wash the surface well several times until the water you are using no longer clouds. Then paint the surface with a stabilizing primer to seal in any remaining distemper and leave it to dry.

Old mouldings were often decorated with distemper, over the years building up a surface that eventually hid most of the design. These mouldings take time to clean but if you have the patience the end result is well worth it. Spray the distemper with water and leave it for about half an hour, then loosen the distemper by gently pushing an old screwdriver into it (**A**). The distemper falls away in lumps. Wash down, allow to dry and repaint.

A

FINAL PREPARATION

For ease when painting or papering, unscrew and loosen light fittings, switches and electrical points (**A**). (Do not remove them completely and make sure you turn the electricity off first.) You can then work far more quickly around them, pulling them slightly away from the wall as you work. Never tuck a foil wallcovering under fittings in this way but trim it around them – foil conducts electricity.

Finally, remove bulbs and cover fittings with a plastic bag secured with tape (**B**).

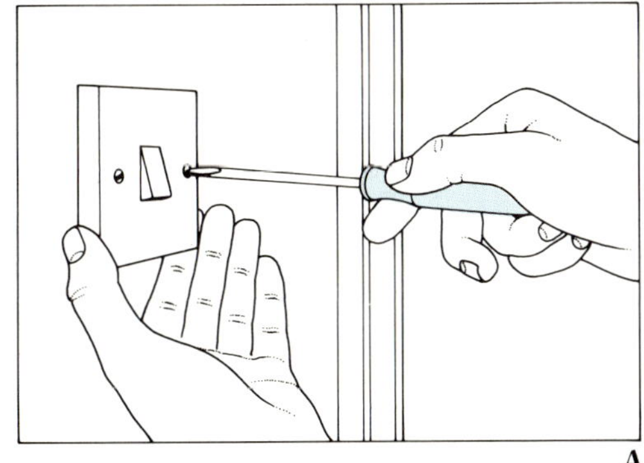

A

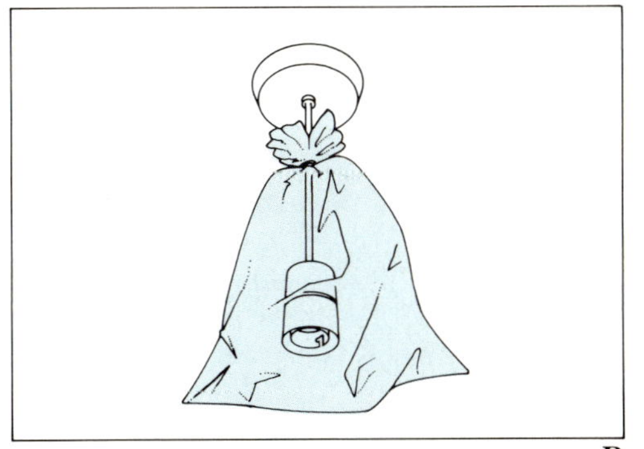

B

PAINTING WALLS AND CEILINGS

Paint is the cheapest, simplest and quickest way to decorate walls and ceilings. A wide range of colours is available, not only ordinary paint in a variety of finishes but also textured paints which can be finished in a number of decorative patterns. You can also create designs on ordinary paint quite simply by using second and third colours on top of the base coat, applied with a sponge, a rag, or even a plastic bag (see pages 69-71)! Or for a finishing touch you can paint stripes or other patterns on a plain painted wall to form a border (see page 91).

Emulsion (latex) and textured paints are dealt with here. See also pages 63-4.

EMULSION (LATEX) PAINT

The types of paint available in Britain and the United States differ somewhat in their composition and terminology, but in both countries there are two main types: oil-based and water-based. Oil-based paints are dealt with on pages 63-4. The commonest type of water-based paint in Britain is emulsion; it comes in both matt and silk finishes – the latter, called vinyl silk, having a slight sheen. The American equivalent of emulsion, latex, also comes in a range of finishes, including a glossy enamel, suitable for woodwork.

These water-based paints are easy to apply, hardwearing and wipe clean with soap and warm water. They dry very quickly, allowing you to apply two or even three coats in a day, if necessary, and are suitable for all rooms.

A matt emulsion (latex) is best for walls that are uneven, as a silk (semigloss) finish will show up imperfections; but silk finish has the advantage of being easier to clean and of resisting condensation better, which makes it more suitable for kitchens and bathrooms where this is a problem.

The choice of emulsion colours is almost endless. If you cannot find the colour you want on the standard charts then a tinting system giving around 500 shades should be able to provide it. Paints tinted on the spot by the shop allow you to match matt and gloss paints if you want to and to use different tones of a colour for a particular effect. For instance a lighter tone of the wall colour used on the ceiling will make a low ceiling appear higher, and a darker tone will make a high ceiling seem lower. If you have a paint mixed by this system buy the quantity you need all at one time as a second batch may not exactly match.

You can now buy extra-thick or 'solid' emulsion (thixotropic latex) in both matt and silk finishes. It comes in its own tray ready for use with a roller or brush. As it is less likely to drip or splash this sort of paint is particularly good for covering ceilings. It comes mainly in white but some pale colours are also available.

Vacuum emulsion paint using the dusting tool and wipe off marks with a soapy cloth.

TEXTURED PAINT

This is particularly useful for covering a less than perfect ceiling as the rough texture will conceal small cracks and blemishes. Do not expect it to turn a badly deteriorated old ceiling into a new one, however; serious faults, such as plaster coming away in chunks, must be remedied before decorating.

The finer-textured coatings available ready to use in tubs will disguise fine cracks and imperfections. In Britain a powder form is available; this can be mixed more thickly for areas with more obvious cracks, hollows and blemishes. Some are rougher than others; choose a finer finish for walls so that people don't scratch themselves. Before you set to work, remember that, although textured paint can be removed, it is a time-consuming task made even more laborious if you have also painted on top of it.

Textured paints are available in white and in a limited range of pale colours.

Clean textured paint surfaces with the small dusting brush attachment on the vacuum cleaner.

SPECIAL PAINTING EQUIPMENT

• Brushes

What brushes you buy should depend on how willing you are to clean and look after them. Expensive brushes, which are thicker, less likely to lose bristles and should retain their elasticity and shape, need cleaning thoroughly. You can now buy fairly cheap brushes which are designed to be thrown away after the job is finished.

When buying brushes check that they are comfortable to hold, that there are no loose bristles and that there is no gap at the base of the bristles. Gaps can cause a sudden flooding of paint and, consequently, runs. If you intend to use the paintbrush for walls or ceilings you will need one about 4 in (10 cm) wide. For woodwork you will probably need three, one about 3 in (7.5 cm), one about 1 in (2.5 cm) and a narrow ½ in (13 mm) size – make this an angled sash brush which will be useful for the accurate painting of narrow window beadings.

• Rollers

You will need a short pile roller for smooth surfaces and a longer pile for rougher surfaces. Make sure the roller comes off the handle easily for cleaning and that it has a plastic base which will not soften even after repeated washings. For painting ceilings it is useful to buy a roller that can take an extension handle. You can also buy small, long-handled rollers for painting behind radiators – and a clean one of these can be extremely useful for wallpapering behind a radiator too (see page 80).

• Paint tray

Pick a tray to suit the size of your roller; you will need a wide roller and tray for painting walls or ceilings. The tray should have a rough grid on the slope to remove excess paint from the roller before you use it.

• Painting pads
These are easy to work with, cover large areas quickly and use less paint than a roller. They come in a number of sizes up to about 6 by 4 in (15 × 10 cm) and the smaller sizes are particularly good for working accurately along skirting (baseboard) edges and around fittings. This is called 'cutting in' and is a useful technique for when you are using a roller to paint a large surface area.

Do not overload pads with paint when using them or you may damage the backing. Small pads can be dipped straight into the tin of paint; use a paint tray for a larger pad.

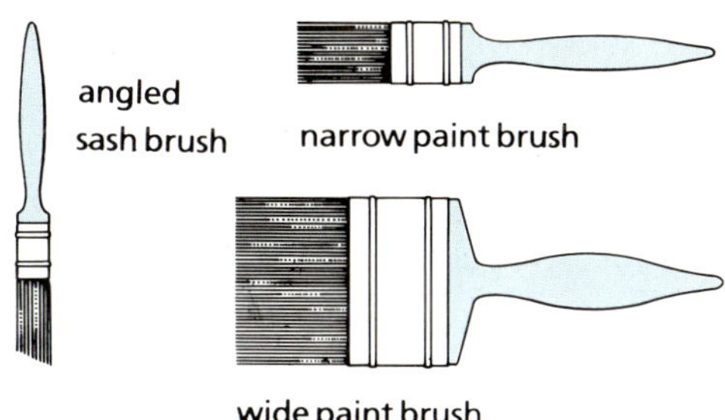

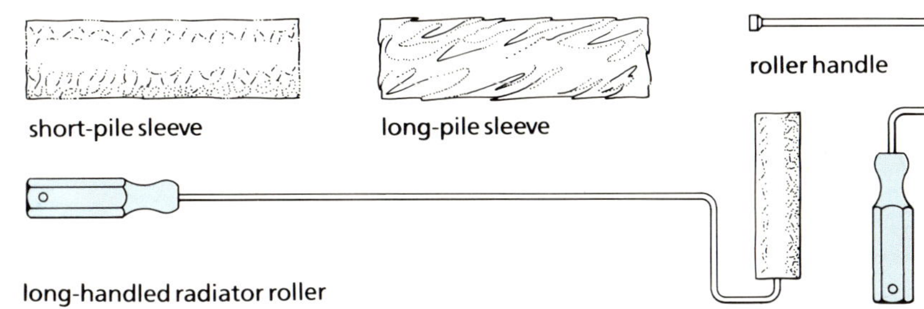

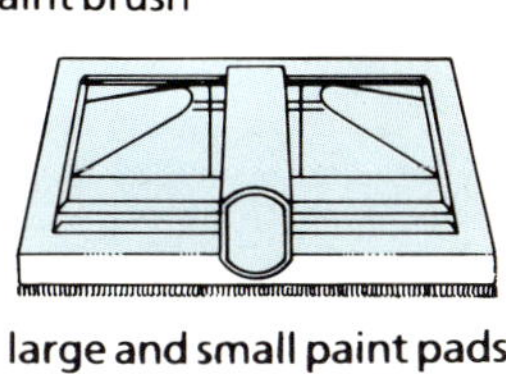

large and small paint pads

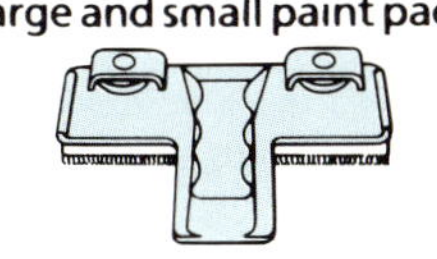

USING EMULSION (LATEX) PAINT

When possible choose a warm, dry day as the paint will dry more quickly and open windows to allow paint smells to disperse; work in a well-ventilated room whatever the weather. Prepare carefully the surface you want to paint following the instructions on pages 54-7.

WHERE TO START
If you are painting the whole room start with the ceiling. Whether painting ceiling or walls, start from the window and work away from the light source. If there is more than one window start from the best-lit area. Allow enough time to complete a wall or the ceiling in one go; if you stop half-way you will leave a tidemark. Start walls from the top.

You will need:
Emulsion (latex) paint
Roller and tray
Small 1 in (2.5 cm) brush or pad
Clean cloth for wiping away smudges or splashes
Two stepladders and one plank, or one stepladder, a plank and a strong box if painting a wall (see page 57).

CALCULATING QUANTITIES

In the UK paint is sold in litres, so it is easier to take all your measurements in metric units to avoid conversions. In America paint is sold in US gallons. The quantity you will need can vary greatly from one brand to another. Cheaper paint is often thinner, covering a large area but needing more coats to obtain a good result. A roller uses more paint than a brush and some paint colours cover better than others. In general, two coats of emulsion (latex) should be adequate. Approximate coverage rates are given in the chart below.

Average spread rates
UK (per litre)

Matt emulsion	12 sq m
Vinyl silk emulsion	15 sq m
Solid emulsion	12 sq m
Textured paint	2 sq m

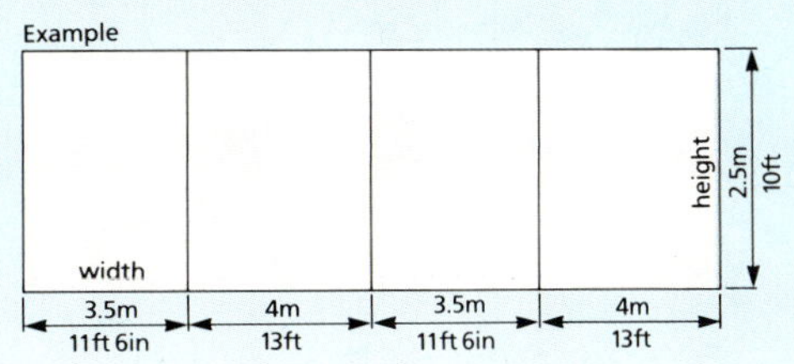

US (per US gallon)

Matte latex	42 sq yd
Semigloss latex	42 sq yd
Thixotropic latex	55 sq yd
Textured paint	9 sq yd

To calculate the amount of paint you require, measure the length of each wall then add these measurements together. Next, measure the height from the skirting (baseboad) to the ceiling, ignoring windows and doors. Multiply length by height to find how many square feet or metres you have to cover. For a ceiling take the measurement in each direction and multiply the two figures to find the total square area you have to cover.

Example
In the room left, two opposite walls measure 11ft 6in (3.5m) each; the other two measure 13ft (4m) each. The total wall length is therefore 49ft (15m). The height of the room is 2.5m (10ft). The two figures multiplied together give a total of 490 sq ft or 54 sq yd (37.5 sq m). For 2 coats of vinyl silk emulsion (semigloss latex) you will need 5 litres or about 1⅓ US gallons.

STARTING WORK

The method given here is for applying emulsion (latex) paint with a roller, which is by far the fastest method. Of course, it is possible to use a brush, if you prefer. Choose a wide brush for speed and apply the paint in broad, horizontal bands. Work downwards and away from the light.

1 First use the brush or pad to paint a border around the ceiling or your first wall (**A**) and around any fittings, lifting the loosened fitting as you work. (Make sure you have turned off the electricity first.)

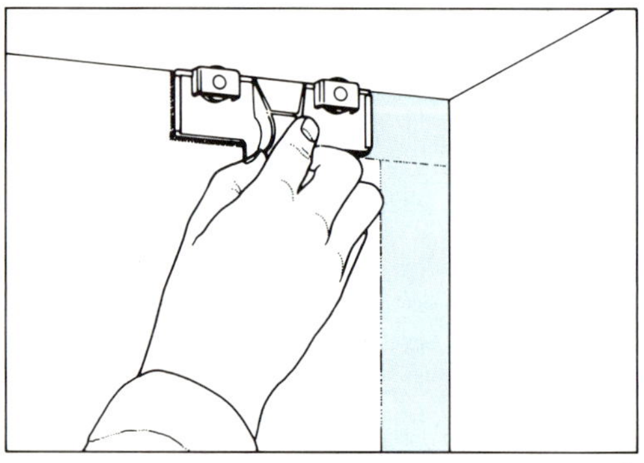

A

B

2 Remove excess paint from the roller by rolling it up the tray slope then paint a strip working in to your border strip (**B**). Take care to apply the paint slowly to avoid spattering. This can also be a problem if you overload the roller or if you jerk it too much.

3 Follow this to-and-fro movement with criss-cross strips to give an even coverage (**C**). Start from the unpainted area and work back into a just-painted one; this will prevent any join marks. When working on the ceiling it is a good idea to cover your head and so avoid painting yourself! Don't forget to protect your clothing, too.

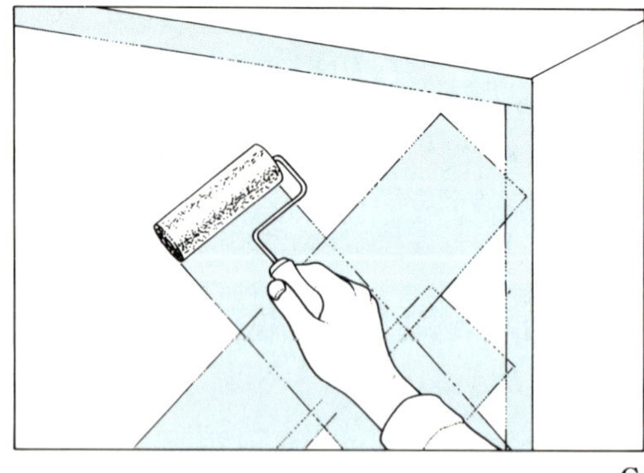

C

4 Continue painting in this way until you have covered the whole area. Leave to dry out thoroughly.

5 Apply a second coat of emulsion (latex) paint following the same procedure.

Alternative
Use a solid emulsion (thixotropic latex) as this will not splash. This type of paint is particularly useful when you are painting ceilings. When painting the border strip around ceilings and fittings just draw your brush or paint pad across the surface of the paint – don't dip it in.

TEXTURED PAINT EFFECTS

Textured paint is applied in much the same way as emulsion and the surface should also be prepared in the same way (see pages 54–7).

If you decide to create a pattern in the texture it is important to have the necessary tool handy as the paint dries within an hour or so and the patterning has to be applied as soon as the paint is in place.

Try out your technique in advance on a piece of hardboard until you are confident of getting the result you want.

DESIGNS FOR A TEXTURED FINISH

Textured paintwork can be given an even more interesting surface by using one of the special tools available to add a pattern. Rollers, brushes, sponges, indeed anything with a texture, can be employed. You could even improvise with any attractively shaped item – a long-toothed hair comb, perhaps – to create an interesting finish.

• Ceilings can take rougher finishes than walls. Don't leave textured paint too bumpy on walls, or people may brush against it and scratch themselves on it.

• A stippling brush with rubber bristles will create a regular stippled effect. Dip it into the coating, press it on, then lift it off the painted area. You can also make deep relief swirls by twisting it. Experiment first to get the best results.

• A paint brush can be used to create the effect of old, uneven plaster if you spread the coating with the flat of the brush in overlapping strokes.

• A special toothed textured tool can be used to form fan shapes, circles or a basket-weave effect. This sort of even repeat pattern is the most difficult to create so practise until you are quite confident before you start on your painted wall or ceiling.

• Use one of the special roller sleeves available to form diamonds, diagonals or a bark effect. These are now available in a wide variety of designs and you are sure to be able to find one to suit both your preference and your decorating scheme.

USING TEXTURED PAINT

CALCULATING QUANTITIES
This will depend on the brand of paint you use and how thickly you put it on, so check when you buy. As a rough guide see the charts on page 59.

You will need:
Textured paint
Roller and tray
Small 1 in (2.5 cm) brush
Cloth for wiping away splashes
Two stepladders and a plank for painting a ceiling, or one stepladder, a plank and a strong box for painting a wall (see page 57)
Plus tool for special effect if wanted

STARTING WORK

Textured paint is at present only available in white and a limited range of pale colours, but you can always go over it once it is dry with ordinary paint in a more interesting shade. The effect created by applying the paint with an ordinary roller is roughly stippled.

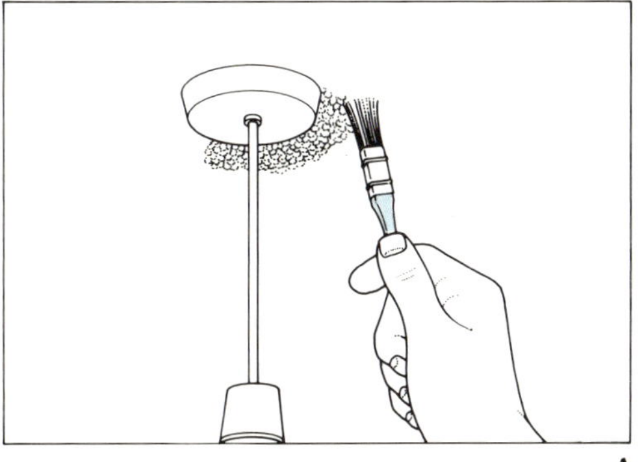

A

1 With the brush, paint the border around your ceiling or wall first, then stipple this paint with the flat of the brush (**A**) to give it a textured finish.

2 Pour paint into the roller tray and load the roller evenly but liberally, then remove excess by rolling it up the slope of the tray before you start painting.

3 Starting at the lightest point in the room, and at the top on a wall, paint a strip with the roller then follow with criss-cross movements as for emulsion (latex) (see page 60). Do not cover more than a square yard (metre) at a time or you will find that the 'seams' are hard to paint over.

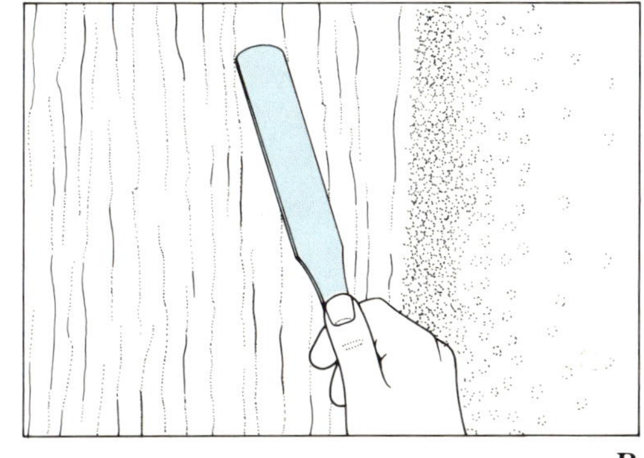

B

4 To create an even finish, lightly roll the roller across the painted surface in one direction. If you want to, finish by forming a design for added interest (**B**). (See above for some suggestions.)

Alternative
Textured paint can also be applied with a brush, in which case you can work straight from the tub or mixing bucket. Coat the brush about half-way up the bristles, but no further or the paint may drip.

PREPARING WOOD SURFACES

If the old paint surface is in good condition it can simply be cleaned with a damp cloth and an ordinary household cream cleaner which acts as a mild abrasive and will provide the key for the new paint.

Where the surface of the paint is loose or chipped you will need to sand it. On a bad surface use coarse, then medium, then fine sandpaper and finish by wiping over with white (mineral) spirit to remove any fine dust before you start painting.

If you are going to replace a dark or bright colour with a light one or if the surface is in very poor condition it is best to strip the paint completely.

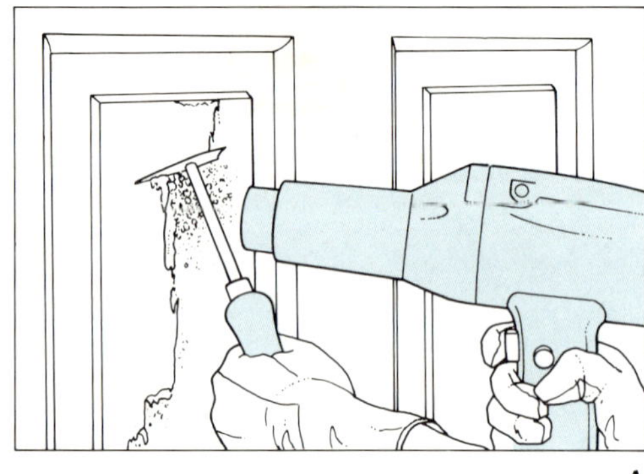
A

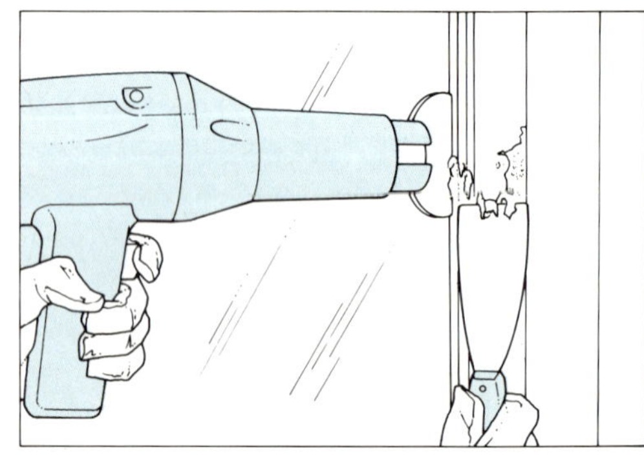
B

STRIPPING PAINTWORK

If you have a blowtorch and are going to repaint then this can be used for stripping the wood, as occasional scorch marks won't show. A hot air stripper (easily hired) is easier to use, however, and much less likely to mark the surface. Wearing thick working gloves for protection, heat the old paint by moving the head of the stripper backwards and forwards across a small area until the paint begins to bubble. Then use a scraper to remove the paint, working in the direction of the grain of the wood (**A**). Remove any paint residue with liquid stripper and finish by wiping over with white (mineral) spirit. A variety of special nozzle attachments is available for working in awkward areas such as window frames (**B**).

STRIPPING FURNITURE

Furniture and doors can be sent away to be stripped by a firm with a caustic soda bath but unfortunately this method has its drawbacks, in that it does tend to dry out and bleach the wood rather drastically.

To strip furniture yourself it is best to use a solvent stripper, with a paste, gel or powder product on mouldings and carvings. Always work in a well-ventilated area (preferably outdoors). Cover your clothes well and wear heavy-duty plastic gloves. Apply the stripper with an old paintbrush and use a thin flat scraper to remove the paint, with wire (steel) wool to get into mouldings and to remove any residue. Always work along the grain of the wood. Finish by cleaning with white (mineral) spirit.

FILLING

Cracks, holes or sunken screw heads should be filled with special wood stopping (sometimes called filler). This allows for some movement: if you use an interior plaster filler it may crack again. Apply the stopping with a knife (**A**) – you may need to apply a second layer in larger holes as the stopping will shrink. Fill proud of the surface and sand back when dry (**B**). It dries quickly.

Stopping is available in a number of wood colours. If you intend to use clear varnish on top make sure you use the correct colour to match your wood.

Use wood filler to fill the grain on open grain wood. This also comes in various wood colours or can be tinted with wood stains (see page 64).

WOODWORM

If you notice any tiny woodworm holes don't ignore them. If the area affected is extensive call in a professional firm. Otherwise, treat by painting the damaged area with a 50/50 solution of paraffin and white (mineral) spirit. Give it several applications. Alternatively, inject and paint with a proprietary product (**A**).

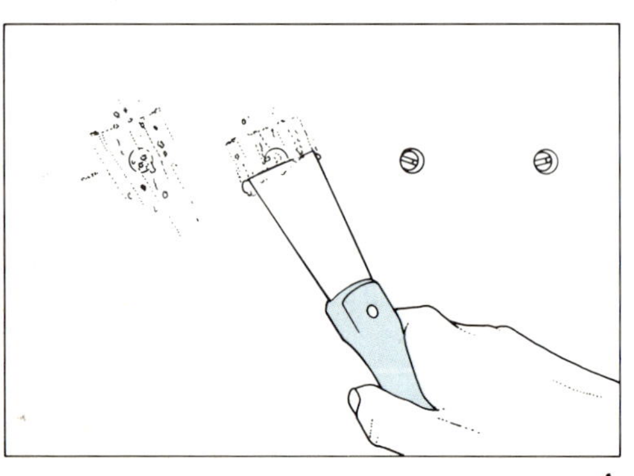
A

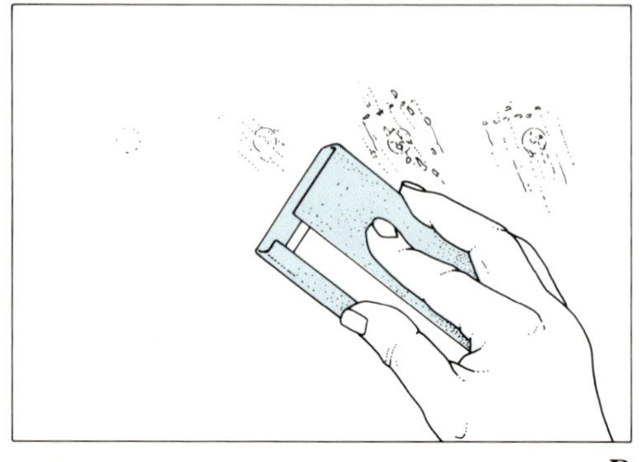
B

A

PAINTS, VARNISHES AND STAINS FOR WOOD

Woodwork finished with gloss paint or varnish not only looks good but is well protected against extremes of temperature, drying out from radiators, damp and condensation.

PRIMER (SEALER)

On bare wood or metal that is to be painted a primer (sealer) must first be used. This is designed to bind firmly to the bare surface, to seal it and to provide a good base for the next coat. Primer (sealer) does not give any protection in itself and should be covered with an undercoat and/or topcoat.

UNDERCOAT (PRIMER)

At least one layer of undercoat (primer in the US) is necessary under a liquid gloss paint. It covers evenly, disguising minor blemishes, and coats well, hiding any colour. It also rubs down well to provide a smooth surface for the less opaque top coat. Undercoat (primer) is not necessary under a non-drip gloss.

OIL-BASED GLOSS PAINT

Although oil-based paints (called alkyds in the US) come in a variety of finishes, the most familiar type is gloss, which is used on woodwork and radiators because it gives a tough, protective finish just where it is needed most. Besides full gloss, there is in Britain a non-drip gloss, which is easier to work with. It comes in a jelly form which is less likely to run or drip; it needs no undercoat and is applied thickly, thus requiring fewer coats.

Full gloss is liquid and because of this provides a smoother finish as it flows and spreads out to form a surface that disguises brush marks and is more hardwearing. Extra shiny gloss paints are available as are satin finishes that provide a sheen rather than a gloss.

LACQUER

This is available in strong colours and with a high gloss finish; it is hardwearing and weather-resistant. It can be used on metal, sanded plastic, glass fibre and glass, as well as on wood. Because the finish is so glossy dust or dirt will instantly show up so brushes need to be kept scrupulously clean. Lacquer is particularly suitable for toys and children's furniture, and is usually lead-free.

Above: Bright gloss paint gives a tough, protective finish and also has a reflective quality which adds interest to plain surfaces, whether they be walls, wood or elegant panelled doors.

*Below: (**a**) undercoat (called primer in the US); (**b**) and (**c**) lacquers; (**d**) non-drip gloss; (**e**) and (**f**) lead-free nursery paints; (**g**) primer (called sealer in the US).*

LEAD-FREE PAINT

It is important to paint children's furniture and toys with lead-free paint in case they suck or chew them. Information on the tin will tell you if the paint is lead-free. On metal toys use a zinc phosphate primer as this is non-toxic.

Furniture which children come into contact with should be painted with a lead-free product.

*(**a**) ebony wood dye; (**b**) mahogany wood dye; (**c**) blueberry clear satin varnish; (**d**) fir green wood stain; (**e**) oak polyurethane gloss; (**f**) pine polyurethane gloss; (**g**) clear satin polyurethane varnish*

AEROSOLS

Spray paints in tins are more expensive to use than other paints but come in very handy for painting wicker or cane which is difficult to cover evenly with a brush.

Aerosols are either oil- or cellulose-based and the right matching undercoat must be used or the paint will wrinkle. Check by trying out in a small hidden place first.

Work outdoors on a warm windless day. Protect surroundings with newspaper and use a number of light coats rather than one thick one that will run. Spray in short sharp bursts from a distance of about 8 in (20 cm).

Spray paints can give a new lease of life to worn cane or wicker articles.

INTERIOR VARNISH

Polyurethane varnish is available in matt, satin and gloss finish. Unlike paint it allows the grain of the wood to be displayed. It provides a tough, clear finish if you want to leave stripped wood its natural colour. Seal the surface of stripped wood with a coat of polyurethane thinned with a little white (mineral) spirit. Brush on two coats of polyurethane, leaving it to dry thoroughly between coats. Before the final coat sand lightly then wipe over with white (mineral) spirit on a cloth to remove any dust.

Polyurethane varnish can be used over stains (dampen the wood to get an idea of what the finished colour coated with polyurethane will be like) or you can apply a varnish stain where the two are incorporated in one product. This needs to be applied very evenly or it will give a blotchy result; successive coats will also add to the strength of the stain colour, so use two coats only and finish with more coats of clear varnish.

STAIN

Wood can be stained to almost any wood tone using one of the wood stains available. These are based on either white (mineral) spirit, methylated spirit (denatured alcohol) or water, so if you are mixing stains to get the exact colour you want be sure to use two of the same type. Stains and bleaches are useful for blending old wood with new.

When using a stain, check the colour first by trying it out on a small offcut or on a hidden part of your piece of furniture. The colour will vary according to the type, age and so on of the wood and will become lighter in tone when dry. The finish you use over the stain will also affect the final colour.

Wood bleach can be used to restore furniture which has darkened with age to its former glory.

WOOD BLEACH

Wood can also be lightened by applying a wood bleach. Don't use household bleach which will damage the wood fibres but buy the proper commercial wood bleach and follow the instructions supplied by the manufacturer.

USING GLOSS PAINT

Doors, windows and skirtings (baseboards) should always be painted and allowed to dry thoroughly before surrounding walls are painted or papered. Choose a dry day with a minimum of wind. Windows will need to be open when you are painting and wind will carry dust; damp weather will slow down the drying time. Tackle the windows first, followed by doors and then skirtings. If you are painting a staircase, treat banisters and hand rail before stairs.

Prepare the surface following the instructions on pages 54-7. Skirtings (baseboards) are likely to suffer from chips more than other areas and may need stripping.

New paintwork can be kept clean with a damp, soapy cloth. Wipe grubby areas with white (mineral) spirit.

CALCULATING QUANTITIES

These are approximate figures, as manufacturers claims vary widely. UK measurements are given in metric only; American measurements are given in US gallons.

Average spread rates

UK (per gallon)

Primer	8 sq m
Undercoat	11 sq m
Liquid gloss	17 sq m
Non-drip gloss	12 sq m

US (per US pint)

Sealer	38 sq yd
Primer	53 sq yd
Liquid semigloss	42 sq yd

To calculate the amount of paint you require, count a standard door, including the frame, as a basic unit of 2½ sq yd (2 sq m).

Windows are calculated in door area, as follows: a small window as 1 door unit, a medium one as 2 door units (4½ sq yd or 4 sq m) and a large one as 3 door units (7 sq yd or 6 sq m).

Skirtings (baseboards) are about 5 in (12.5 cm) deep. In an average room this will give a total area of about one door unit.

Example

In an average room you might have:

1 door	2½ sq yd (2 sq m)
2 windows	
1 large	7 sq yd (6 sq m)
1 small	2½ sq yd (2 sq m)
Skirting (baseboard)	2½ sq yd (2 sq m)
TOTAL GLOSS PAINT AREA	14½ sq yd (12 sq m)

Allowing for some touch-up paint you would therefore need about half a US gallon or 2 litres of primer (sealer), a little less undercoat (primer), and one-third of a US gallon for a coat of semigloss or 2 litres for two coats of liquid or non-drip gloss.

A

B

C

GLOSS PAINTING TECHNIQUES

The technique used for painting with non-drip gloss is quite different from that used for painting with liquid gloss. Here is how to use each for the best possible result:

Non-drip gloss

Do *not* stir the paint. Dip the brush into the paint then, as you start painting, flex the bristles against the woodwork so the paint runs down to the tip of the brush (**A**). Using the brush lightly, dab on paint in a horizontal direction first (**B**), and then spread the paint out by brushing over this vertically (**C**).

Non-drip gloss is designed to cover in one generous coat so do not spread the paint out too thinly or you will just end up with an unsatisfactory streaky effect – this sort of gel paint was developed specially to do the job of undercoat (primer in the US) plus topcoat(s) all at one go. Two coats may, however, be needed.

Liquid gloss

Stir the paint well before you start. Then dip the brush into the paint so that about one-third of the bristles is covered. Take any excess paint off on the inside rim of the paint tin or, even better, against a piece of string stretched between the tin handles. When you start painting flex the bristles against the woodwork in the same way as when painting with non-drip gloss but with liquid gloss put the paint on in a vertical direction first, covering a small area only (**A**). Then paint across this horizontally to distribute the paint (**B**). Finish by applying light, vertical strokes; this is 'laying off' (**C**).

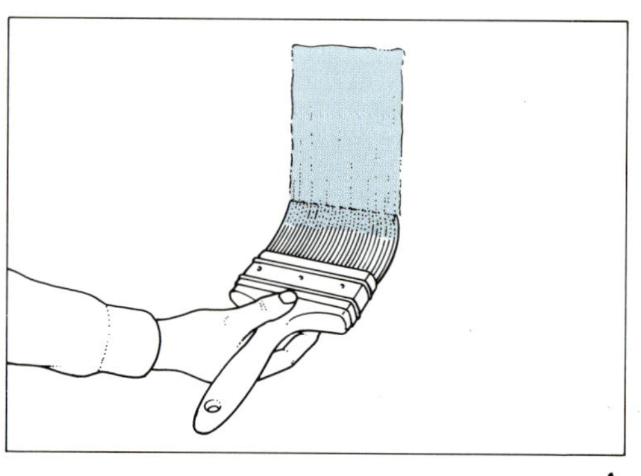

A

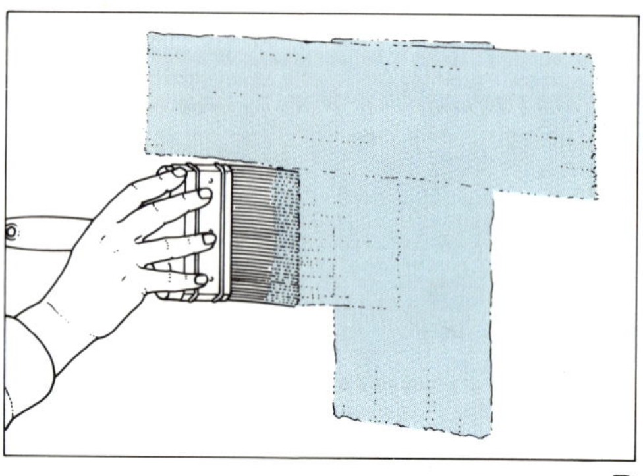

B

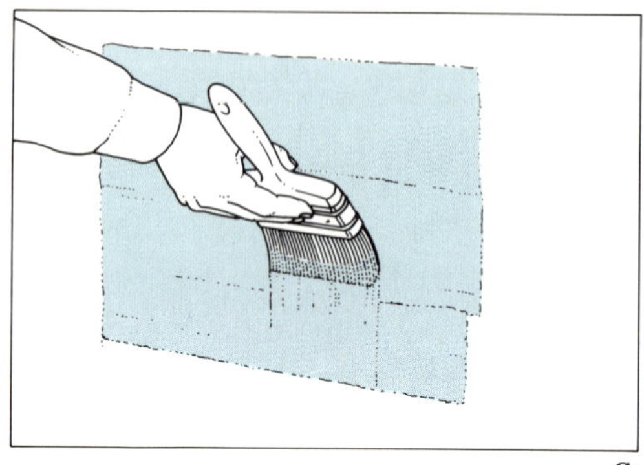

C

PAINTING SKIRTINGS (BASEBOARDS) AND RADIATORS

Where possible pull back the carpet before you start or cover with a dust sheet and use a piece of rigid cardboard as a mask (**A**). Check regularly that no paint has got on to the clean side of the card and wipe it or change it immediately if this happens. Avoid using this room while the paint is drying, as any movement can stir up dust

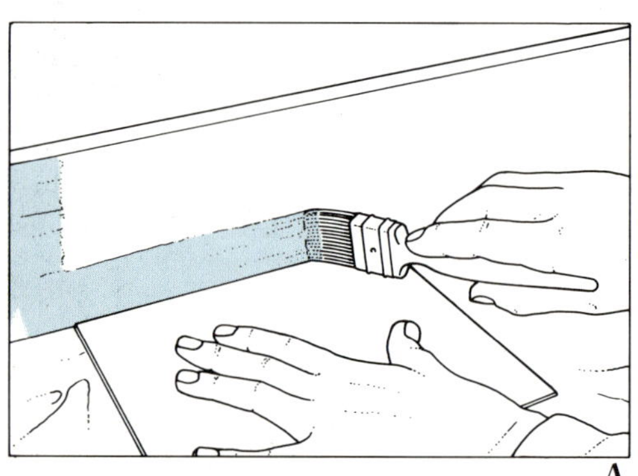

A

which will then settle on the wet paint, particularly on skirtings.

Gloss paint can reduce heat output on a radiator by up to 20 per cent; matt paint will not reduce it as much. If you want a radiator to remain sparkling white use the special radiator enamel available. Do not use an undercoat (primer) on a radiator.

Paint radiators when they are cold.

You will need:
Paint of required finish
Brushes, one about 3 in (7.5 cm) and one about 1 in (2.5 cm)
White (mineral) spirit and a cloth
Fine grade glass (sand) paper
Plus primer (sealer) and undercoat (primer) if necessary

STARTING WORK

1 Paint bare wood with a coat of primer (sealer) and leave to dry overnight. Wood primer helps to give good adhesion for the next coat to be applied.

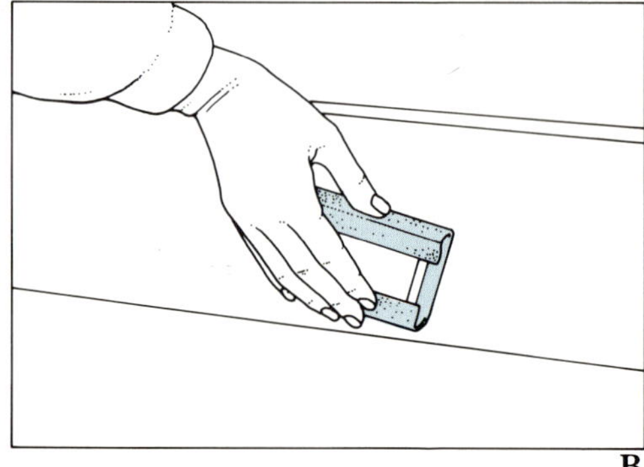

B

2 Under liquid gloss use an undercoat (primer). When this is completely dry, sand lightly (**B**) and wipe with a cloth dampened with white (mineral) spirit to remove dust.

3 Paint with gloss, following the technique appropriate for the paint you are using (see above).

CLEANING EQUIPMENT

Always clean brushes, rollers and pads thoroughly. Use hot, soapy water for emulsion (latex) paint, white (mineral) spirit or a proprietary cleaner for other paints and varnishes. If you need to soak brushes, use a container like the one below, so as not to damage the bristles.

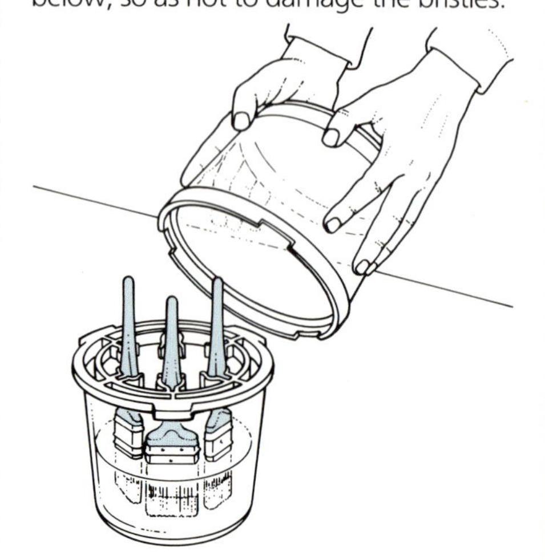

PAINTING DOORS

Prepare following the instructions on page 62. Remove door furniture (hardware) before you start, tape the screws to it and keep in a safe place. Slide a protective covering underneath the door and prop it half open. Do not close the door or paint the frame until all the paint is completely dry.

FLUSH DOORS

You will need:
Paint
3 in (7.5 cm) brush for the main area and 1 in (2.5 cm) brush for edges
White (mineral) spirit and a cloth
Fine grade glass (sand) paper
Plus primer (sealer) and undercoat (primer) if necessary.

Divide flush doors into smaller sections for painting, and they will be easier to cope with. It is important to work quickly to avoid a tide mark between the sections, which will be very hard to remove.

STARTING WORK

1 Sand unpainted doors and apply a coat of primer (sealer); allow to dry thoroughly before you add the next coat.

2 Apply undercoat (primer) if using liquid gloss.

3 Paint on the topcoat section by section, as numbered **1-6** in the illustration. The expanse of the door needs to be divided up into manageable sections of about 16 in (40 cm) square; working in larger sections could mean one starting to dry before the next one to it is painted, resulting in a tide-mark between the two. Start work at the top to avoid the risk of touching newly painted areas.

4 Paint the top and then the side edges of the door (**7**).

5 When the door is dry paint the frame in the same way (**8**).

PANELLED DOORS

You will need:
Paint
Brushes of 2-3 in (5-7.5 cm) and ¾ in (2 cm)
White (mineral) spirit and a cloth
Fine grade glass (sand) paper
Plus primer and undercoat if necessary

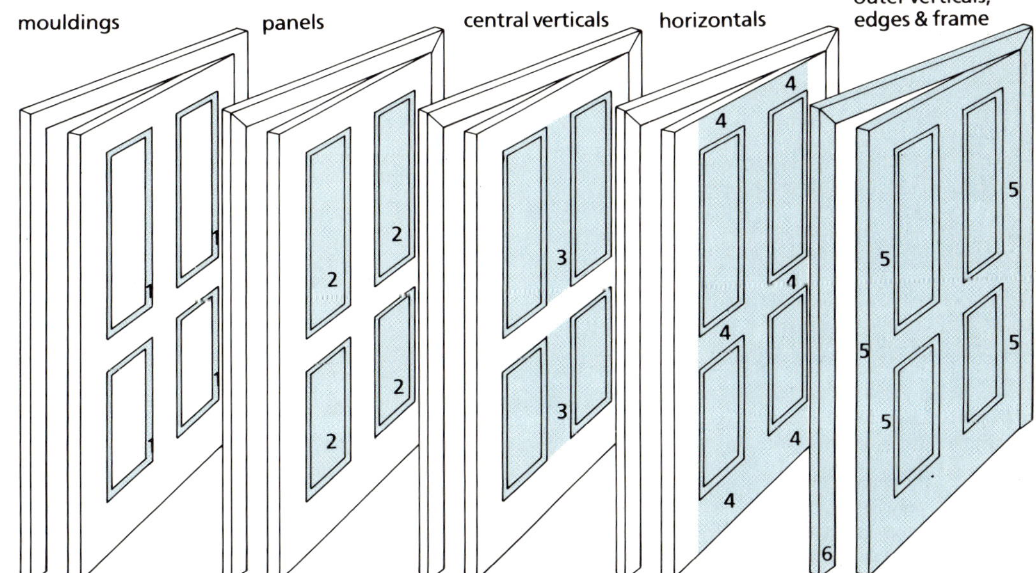

STARTING WORK

1 Prime and undercoat (seal and prime), as above, if necessary, as shown right.

2 Sand lightly, then paint with gloss, again following the same sequence. Paint mouldings with the small brush and look out for drips. If they do occur, allow the paint to dry, sand with fine glass or sandpaper then touch up. Begin each panel at the top and start with the top panels, this time using the larger brush for best results.

3 Finally paint top and edges.

4 When the door is dry paint the frame.

PAINTING WINDOWS

Prepare the window frame as described on page 62. Remove any handles and locks before you begin and keep them in a safe place. Always paint windows in the open position. The type of window you have will determine the order you work in, so follow the sequences described below, for best results.

Keep paint off the windows when using primer and undercoat (sealer and primer) by slipping a rubber band around the bristles of your narrow brush. If you have an unsteady hand, use masking tape on the glass when you apply the gloss paint. Place the tape on the glass, leaving a space of about ⅛ in (3 mm) between the tape edge and the rebate – the paint will then extend slightly on to the glass, protecting the putty.

Alternatively, you could try using a paint shield to keep paint off the glass. If you do get any paint on the window pane, scrape it off carefully, using a razor blade, and then wipe clean with a little white (mineral) spirit on a clean piece of rag.

You will need:
Paint
Narrow ½ in (13 mm) paintbrush and a 1 in (2.5 cm) brush
White (mineral) spirit and a cloth
Fine grade glass (sand) paper
Paint scraper
Elastic band
Masking tape
Plus primer (sealer) and undercoat (primer) if necessary

Casement windows
Start by painting the rebates **(a)** *and then move on to the horizontal and vertical crossbars* **(b)**. *Next paint the crossrails* **(c)** *and then the vertical sides and the edges of the window* **(d)**. *Tackle the frame and the sill* **(e)** *but leave the stay until last, as you will probably need to use it to change the window's position while painting.*

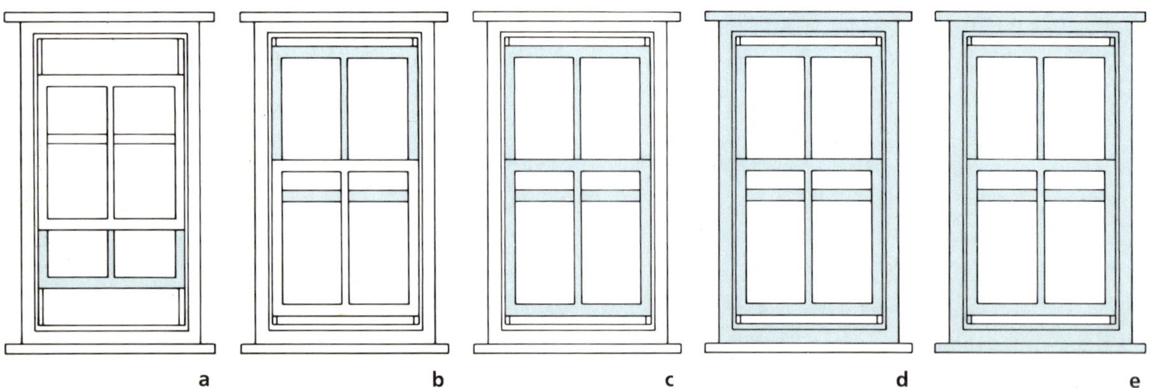

Sash windows
Push the top sash down and the bottom sash up to overlap by 8 in (20 cm). Paint the bottom rail of the top sash and any vertical parts of the top sash in reach **(a)**. *Almost close the window and paint the rest of the top sash* **(b)**. *In the same position, paint the bottom sash and let it dry* **(c)**. *Paint the frame* **(d)**, *then the runners* **(e)**. *Leave the sill until last.*

OTHER WINDOW SHAPES

Windows come in many different designs, in addition to those above. They may be pivoting windows, louvred windows, sliding windows, French windows or sealed windows. The latter may have a small opening section at the top.

Paint any window that opens as early in the day as you can, as this will allow the longest drying time. Tackle areas nearest to the glass first, followed by crossbars. Horizontal rails are best painted before vertical ones. Finish the opening part of the window by doing the sides and edges. Finally paint the frame.

If you are planning to put in new windows, bear in mind that pivoting ones are easy to clean, but can be dangerous if there are small children in the house. When open, they can get in the way of curtains and blinds. Glazed double opening doors (or French windows) cannot be used to provide a complete wall of window but they do open over their entire width. Sliding windows can only open over half their width. Louvred windows can be a security hazard.

Pivoting window

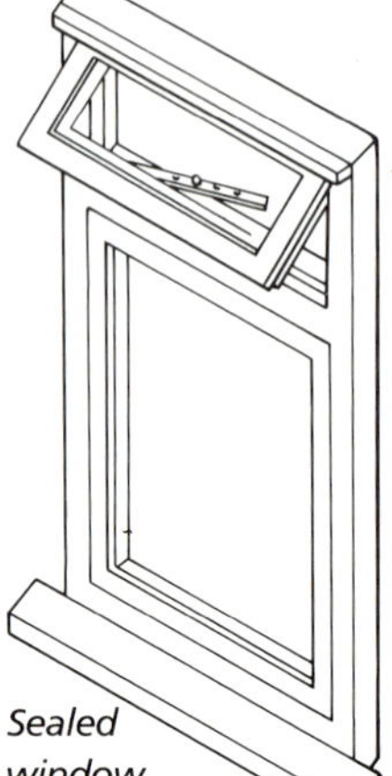

Sealed window

CREATING DECORATIVE PAINT FINISHES

Subtle multi-colour patterns can be added to plain painted walls by using a sponge, a rag or a plastic bag to dab second, third or fourth colours over the base colour. The irregular patterns that are created look professional and yet are very simple to do. They also take surprisingly little time and are inexpensive as on the whole they use materials that you already have around the house. Very little paint is needed: you can use leftover paint from walls, skirting (baseboard), doors and windows and mix it if you want; beg a new colour from friends; add white to your colours to create softer tones or simply buy a couple of small tins of paint in the colours you require.

If you want to achieve a coordinated look with curtains and upholstery, pick colours featured in these for decorating your walls or ceiling in a special finish.

Oil-based paints create the most subtle blended effects if you are sponging and they can be made even more subtle if the paint is thinned with white (mineral) spirit. Use emulsion (latex) for ragging on and for bag graining and thin with water. Practise on large sheets of paper before you start on your wall – both to perfect your technique and to give yourself a chance to try out different colour mixes. When your samples are dry, pin them up on the wall and see which mix is going to be the most effective. A strong colour for the base softened back with paler additions works well for ragging on but sponging and bag graining probably look most effective on a pale base coat.

For extra protection paint over a ragged or bag grained surface when dry with a coat of polyurethane varnish, thinned 3 parts white (mineral) spirit to 1 part varnish. Remove any marks from treated surfaces with a damp, soapy rag or sponge.

Sponging, bag graining and ragging on are dealt with here as they are simplest finishes. If you enjoy doing these you can advance to rag rolling and dragging, even marbling.

Furniture

The above finishes can also be used on furniture. Prepare and paint the surface following the instructions on pages 62 and 65-6. When the painted surface is completely dry (about three days) apply the decorative finish, using an oil-based paint.

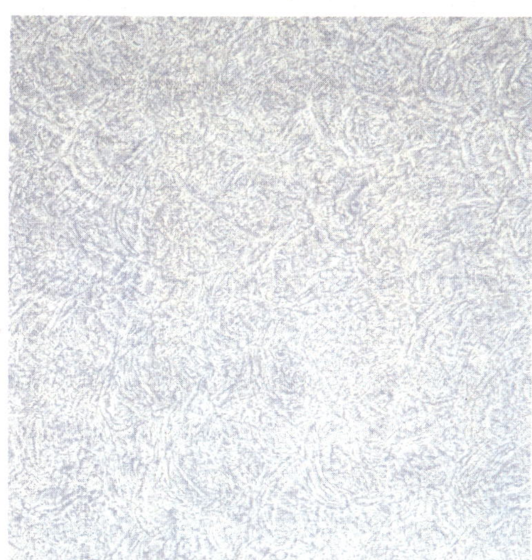

SPONGING

A soft mottled effect is achieved by dabbing the surface lightly with a natural sponge which has first been dipped into paint. You have to 'knock back' the paint first – that is, dab the sponge on to scraps of paper (newspaper will do) until it makes only a light feathery impression on the paper. It is then ready for use on the surface to be sponged. You can use one colour only – I have used pale grey on soft cream to great effect – or you can use up to four sponged colours on a base coat.

BAG GRAINING

A random pattern is created by putting a rag into a plastic bag and then using this lightly scrunched up and dabbed into paint. The effect is slightly stronger than you get with a sponge and two colours give the best result. Throw away and replace the bags when they start to become clogged or you may end up with solid clots of colour rather than the attractive subtle and irregular markings you are supposed to be aiming for.

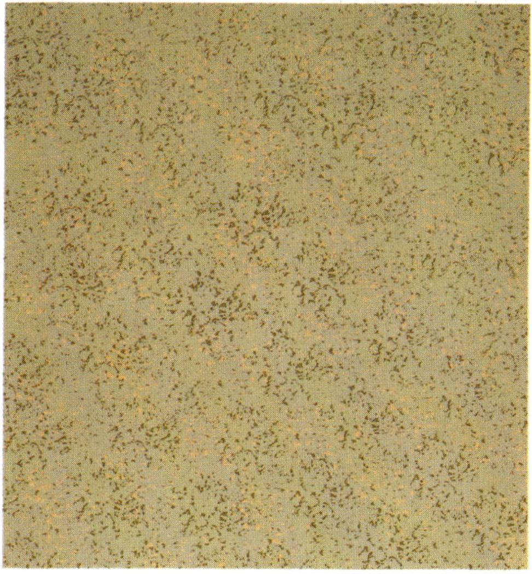

RAGGING ON

The ragging on technique described on page 71 is not difficult to do, consisting simply of dipping a crumpled-up cotton rag into small amounts of a 'second' paint colour and then rolling it over the base surface in overlapping stripes until you have covered the whole area with a continuous pattern. (A more skilled ragging method involves painting the surface with the second colour, or glaze, and working on this with a rag to create a pattern – this is called 'ragging off'.) It needs a very smooth surface, however.

SPECIAL PAINT TECHNIQUES

CALCULATING QUANTITIES
The amount of paint needed for any of these finishes is small, 1 pint (0.55 litre) at most of any colour to decorate an average-sized room and less for sponging. It is therefore an ideal way to use up leftover gloss or eggshell (semigloss) paint. If a skin has formed on the paint and you cannot remove this in one piece strain the paint through a good part of an old stocking or tights. Tie this loosely over the top of a clean tin and pour the paint slowly through, allowing it to filter into the container below. Carefully remove and discard the strainer and the bits it has retained before you start.

This period bathroom has been attractively bag-grained in pale and darker greys. It is a good example of how this type of subtle paint treatment allows other elements of a room's design – brass fittings, bust and windows, here – to speak for themselves, without competing for attention.

PREPARATION
Prepare and paint the surface with matt or silk (semigloss) emulsion (latex).

SPONGING

You will need:
Paint
Natural marine sponges, one per person (the unevenness of the holes in the natural sponge creates by far the most interesting effects)
Test card of the colours you are going to use
Sheets of paper for dabbing off (newspaper will do)
Piece of cardboard to use as a mask
Old saucer and old spoon
White (mineral) spirit and a cloth for removing splashes
Rubber gloves

STARTING WORK

1 Mix up the colours you are going to use as necessary.

2 Cut off a small piece of sponge, about 1½ in by ¾ in (4 × 2 cm), and put it on one side for use at a later stage.

3 Stir the paint well and spoon a little into the saucer.
Alternatively, if you are not mixing colours you can simply use the paint left on the tin lid after shaking.

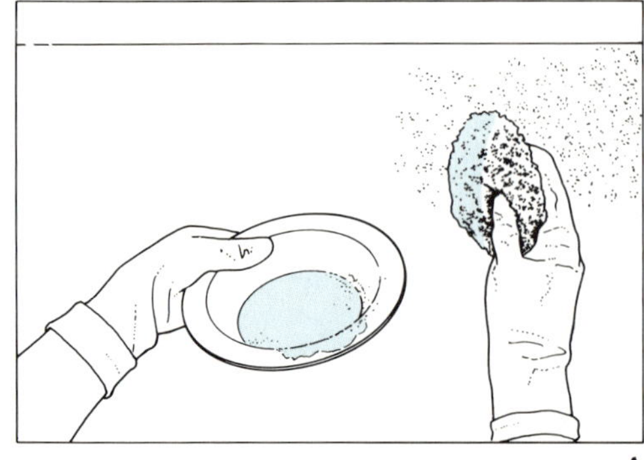

A

4 Dampen the sponge with water; dab it into the first paint colour. Using your sheets of paper, quickly dab the sponge up and down on this until the imprint left is light and feathery and not too heavy. Transfer to the wall and, starting from the top, sponge in quick, light dabbing movements (**A**), not pressing on too hard.

If you are using only one colour leave about two to three times as much base coat showing through; however, it's probably better to leave slightly more if you are going to add more colours.

If the sponge becomes clogged clean it with white (mineral) spirit, wash it out, squeeze and start again. (Do the same when the first sponged coat is completed.)

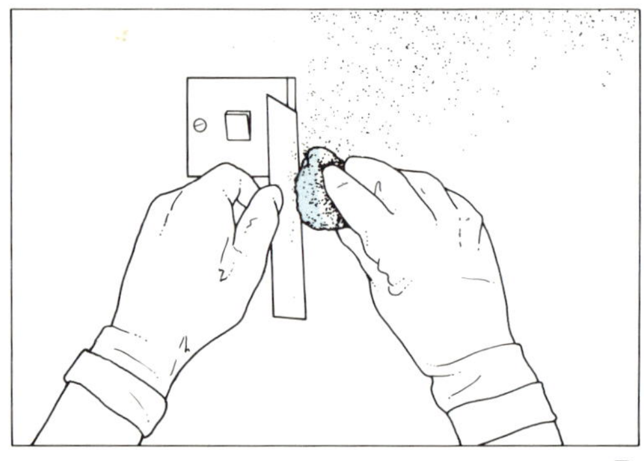

B

5 Using the small piece of sponge in the same way, do the corners, along the skirting (baseboard) edge and around fittings. Use your masking card carefully so that the sponging doesn't go where it is not wanted (**B**) and spoil the effect.

6 It is not necessary to leave the first sponged coat to dry before you start on the second. If two of you are working together, the second person can even follow on behind the first, sponging on the second colour. If you are using the same sponge for both coats use a different part of the sponge each time to vary the impression produced by the natural pattern of the holes.

7 When you have finished all the sponging stand back to check the effect. If you have lost too much of the base coat simply sponge some of this on top; if the colours appear too strong you can correct this by sponging on some white.

8 Remove any paint marks as soon as possible from the surrounding walls or woodwork with white (mineral) spirit and leave to dry overnight.

BAG GRAINING

You will need:
Emulsion (latex) paints
Plastic food bags
Cotton rags
Paint tray and old spoon
White (mineral) spirit and cloth
Sheets of paper for dabbing off (newspaper will do)
Rubber gloves
Cardboard for masking
Test card showing the colours you are going to use

STARTING WORK

1 Half fill a plastic bag with rags (**A**), press the air out and grasp the bag with the opening held together in your palm.

2 Pour a few spoonfuls of paint into your tray (**B**). Dip in the bag, then dab it on the shallow end to remove excess and on to the paper until the impression is clear.

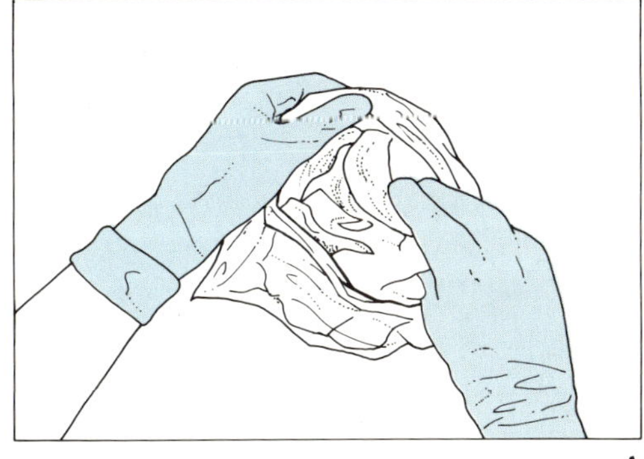

A

B

3 Starting at the top of the wall, dab the bag lightly onto the wall. Aim to end with about two to three times as much base colour showing as bag colour. Thin the paint slightly with water if the colour is too harsh.

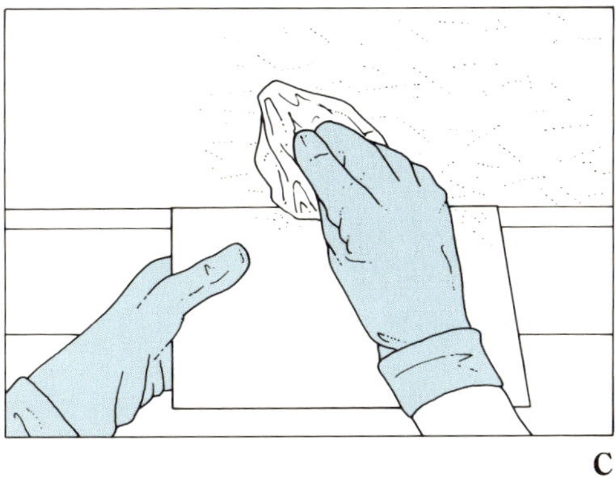

C

4 Use the mask card when doing edges to protect the skirting (baseboard), etc. (**C**).

5 Repeat steps 2, 3 and 4 with a second colour. (When the bag becomes clogged, throw away and transfer rags to a new one.) When you are happy, leave to dry.

RAGGING ON

You will need:
Emulsion (latex) paint
Pure cotton rags
Paint tray and old spoon
Large pieces of paper (newspaper will do)
Cloth for wiping away splashes
Rubber gloves (lightweight ones)

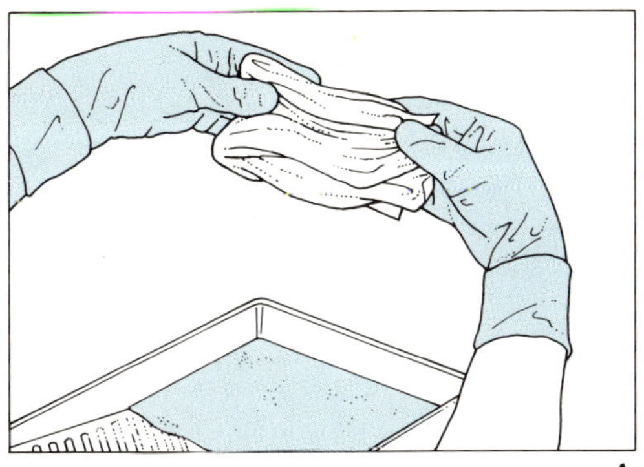

A

STARTING WORK

1 Pour about two large spoonfuls of paint into the tray and dip the rag into this. Bunch up the rag so it creases and forms a lightly rolled sausage shape (**A**).

2 Try out your technique by lightly rolling the rag over your spare paper. Refold the rag if necessary to get an interesting impression. Use the rag almost dry to avoid runs in the paint.

3 Hold the rag in your fingertips and, starting at one end of a wall, lightly roll it from skirting (baseboard) to ceiling.

4 Move slightly to one side and roll on another stripe with the edge just overlapping that of the first so that the pattern is continuous.

5 Continue until the whole area is covered. Fill any small missed areas by dotting with the tip of the paint-covered rag.

OTHER DECORATIVE PAINT FINISHES

- **Dragging** A brush is dragged through a coat of freshly applied glaze, leaving a pattern of fine lines where the base coat shows through.
- **Stencilling** Currently undergoing a revival, this technique is not difficult. You can either buy a ready-cut stencil kit or design and make your own – helpful kits are available. Just fill in your chosen colour with a special stencil brush.
- **Stippling** Use a special brush to break up your colour into thousands of tiny dots for a soft, smooth effect.
- **Spattering** This is great fun to do and brightens up plain surfaces with spots and splashes of colour (see page 51).

CHAPTER 4

Coverings for walls and ceilings

Many wallcoverings now come with matching or coordinating fabrics, curtains and draperies, bedding and other accessories which makes planning a room scheme easy.

When choosing a wallcovering it is difficult to envisage exactly what it is going to look like in your room. Most pattern books include photographs which help to show you the overall effect but if you are at all worried about your choice start by buying enough to cover one wall only and ask the shop to reserve the rest for you.

If you are looking for a more durable surface, tiles can be invaluable. Smart yet easy to maintain, they have a time-honoured role in kitchens and bathrooms.

Papering a ceiling, either to complement or contrast with your wallcovering, gives a coordinated and well-thought-out look, and coving provides a neat finish between wall and ceiling.

And to add a touch of style to your new room, why not consider a border – paint, paper or stencil?

MATERIALS FOR WALLS AND CEILINGS

Apart from the enormous range of colours and patterns available, there is also a wide choice of types of wallcovering. Besides choosing a wallcovering for its looks, consider its suitability for the room you are decorating. Here are some points to bear in mind when making your selection.

WALLPAPER

Standard wallpaper has its pattern printed on the paper. Some can be lightly wiped over with a cloth; others should only be vacuumed so are not really suitable for areas subject to heavy wear. The cheaper the paper the more difficult it will probably be to hang as thin papers tear easily when damp.

Washable, vinyl-coated wallpaper is ordinary printed wallpaper with a transparent water-resistant coating that can be wiped with a damp soapy cloth or sponge. Washable wallpapers are more difficult to strip than other kinds when you come to redecorate: the surface has to be scored to allow the water to soak through to the backing (see pages 55-6).

TEXTURED PAPERS FOR PAINTING

The cheapest of these is woodchip, which has tiny chips of wood embedded between two sheets of paper. It is therefore thick and makes a good covering for old cracked or uneven walls and ceilings. In Britain, various embossed patterns are also available: Anaglypta, made from thick paper (wood pulp); Supaglypta, which is thicker, made from cotton fibres, wood pulp and china clay; and luxury vinyl Anaglypta, a three-dimensional blown vinyl covering with a flat paper backing which is left behind when the vinyl is stripped off the wall for redecorating.

Leave embossed papers to soak well after pasting to prevent bubbles from appearing when they are hung. When hanging, take care not to press out the pattern (not a problem with the vinyl Anaglypta). Embossed papers are not difficult to hang, except on ceilings because they are heavier than other wallpapers.

Woodchip and embossed paper that has been painted is difficult to strip.

Clean with the dust attachment on the vacuum cleaner and gently rub off greasy marks with a damp cloth.

VINYL

Vinyl containing the design is bonded to a paper backing. This makes the covering very hardwearing (it can virtually be scrubbed) and is therefore suitable for busy areas such as halls and stairways and children's rooms. It is also a practical choice for rooms with a steamy atmosphere such as kitchens and bathrooms.

Vinyl is easy to hang as it does not expand like paper. Use a fungicidal paste as it has a very low water permeability and ensure that the wall beneath is completely dry or you will run into trouble.

Both ready-pasted and unpasted vinyls are available. Stripping when you want to redecorate is easy as the vinyl layer can be pulled away, leaving the backing on the wall, and you can use this as a lining paper for a new wallpaper.

Blown and sculptured vinyls are also

available. The manufacturing processes used to produce them are slightly different but in each case the design is put on first and then the covering goes into an oven where the heat expands certain areas of the design to form a three-dimensional texture. Both these vinyls have some insulating properties, which can be useful.

Sculptured vinyl is particularly tough. It is often produced in tile designs and used in place of ceramic tiles on bathroom and kitchen walls. It is scrubbable and very suitable for areas that suffer from condensation.

Blown vinyl, which can be sponged but not scrubbed, is not quite as tough as sculptured vinyl. It comes in designs more suited to living areas and bedrooms and in white for painting over.

NOVAMURA

This is a unique wallcovering which resembles thin, unwoven fabric but is printed like wallpaper. The adhesive (use the special fungicidal type recommended) is applied to the wall and the wallcovering is then hung dry over it. Novamura is very light in weight and has a matt appearance. It can get scuffed in areas of wear such as outside corners.

Marks can be removed with a damp, soapy cloth and Novamura can be dry-stripped when you redecorate.

METALLIC PAPERS

The design on this type of paper is printed on to a metallized plastic film on a paper backing which produces a highly reflective wallcovering. It needs to be used on a good, flat surface as it will highlight any imperfections. It is washable and waterproof but should *never* be hung behind light switches, power sockets or in any place where it could come into contact with electric wiring because foil conducts electricity.

Similar in appearance, light-reflecting vinyls are not a problem with electricity but are not suitable for humid areas.

FLOCK

Modern flocks, made of durable PVC (polyvinyl chloride) film on a paper backing and textured with viscose rayon fibre, have the velvety appearance of old flocks but are more practical. They are heavy and need to be soaked well after pasting with a fungicidal adhesive. Sponge off marks with warm, soapy water or use methylated or white spirit (denatured alcohol or mineral spirit) on stubborn stains, followed by a rinse. When it is thoroughly dry brush the surface lightly to align the fibres of the flocking.

FABRICS

Hessian (burlap), silk, wools and grasscloths are all available on a paper backing. They are best put up by someone with a lot of paper-hanging experience as it is important not to get adhesive on the fabric.

TILES

See pages 82-5.

Pattern matching

If you are worried about being able to match the pattern perfectly in adjacent strips then choose one of the newer random pattern or no-match papers. These are designed so that the pattern matches wherever you place the paper, and are therefore cheaper.

INTERNATIONAL WALLPAPER SYMBOLS

CLEANING AND MOISTURE RESISTANCE PROPERTIES

Spongeable: Domestic stains, either water or solvent-based, cannot normally be removed. Not resistant to oils or fats.

Washable: Suitable for rooms with occasional high humidity (e.g. kitchens and bathrooms). Use a damp cloth and mild soap to clean while stains are still fresh.

Super-washable: Suitable for rooms with occasional high humidity (e.g. kitchens and bathrooms). Use a wet cloth and mild soap to clean. Most water-based stains, domestic grime and dust can be removed.

Scrubbable: Wash down with a sponge or soft brush with a mild detergent or mild abrasive. Domestic grime and dust, most water-based and some solvent-based, oil and fat stains can be removed.

COLOUR FADE-RESISTANCE

Moderate light fastness: Not significantly affected by sunlight, except over a long time.

Good light fastness: Can be used throughout the home without risk of colour fading.

APPLICATION METHODS

Paste-the-wall: Apply adhesive to the wall and not the wallcovering.

Ready-pasted: The adhesive is factory-applied and is activated by immersion in water before hanging.

ACCESSORIES

Co-ordinated fabric available: Co-ordinating furnishing fabrics are available.

REMOVAL

Strippable: Can be dry-stripped by lifting a corner and pulling firmly away.

Peelable: The front surface can be dry-stripped by lifting a corner and pulling away from the base which can be left on the wall.

PATTERN MATCHING

Free match: No need to match the pattern at the join between lengths.

Straight match: The pattern is repeated horizontally at the join between lengths.

Offset match: The pattern repeat is offset from the horizontal, giving a 'stepped' pattern match.

Design repeat/Distance offset. 'Design Repeat' shows the size in cm of one pattern repeat along each length. 'Distance Offset' gives the distance by which each length should be adjusted to give a correct match.

PATTERN DIRECTION

Direction of hanging: The top of the pattern is indicated by the arrow on the reverse side of this wallcovering.

Reverse alternate lengths: Hang each length the opposite way up to the previous one.

CONSTRUCTION

Duplex: Made by combining two papers together during the embossing process.

(a) *pink hessian*
(b) *marbled fabric and border*
(c) *grey suedette*
(d) *white Anaglypta*
(e) *pink vinyl*
(f) *metallic wall covering*
(g) *candy-striped paper*
(h) *flock*
(i) *marble-textured paper*
(j) *Novamura*

PREPARING TO HANG A WALLCOVERING

Prepare the walls for papering as described on pages 54-7. Once prepared it is best to size them unless they are already lined. You can use a proprietary brand of size or diluted wallpaper adhesive, following the manufacturer's instructions on mixing. Size seals the wall and stops the wallpaper paste from being absorbed too quickly. This gives you time to position the paper correctly, allowing you to slide the paper up, down or sideways as necessary.

Lining the walls provides a perfect backing to which wallpaper will stick smoothly. In some cases it is particularly helpful to line the walls first – for instance under very heavy or highly textured papers as these can shrink back on drying, leaving a small space at the seams. This is much less likely to happen if the walls are lined. Lining the walls will also disguise a poor surface and act as an insulating layer. Walls are usually lined horizontally as this gives a smoother finish under vertically hung wallpaper. If you use the lining paper left after stripping vinyl make sure that the seams fall in a different place when wallpapering or they will become too obvious.

CALCULATING QUANTITIES

For the walls, measure the distance around the room in feet or metres including doors and windows,. Then measure the height from skirting (baseboard) top to ceiling. Multiply these two figures, then divide by five. This calculation is based on a standard (US double) roll, 20½ in × 33 ft (52 cm × 10.5 m). See the charts below. You should allow an extra roll for matching a small pattern, two extra for a large pattern, plus another extra roll if you are a first time decorator to allow for any disaster during the hanging process.

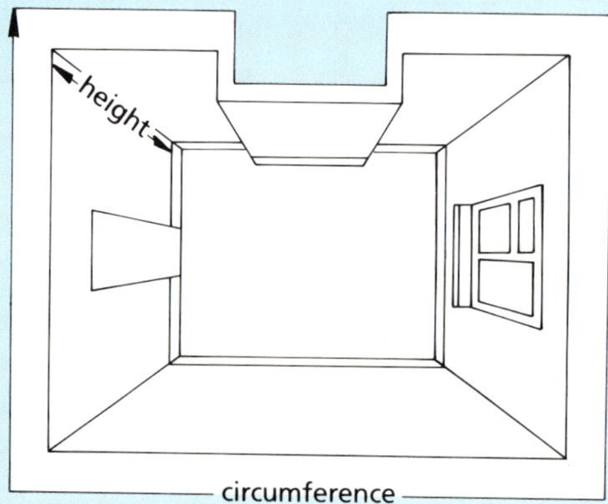

For a ceiling, measure the distance around the room and then use the charts below to work out the number of rolls you need.

Buy all the rolls you need at the same time to ensure that they come from the same batch. The batch number is printed on the roll covering. Slight colour variations can occur because not all the paper can be printed in one continuous run, inks must be replenished and new reels of paper used. If there is any variation keep light rolls for one wall, darker ones for another and use the darker ones nearer the natural light source.

Calculating number of rolls for walls

	Distance around room												
Height from skirting (baseboard)	27ft 9in (8.53m)	31ft 8in (9.75m)	35ft 8in (10.97m)	39ft 7in (12.19m)	43ft 7in (13.41m)	47ft 7in (14.63m)	51ft 5in (15.83m)	55ft 6in (17.07m)	59ft 5in (18.29m)	63ft 5in (19.51m)	67ft 4in (20.73m)	71ft 4in (21.95m)	75ft 3in (23.16m)
7ft-7ft 6in (2.13-2.29m)	**4**	**4**	**5**	**5**	**6**	**6**	**7**	**7**	**8**	**8**	**9**	**9**	**9**
7ft 6in–8ft (2.30-2.44m)	**4**	**4**	**5**	**5**	**6**	**6**	**7**	**8**	**8**	**9**	**9**	**10**	**10**
8ft-8ft 6in (2.45-2.59m)	**4**	**5**	**5**	**6**	**6**	**7**	**7**	**8**	**8**	**9**	**9**	**10**	**10**
8ft 6in-9ft (2.60-2.74m)	**4**	**5**	**5**	**6**	**6**	**7**	**8**	**8**	**9**	**9**	**10**	**11**	**11**
9ft-9ft 6in (2.75-2.90m)	**4**	**5**	**6**	**6**	**7**	**7**	**8**	**9**	**9**	**10**	**10**	**11**	**12**
9ft 6in-10ft (2.91-3.05m)	**5**	**5**	**6**	**7**	**7**	**8**	**9**	**9**	**10**	**10**	**11**	**12**	**12**
10ft-10ft 6in (3.06-3.20m)	**5**	**5**	**6**	**7**	**8**	**8**	**9**	**10**	**10**	**11**	**12**	**12**	**13**

Calculating number of rolls for a ceiling

Measurement around room	32ft (9.75m)	32ft 10in (10m)	36ft (11m)	37ft 9in (11.5m)	39ft 4in (12m)	42ft (12.8m)	44ft (13.4m)	46ft (14m)	47ft 6in (14.5m)	51ft 10in (15.8m)
Number of rolls required	**2**	**2**	**2**	**2**	**2**	**3**	**3**	**3**	**3**	**4**
Measurement around room	54ft 2in (16.5m)	55ft 10in (17m)	57ft 5in (17.5m)	59ft (18m)	62ft 4in (19m)	64ft (19.5m)	65ft 8in (20m)	67ft 3in (20.5m)	69ft (21m)	73ft 10in (22.5m)
Number of rolls required	**4**	**4**	**4**	**5**	**5**	**5**	**5**	**6**	**6**	**7**

SPECIAL EQUIPMENT

• Plumb line
This is an important tool as walls are rarely straight and cannot be used as a guide. The plumb line – a heavy weight on a length of twine – will give you a perfectly straight line to act as a guide for hanging your first length of wallpaper. You can buy one or make your own by tying a small heavy object – an old metal door knob for instance – to a length of string long enough to reach from the ceiling to the top of the skirting (baseboard).

• Scissors
Use long-bladed sharp scissors suitable for cutting wallpaper and other coverings.

• Paperhanging brush
This is a large, soft brush without a handle for smoothing down the lengths of wall-covering on the wall, removing wrinkles and bubbles. A good one should last forever.

• Seam roller
This is not always necessary but is used for rolling butted edges of wallcovering down to ensure a neat seam.

You will also need the following:

• Stepladders
Two stepladders with a plank between them produce an ideal platform from which to paper ceilings or walls. A plank over 6 ft (2 m) long should be supported by a box in the centre. For the walls you can use one stepladder, a plank and a strong box (see pages 57 and 81).

• Chalk and pencil
Use the chalk with your plumb line and the pencil to mark the wallpaper lengths.

• Measuring tape
You will need this for measuring lengths of wallcovering and so on. A steel tape is best.

• Sponge
Use a damp sponge to mop up any adhesive which gets on to the wrong side of the wall covering before it dries.

> **PASTING EQUIPMENT**
>
> If you are using a wallcovering that needs pasting, you will need, in addition to the items above, adhesive (see page 76), a bucket in which to mix it, a pasting brush and a pasting table. Buy a decorator's large pasting brush with a firm handle. It should last for years if you look after it properly.
>
> Folding pasting tables can be bought from do-it-yourself shops. They are usually 6 ft (1.8 m) long and slightly wider than a standard width of wallpaper. Because they fold, they stack neatly away when not in use. Alternatively, use a rectangular table if you have one, or put a board or an old flush door on top of a protected table covered with a plastic sheet.
>
> If you are using a ready-pasted paper, you may need to buy a trough to soak it in, although wallpaper manufacturers often provide one with their product.

STARTING WORK

> **You will need:**
> Wallcovering
> Dust sheets
> Plumb line and chalk
> Soft pencil
> Steel tape measure
> Paperhanger's brush
> Large and small scissors
> Sponge
> Seam roller
> Stepladder and plank
> *Either,* if you need to paste the paper, a pasting bucket, pasting table, pasting brush and adhesive
> *Or* if you are using a ready-pasted paper, a trough and water

LINING WALLS HORIZONTALLY

1 You will probably be dealing with long lengths of paper for this. Paste the rough side and fold without creasing to form a concertina or accordion pleats, pasted side folded to pasted side. Leave to rest.

2 In adjacent corners, measure down from the ceiling the width of your lining paper minus ½ in (13mm). Join the two marks with chalked string. Pluck it so that it leaves a straight line to follow.

3 Carry the paper over one arm and start work at the top right-hand end of the wall if you are right-handed, top left if left-handed.

4 With the folds in your left hand, position the end in the corner with your right hand and brush to the wall. Continue along the wall, lining the paper edge up to your chalk mark. Gradually undo the folds. Trim at top and ends as for top and bottom of wallpaper.

5 Place the second strip in position in the same way, butting it up to the first.

6 When you paper the second wall, butt up in corners leaving no overlap.

CUTTING THE LENGTHS

1 Check carefully that you are working with the wallpaper design the right way up and then cut the top of the first length, allowing 2 in (5 cm) trimming above the design, so that it starts at the top of the wall.

2 Measure the drop, allowing 2 in (5 cm) extra again at the skirting (baseboard) for trimming. Cut this length and pencil number 1 on top back. Cut a number of exactly matching lengths and number with consecutive odd numbers, 3, 5, 7 and so on, as numbered on the illustration right.

3 Place the second roll of paper beside the first length and slide it up and down until the pattern matches exactly. Mark the top and bottom of the length and cut these at your marks. Number this length 2 at the top and continue cutting matching lengths, marking each with an even number until you have used the whole roll.

4 Set the last odd and even numbered lengths on one side to use as patterns to cut following lengths from.

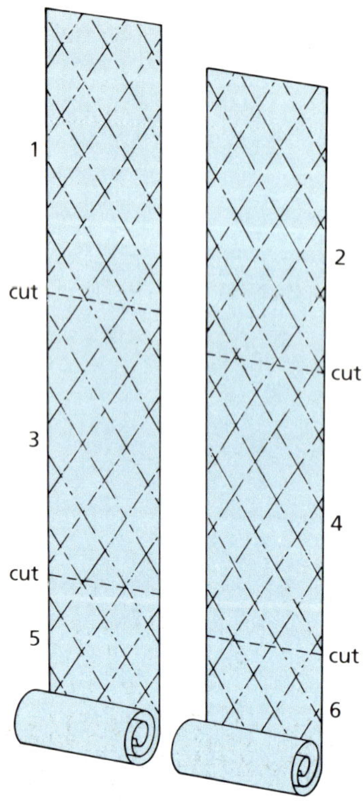

PREPARING READY-PASTED COVERINGS

These coverings usually come with their own water trough.

1 Place the trough at the base of the wall where you intend to start papering and three-quarters fill with water.

2 Line up your cut wallpaper lengths in numerical order on one side. Loosely roll the first length with wrong side outside and top edge uppermost and place in the trough (**A**) or follow the manufacturer's instructions if different. Make sure that the entire length is well soaked and then slowly draw the paper out of the trough, draining surplus water into the trough as you do so. It is now ready to hang on the wall.

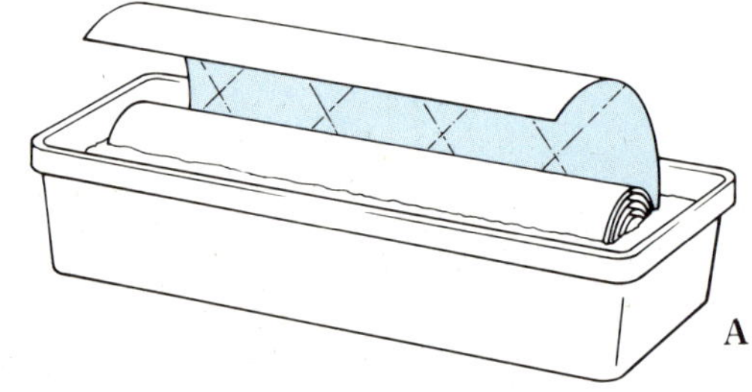
A

ADHESIVES

Make sure that you buy the type of adhesive recommended on the wall-covering you are using. Mix it up about 20 minutes before you want to start work and use a complete packet so that you make sure you get the consistency right.

When using adhesives containing fungicide use rubber gloves as these are harsh on the skin. Wash well afterwards anyway and keep children and pets out of the room.

PASTING

Not necessary for ready-pasted and paste-the-wall coverings

1 Check that you have bought the correct adhesive for the wallcovering you are using, then mix up following the manufacturer's instructions and leave for 15 to 20 minutes.

2 Line up your wallpaper lengths in numerical order (see above). To flatten, roll up each length loosely in the opposite direction of the original roll.

3 Put your first length, wrong side up, on your pasting table and apply the adhesive liberally down the middle, then brush the paste out towards the edge farthest away from you, keeping that edge of the paper flush with the table edge. Pull the paper towards you and do the same to the near-side edge (**A**).

4 Fold the pasted paper over on itself without creasing it and slide the unpasted end on to the table (**B**). Paste in the same way as the first half then fold to first edge.

5 Leave to rest for the recommended time and paste the second length in the same way.

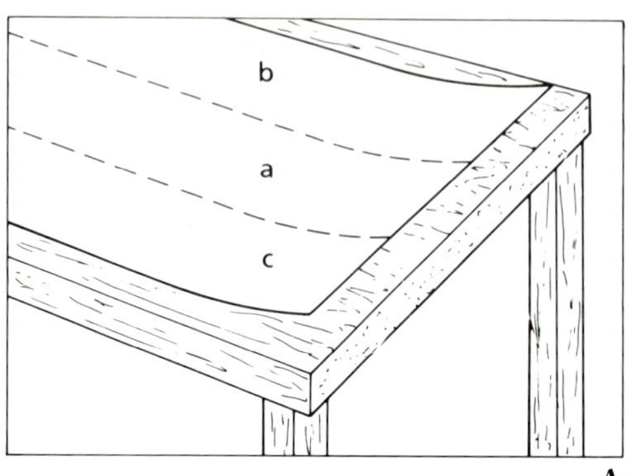

A

B

PREPARING THE WALL FOR PASTE-THE-WALL-COVERINGS

For some wall coverings, such as Novamura, you should apply the adhesive to the wall, not to the back of the covering. Use the special fungicidal adhesive recommended on the rolls and mix it following the instructions.

1 Size the walls with the adhesive first and allow this to dry. Use the pasting brush or a large paintbrush to do this for the main wall (**A**) and a smaller brush or pad for the edges and corners (**B**), so that the adhesive doesn't spatter all over the place.

2 When it is dry, paste one wall again and place the wall covering in position while the paste is still wet. As it is very light, you can apply this type of covering straight from the roll on to the wall. You do not need to cut it into lengths first. Start at the top, unroll and smooth out with the brush then trim as for other wall coverings (**C**). Try not to get adhesive on the front of the covering. Paste each wall as you are about to put the paper on it, not too far in advance.

A

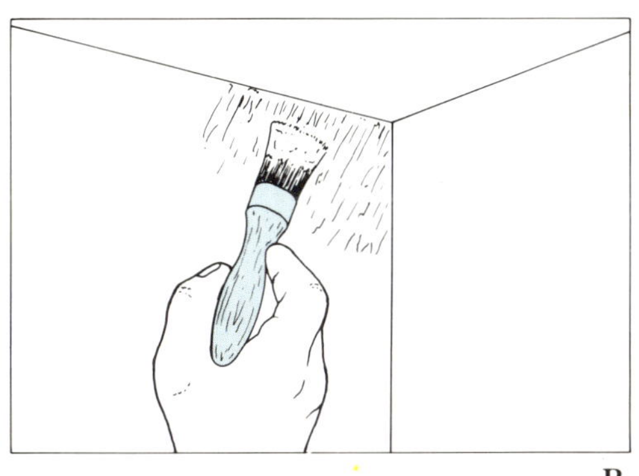

B

C

WHERE TO START

This will depend on whether your wall-covering has a bold design or not.

If the design is small, you are using a random pattern, or a texture, then it is best to begin on the longest unobstructed wall, in the corner nearest the window, then continue along this to the end of the wall farthest from the window. Return to the window wall and hang lengths from there around the room in the opposite direction.

If you are using a bold design, start from a focal point such as the centre of a chimney breast or the centre of a large unobstructed wall. You can either make this centre point the centre of a length of paper or arrange things so that a seam runs down this line. Before you decide, however, make sure that you will not end up with a narrow final strip in a prominent position.

It is usually best to have a complete pattern starting at the top of the wall and any part pattern at the bottom.

Do a little advance planning when using a wallpaper with a strong design – the first length should be hung to suit a focal point.

A smaller pattern enlarges space visually. In this narrow hall a geometric pattern tones with blue paint on skirtings (baseboards).

PUTTING UP THE WALLCOVERING

Most wallcoverings are put up with lengths butted up to each other except in the corners. If you do have to overlap do so towards the light and smooth well with a seam roller.

It is vital to get the first strip absolutely straight because all the others will follow the same line as this one, so use your plumb line to get a true vertical. Don't rely either on your eyes or on the apparently vertical line of the wall of the room.

So that you can easily relocate the screw holes of any shelves and other wall fittings you may have taken down push a short length of matchstick into each hole so that it stands just proud of the wall. As you paper over the hole, the match will push through the paper, marking the hole's position.

HANGING THE LENGTHS

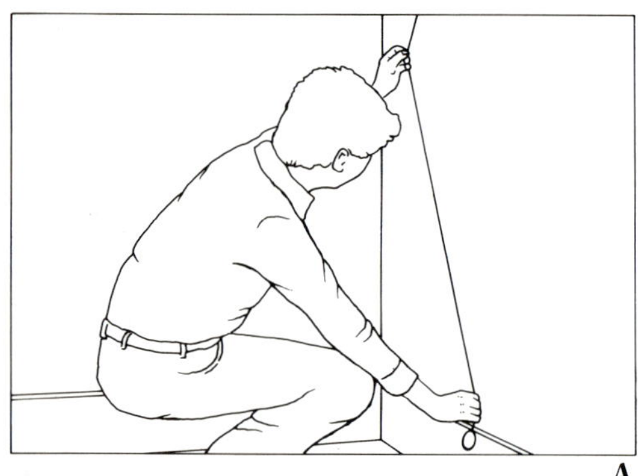

A

1 Chalk the string on your plumb line and hang it at your starting point. The plumb line should hang one wallpaper width, less ½ in (13 mm) away from the corner. When the line hangs straight tape it top and bottom then pluck it so that it marks a line (**A**).

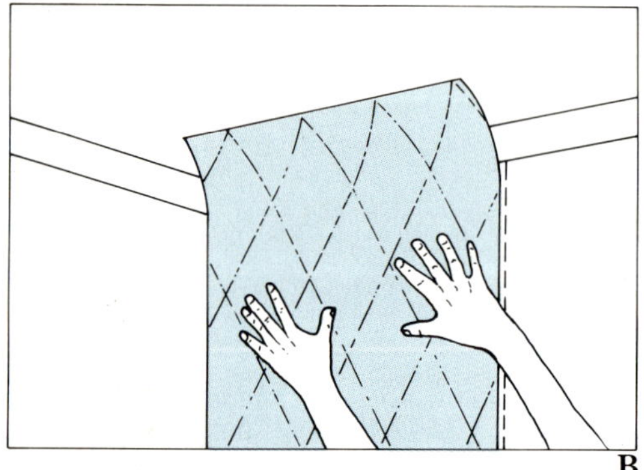

B

2 Take your first length of paper by the top corners. Don't hold it too close to the edges or the paper may tear. Position it so that your 2 in (5 cm) trimming edge overlaps the ceiling and your pattern starts at the top of the wall. Line up the side of the length with your chalk line (**B**).

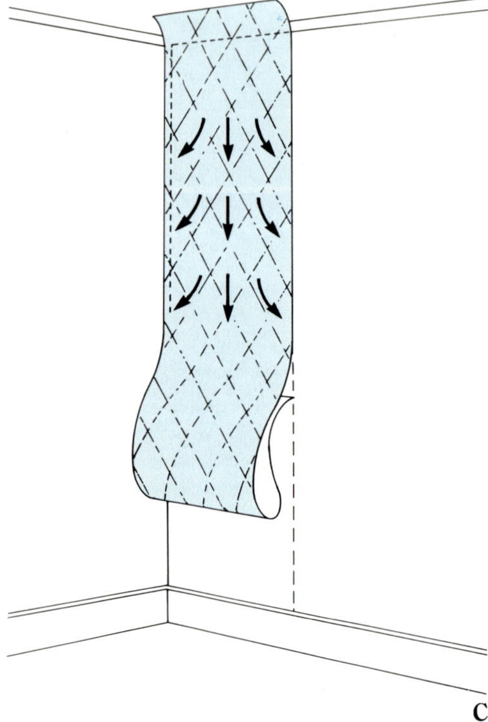

C

3 Smooth along the top edge with your brush to hold in position, then smooth down the middle and brush out towards the edges; this ensures that you remove any trapped air (**C**).

4 Open the bottom fold and smooth this down in the same way, checking that you are keeping straight against the chalk line. Brush the bottom edge with its 2 in (5 cm) trimming margin against the skirting (baseboard) edge. If the paper does not line up pull it gently from the wall, then reapply.

5 When it is aligned correctly, push the wallcovering into the crease between the wall and the ceiling using the back of the scissors to form a mark line. Pull away and cut along this line (**D**). Brush down again.

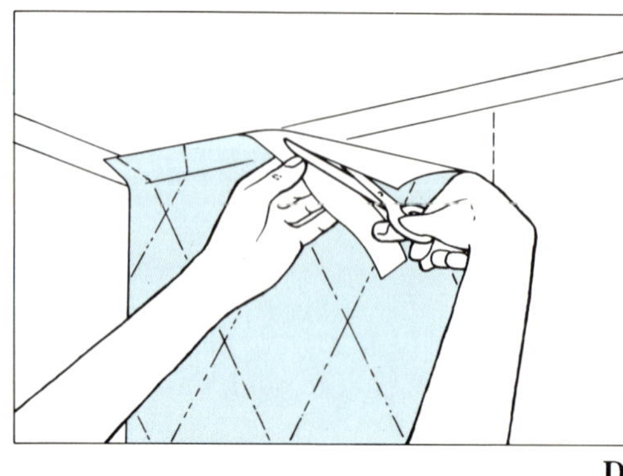

D

6 Repeat to remove the overlap at skirting (baseboard) level.

7 Take the pasted length marked 2 and position it next to the first one, butting it up to the side. Make sure that any pattern matches exactly (**E**). Brush in position in the same way as the first length, working out from the centre towards the edges. Wipe off excess paste with a damp sponge. If the edges do not lie flat you will need to use the seam roller on them. Leave for 15 to 20 minutes before you do this (**F**).

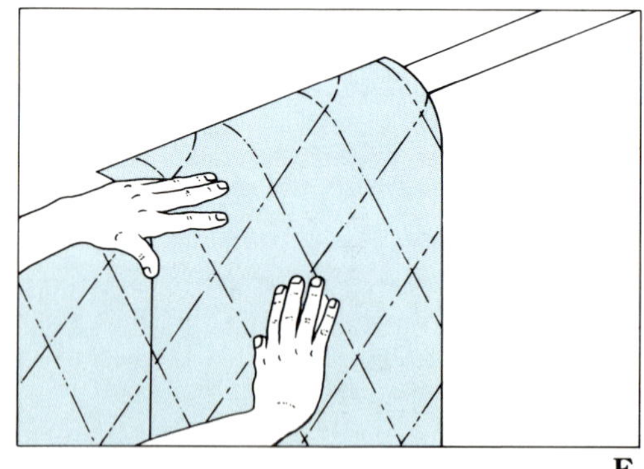

E

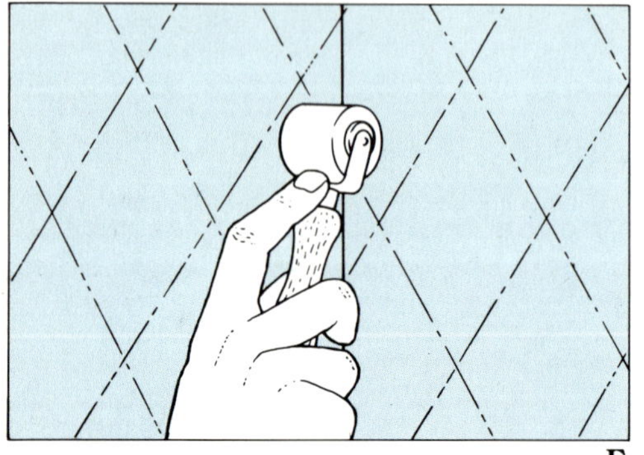

F

CORNERS

When you come to a corner cut a strip of paper that is about ½ in (13 cm) wider than the distance left to the corner. As corners are rarely absolutely vertical it is important that this strip just overlaps the corner. The first strip on the new wall should then overlap this piece (**A**). Only when lining a wall horizontally do you butt up in corners as any overlap would show through the top paper when this is later applied.

The length of paper nearest the main source of light should always be underneath as the overlap will show less this way. It may be necessary to use your plumb line again on the new wall to establish a true vertical, so that your next length of wallpaper is perfectly straight.

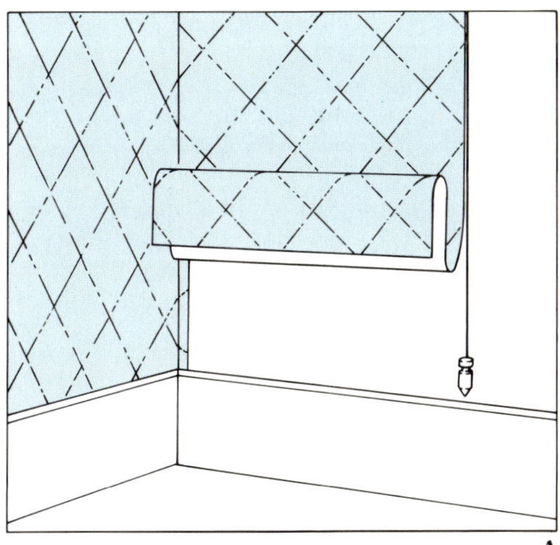

A

DOORS

Place a full width piece of your wallcovering against the wall, brushing down at the top in the normal way (**A**). Cut around the door leaving a 2 in (5 cm) overlap on both sides (**B**), then at the corner make a 2½ in (6 cm) diagonal cut (**C**). Press the paper well against the wall with the brush to form crease lines at the top and side of the frame (**D**), pull away and cut along these crease lines, removing all overlaps (**E**). Wipe all paste off the woodwork before it sets.

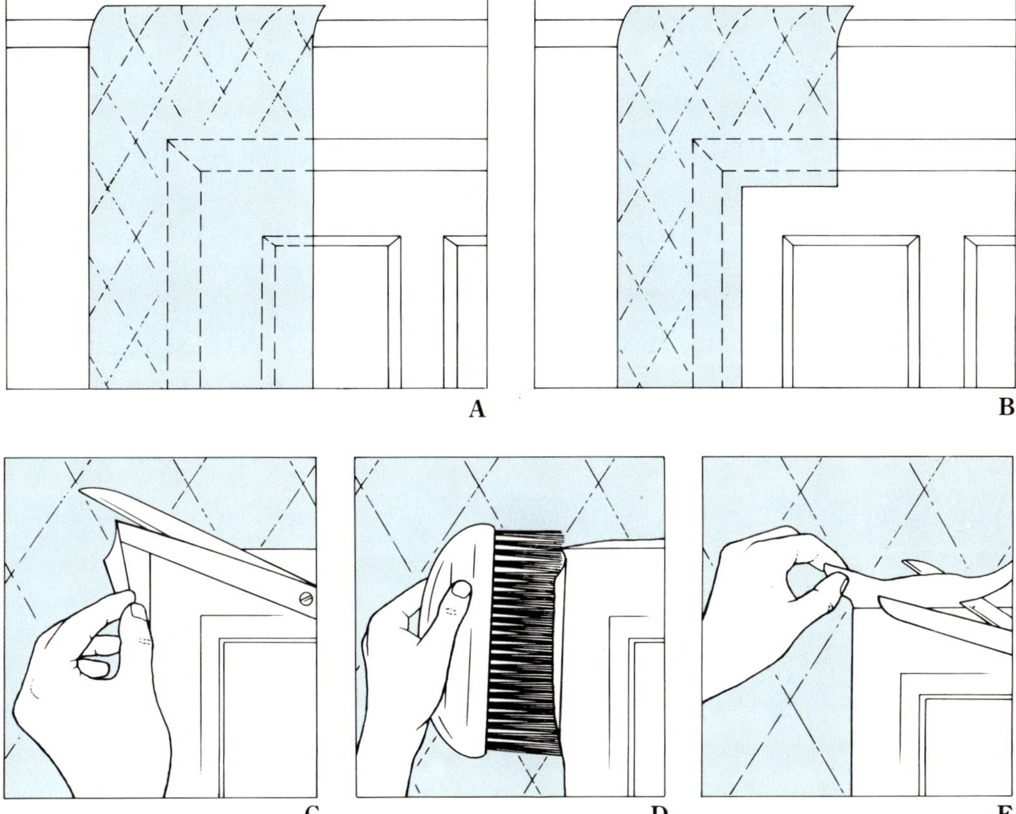

A B C D E

ELECTRIC OUTLETS

Switch off the electricity before you start work. Smooth the wallcovering down lightly over the fitting. Using small scissors, pierce at the centre then make a cut out to each corner, forming a cross shape – these cuts should extend just beyond the corners of the fitting (**A**). Press the covering down on all four sides to form creases at the edge of the fitting. Pull it away again and then cut off the overlap ½ in (13 mm) on the inside of these creases (**B**). Ease the partially unscrewed fitting away from the wall and brush the edges of the wallcovering underneath all round. Screw up the fitting. Wipe away all the adhesive before it has time to dry and switch the current back on.

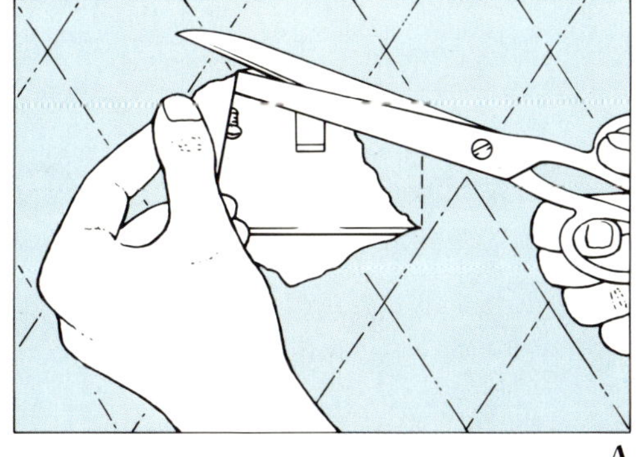

A

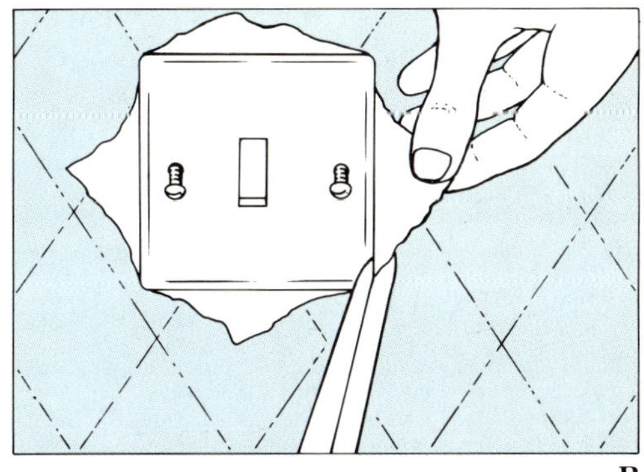

B

If you are using a foil wallcovering cut to fit around the outside edge of the plug or switch. As the foil is a conductor of electricity it must not be tucked inside. Follow the instructions above for trimming ordinary papers, but simply trim without tucking it in.

WINDOWS

If the window has a frame like that of a door, paper around this as described on page 79.

If the window is in a recess then proceed as follows.

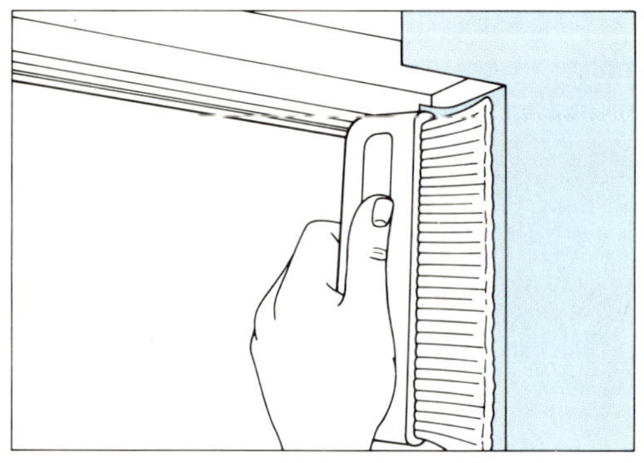
A

1 Measure from the last length of wall-covering to the back of the recess, adding ½ in (13 mm) for trimming; cut and hang a length of paper to this width. Brush down the area above the window. Make a horizontal cut ¼ in (6 mm) below the top of the recess edge to the width of the recess, brush down and trim (**A**).

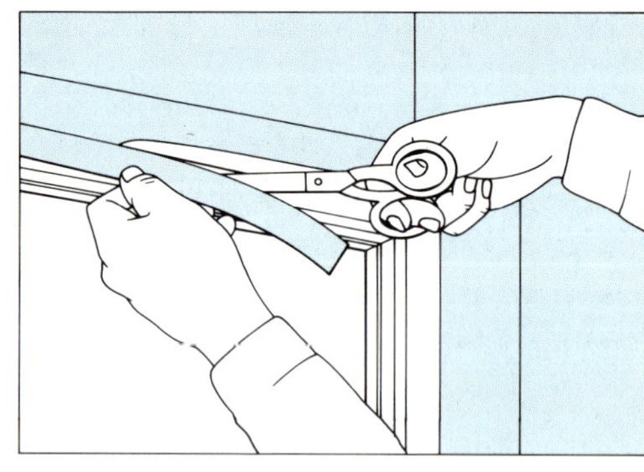
B

2 Cut a short length to go above the window and into the recess, plus trimming allowance of ½ in (13 mm) as before. Match the pattern carefully. Position, brush down into the recess and trim top and bottom (**B**). Add further short lengths as necessary.

3 When you come to the far side of the recess cut and fit in the same way as in Step 1. You will now be left with two small spaces in each top corner of the recess.

4 Matching the pattern, cut two patches to fit these corners exactly, paste them in

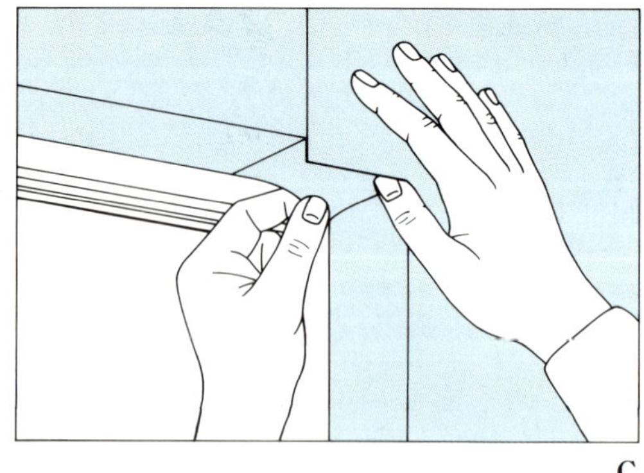
C

place (**C**) and press down the ¼ in (6 mm) flap at the top corners over them.

Alternative

Paper around the window recess but allow ½ in (13 mm) excess on each side and along the top. Paper the recess with a separate strip, matching the pattern carefully. This may mean cutting strips horizontally so your pattern matches correctly. Remember to leave a trimming at the window edge. Finally, paste down the excess over the alcove strips, making cuts into the corners. Deal with other room alcoves similarly.

RADIATORS

Paper behind radiators when they are turned off. Butt seams in the usual way, pushing them down behind the radiator with a small paint roller, or a length of wood or broom handle with the end wrapped in clean rag (**A**). Alternatively, use a special radiator paint roller to push the paper down into place. You may need to slit the lengths so they fit round the radiator brackets, butt-joining them again below the radiator.

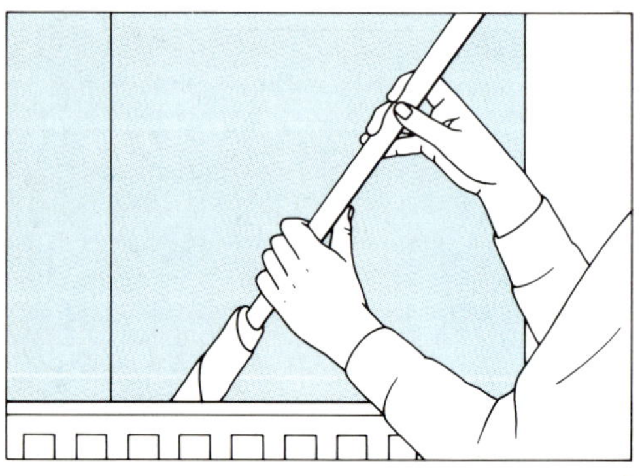
A

VERTICAL PIPES

Paste the length of paper and hang it over the pipe. Smooth down lightly to make a crease. Cut the paper from the bottom in a straight line up the centre of the pipe. Ease the two sections apart and slide them so they fit neatly behind the pipe. Press down gently with the brush (**A**). (Horizontal pipes, of course, present less of an obstacle. Concertina the paper and slip it gradually behind the pipe, brushing down.)

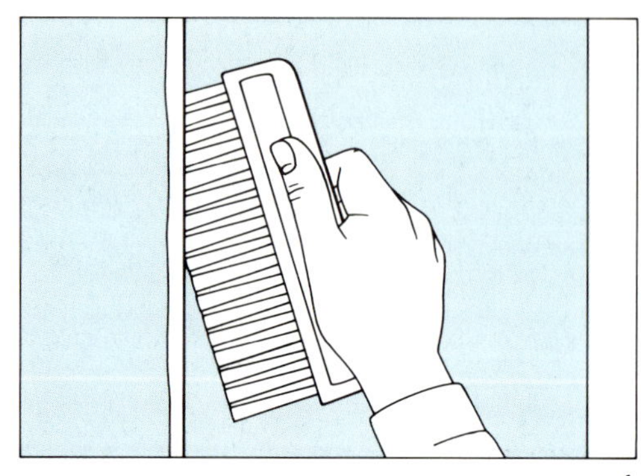
A

MANTELPIECES

If your mantelshelf runs the full width of the chimney breast, treat the wall above and below separately. Work down to the shelf, then paper any areas below, making sure the pattern matches with adjoining lengths.

If the wall continues either side of the mantelpiece and shelf hang paper as one length, as around a doorway (see page 79). Brush into the back of the shelf, then cut to fit around the contours of the fireplace (**A**).

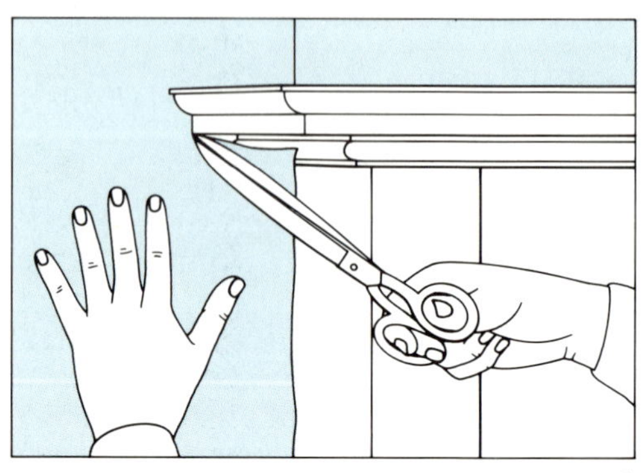
A

DECORATING IN A STAIRWELL

Decorating a stairwell invariably poses a few problems which are worth sorting out before you start work. It is advisable to work with a partner if at all possible. Not only will you have to deal with lengths of wallpaper which are much longer than usual, but you will also have to solve the problem of access. It is foolhardy to try to perch ladders at precarious angles in a desperate attempt to reach the top. Personal safety is paramount and it is quite possible to combine safety with reasonable access these days because there are several special ladders and aids which help make stairwell work easy. And they needn't cost you a fortune because most can be hired.

SAFETY FIRST

Staircase stepladders

These are the most manageable option if you have a straight flight of stairs. The legs of these ladders can be adjusted to different heights so that you can stand them on different treads of the staircase.

When you use a staircase ladder, play safe and anchor the legs to the steps. One way of doing this is to fix a couple of screw eyes or stout nails into the treads and to lash the legs of the ladder to these with rope.

Once you have secured the legs, create a stable work platform by laying scaffolding boards (which you can also hire) between the top of the ladder and the landing. Tie the boards to the ladder and nail the other ends to the landing floorboards.

Stair scaffolding

This is usually worth hiring only if you have a lot of work to do on the walls – plastering, for example. Like stair ladders, this type of scaffolding has legs that can be adjusted to various heights. One of its advantages is that it provides a hand rail and a work platform at the same time.

Home-made platforms

These are usually necessary if you are decorating a dog-leg staircase. With home-made platforms, ladders, stepladders and scaffolding boards are combined to create a sturdy work base. Here are some tips which will help you to make a home-made platform secure and easier to use.

- Screw wooden battens to the treads of stairs to prevent ladders from slipping.

- Use clamps or rope to anchor the boards to the ladders.

- Tie the tops of ladders to newel posts to prevent them from slipping sideways.

Other useful equipment

In addition to ladders and platforms, there are a number of gadgets you can hire, or improvise yourself, which make decorating less of a chore.

- Paint kettles have wider mouths than the average tin and carry more paint. Consequently they allow you to use a wider brush and cut out some of the running up and down ladders to pick up paint.

- Foot rests clamp on to the rungs of a ladder and provide a wider base.

- Tool trays also clamp on to ladder rungs and allow you to keep essential bits and pieces up there with you.

- A butcher's hook will enable you to hang a pot of paint on a rung.

- Padding, wrapped around the top of a ladder, will prevent damage to the wall.

- Ladder stays keep the top of the ladder away from the wall, allowing better access.

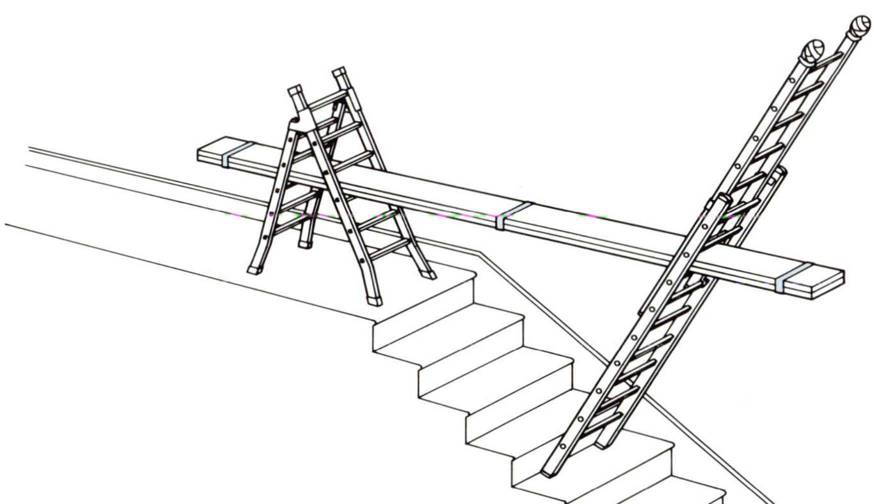

Setting up a safe work station when decorating a stairwell is of paramount importance. Prop a ladder against one wall – padding the ladder top to protect the wall – and run stout planks between it and a second ladder or set of steps, securing everything firmly.

PAPERING A STAIRWELL

On a sloping wall cut each length to fit – measure its longest side plus 4 in (10 cm) to trim (**A**). Mark its position on the wall. At the bottom trim diagonally to follow the line of the skirting (baseboard).

A

TILING A WALL

Tiles are one of the most universally popular decorating materials. This is hardly surprising as they come in a multitude of colours, shapes and sizes, are easy to clean and last almost indefinitely. Putting them up is straightforward if you follow a few simple rules.

There are hundreds of different types of tile. Some are mass produced and therefore relatively inexpensive; others are handmade to order.

In addition to tiles you will also need adhesive and grout. Adhesive is generally sold ready mixed in tubs that state the area the contents will cover. Make sure that the adhesive is suitable for the tiles you are fixing and the area you are tiling.

Grout is also sold in tubs and is essential to seal the gaps between ceramic tiles. You don't have to settle for plain white grout as it is now available in a variety of colours. If you are fixing tiles in a kitchen or bathroom where the atmosphere is damp, consider buying a waterproof grout which also contains a fungicide.

Tiles themselves need little maintenance other than a periodic wipe with a damp, soapy cloth then a rub dry. The grouting between them, however, may require touching up from time to time. You can cleanse and brighten white grouting by scrubbing it down with bleach but a better solution is to brush on a proprietary 'grouting paint'. You can buy this from many do-it-yourself shops in kits containing everything you need, including an application brush. Most makes are water- and mould-resistant and there is a choice of colours to suit your scheme.

Ceramic tiles provide a decorative and extremely hardwearing wall covering that is particularly suited to bathrooms. Here, the red and grey diagonal stripes detract from the coldness of plain white and make a smart, colourful impact. If you are tiling a shower area make sure that you use the special water-resistant adhesive and grout recommended. Choose towels and other accessories carefully for their decorative as well as practical value.

CERAMIC TILES

These are made from fired clay and are usually glazed which makes them easy to maintain. Most glazed tiles are now 'universal' which means that they have chamfered edges that can be butted up against each other to leave a narrow 'grouting line'. If you want a wide grouting line, you can insert spacers between the tiles. A few traditional tiles have built-in spacer lugs around the edges but with most you have to insert plastic slips to provide a grouting line. Generally speaking, it's best to go for the universal type because they are the easiest to fix and there is no shortage of choice. Although some universal tiles come in hexagonal and diamond shapes, square or rectangular types are the most popular. Square tiles are usually 4 in (10 cm) or 6 in (15 cm) square – also 8 in (20 cm) in the US – rectangular ones 6 × 4 in (15 × 10cm).

QUARRY TILES

Quarry tiles are not glazed and are thicker than ordinary ceramic tiles. They are traditionally used on floors but there's no reason why you can't put them on a wall. The choice of colour and size is limited, however: they are usually in tones of brown, from cream to russet red and are 5 in (12.5 cm) square.

MOSAIC TILES

These are simply small ceramic tiles glued to a backing (face up) sheet of hessian (burlap) or paper. They give a wall an interesting texture but require a special technique: the sheet of tiles is glued to the wall and when the adhesive has set, the backing is peeled off and the tiles grouted.

CORK AND VINYL

Cork and vinyl tiles can be used on walls as well as on the floor and are especially good if you want to cover an entire wall – in a bathroom for example. They are usually around 12 in (30 cm) square and are fixed with special adhesive.

MIRROR AND METALLIC TILES

These tiles come in any number of different sizes. Some have a self-adhesive backing. Use these reflective tiles sparingly.

MARBLE TILES

These come in lovely tones of cream, pink, green, grey, black and terracotta but they are heavy, expensive and difficult to cut.

CALCULATING QUANTITIES

Most tiles are sold in packs which clearly state the area that the contents will cover. This makes estimating a great deal easier.

If you want an accurate figure, calculate the area you want to cover by multiplying together the height and the width, then divide into this figure the area of one tile – this will give you the number of tiles you need. The most common tile sizes are given above, but always check your particular design first. It's as well to add an extra 5 per cent on to your total to allow for cut tiles and breakages. Most suppliers are happy to sell individual tiles if you need a few more or less than the quantity in a pack.

FIXING CERAMIC WALL TILES

You will need

- Tiles
- Adhesive and grout
- Two straight 2 × 1 in (5 × 2.5 cm) timber battens
- 2 in (50 mm) nails
- Caulking for sealing joints
- Cellulose filler for preparation
- Tenon saw
- Spirit level
- Try square
- Tile cutter
- File saw
- Hammer
- Filling knife
- Serrated adhesive spreader
- Offcut (short lengths) of dowelling
- Sponge
- Spacers, if you are using them
- A damp rag

a b c d e f g h i

Tiles are available in a wide variety of materials, ranging from sturdy quarry to decorative mosaic and mirror. It is important to choose the right type to suit your situation if you are to get the maximum of wear from them. On the right we show a selection of tiles to indicate some of the types you may like to consider when you make your purchase.

(a) *mosaic ceramic*
(b) *mirror*
(c) *vinyl*
(d) *cork*
(e) *marble*
(f), **(g)** *and* **(h)** *plain, patterned and border ceramics*
(i) *quarry*

STARTING WORK

1 Prepare the surface by stripping off any old wallpaper and filling any depressions or dents in the wall (see pages 54-7). If you are tiling over a painted or already tiled wall, check that the paint – and especially the tiles – are not in danger of peeling off. The wall should be flat, true and dry.

2 Before you set out the wall, make your own gauging rod from 2 × 1 in (5 × 2.5 cm) battening the length of the area you are going to tile – it's an invaluable tool which you will use time and again. Lay the batten on the ground and butt a row of tiles up against it. If you are using spacer lugs, don't forget to include them. Mark off the grouting lines on to the batten (**A**).

A

3 Don't start tiling at the bottom of a wall against a bath or skirting (baseboard). The chances are that neither is truly level and the result will be that the completed tiling looks askew. Tile the bulk of the wall first, working from a true horizontal, and fit cut tiles along the bottom. Draw a horizontal line where the top of the tiling is to fall (**B**), checking it is perfectly level.

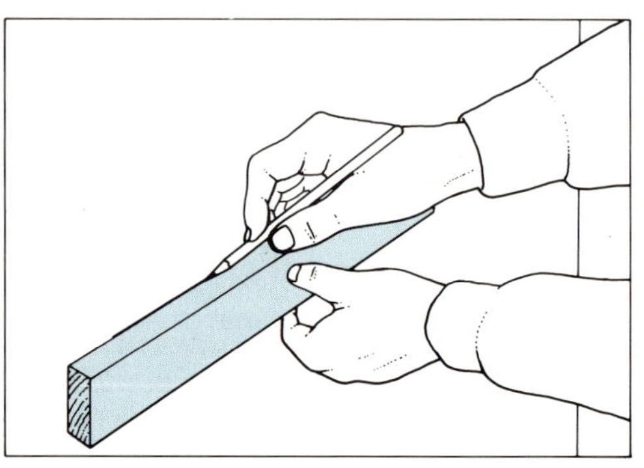

B

4 Use your gauging rod to measure down from this line to the bottom of the area to be tiled (**C**). Almost certainly you will have to cut a row of tiles to fit – and this row should be at the base, not at the top. Mark a line for the bottom of the last row of complete tiles. Check that this line is horizontal with the help of a spirit level (**D**) and nail a batten against it (**E**). This batten will support the first row of tiles until the adhesive dries.

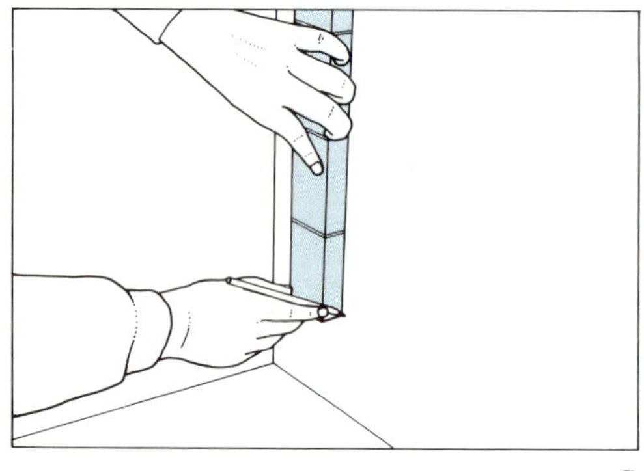

C

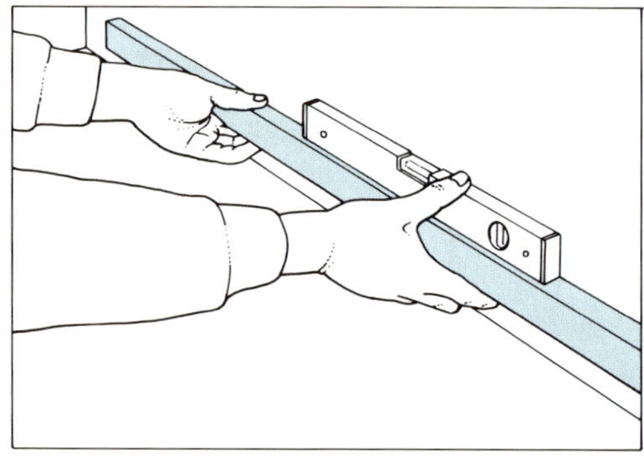

D

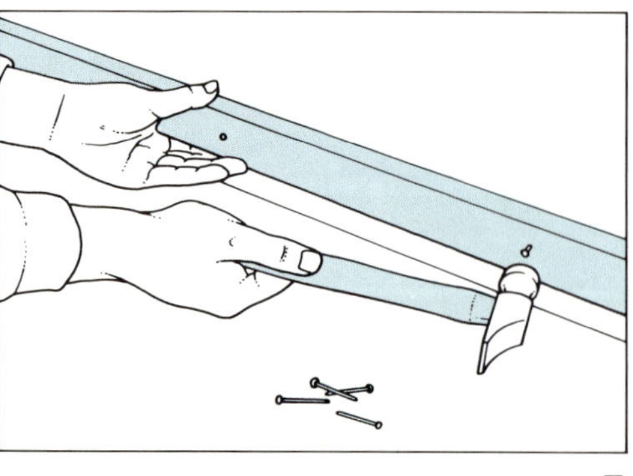

E

5 You will probably find that the width of the area to be tiled doesn't coincide with a number of whole tiles either. Use your gauging rod to judge how best to arrange the tiles. If you are tiling into an internal corner, plan for a cut row of tiles to run up against the corner; if you are tiling within an alcove, run a row of cut tiles up each side; if you are tiling to an external corner, use whole tiles at the corner and cut tiles at the other end. When you have decided on the layout, mark off the horizontal batten accordingly.

6 Draw a line up the wall to mark the last vertical row of whole tiles, check it with a spirit level and nail a straight batten against it. This, with the horizontal base batten, marks the edge of the area to be tiled (**F**).

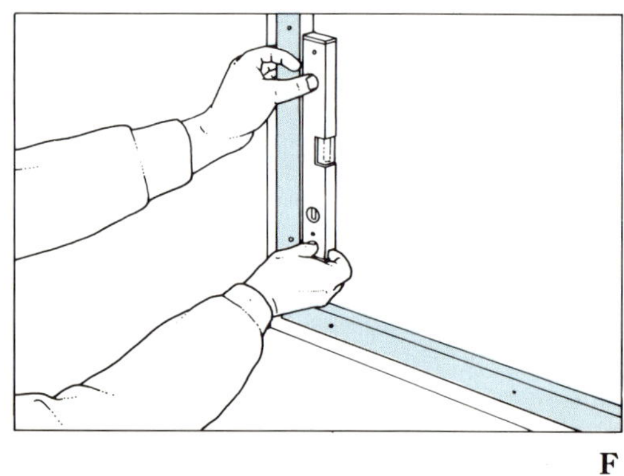

F

7 Where the two battens meet at right angles, spread a layer of adhesive over an area of about 1 square yard (1 sq m), using the serrated spreader provided with the adhesive. Position the first tile tightly in the corner and press it firmly into the bed of adhesive (**G**). Continue adding tiles and spreading adhesive until you have covered the bulk of the wall; if you want to use spacers, insert them as each tile is laid. Wipe off any adhesive on the tiles with a damp rag (**H**) and leave for a day to set.

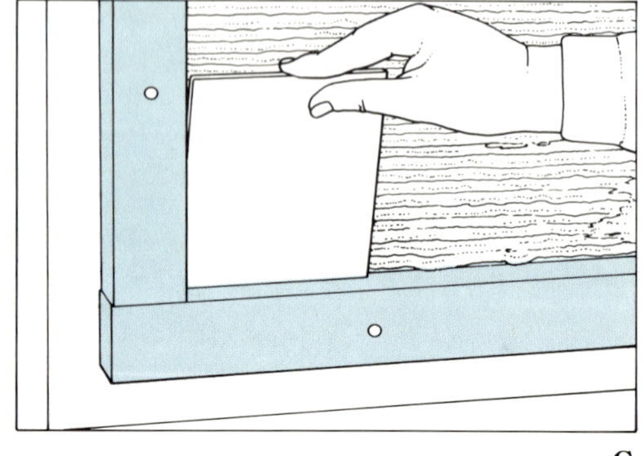

G

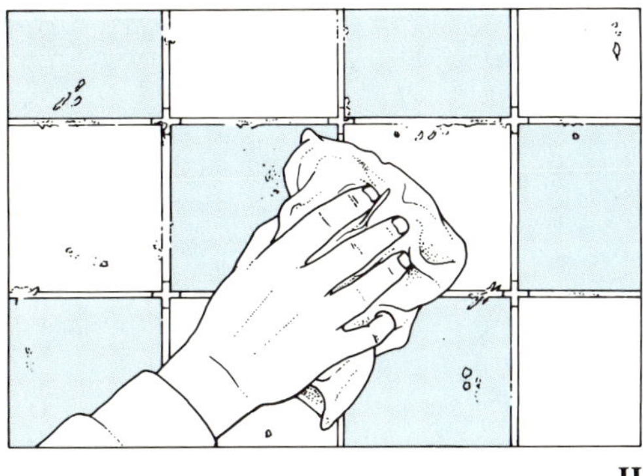

H

8 Gently lever off the battens when the adhesive is hard and start cutting tiles to fit around the borders. To measure up a tile for cutting, hold it upside down over the last whole tile in a row with one edge against the wall (**I**). Make allowances for spacers if you are using them and then scribe a cutting line. Cut the tile by scoring a straight line through the glazed surface using a proprietary tile cutter (**J**). You could use a simple tile cutter with a tungsten carbide tip or a more complicated device with a measuring and marking gauge. Break the tile in two over a pair of matchsticks or in the jaws of the cutter (if it has them) (**K**).

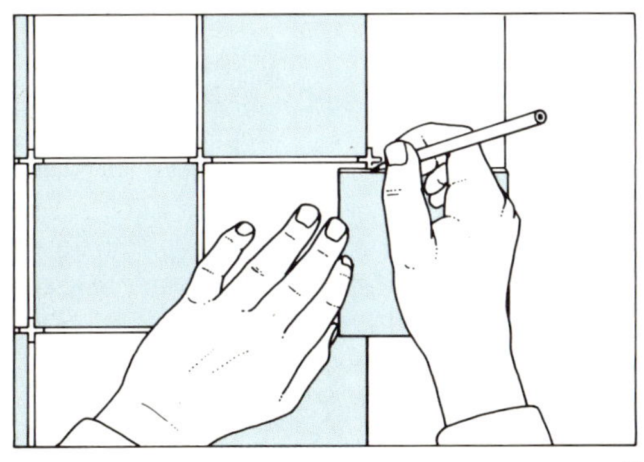

I

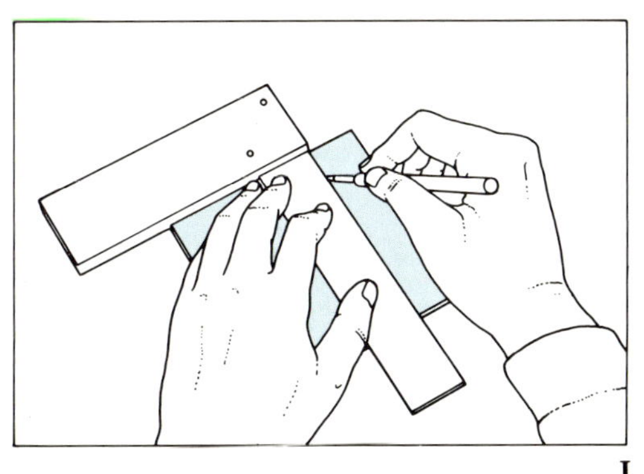

J

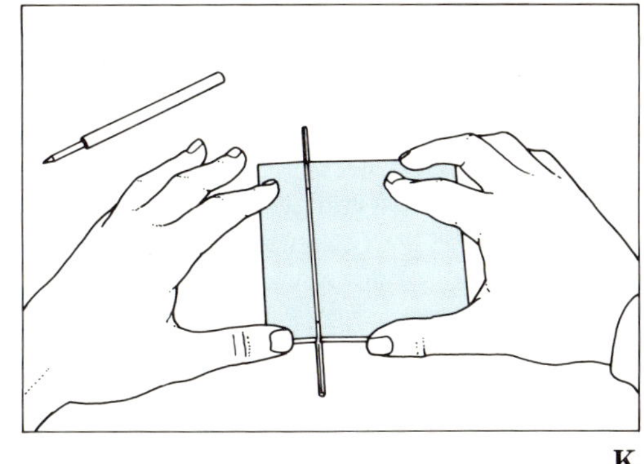

K

9 Fix the cut tiles in place with adhesive and leave for a day or so.

10 If you have to shape a tile to fit around a fitting such as a light switch, mark the waste area and cut it out with a saw file held in an ordinary coping saw frame (**L**).

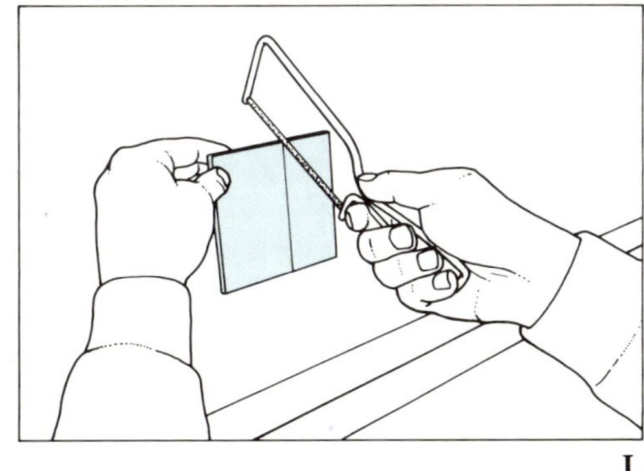

L

11 For pipes, mark the tile by aligning it with the centre of the pipe (**M**). Draw a true horizontal line. Measure from the edge of the last stuck tile to the centre of the pipe. Draw a vertical line on the tile. Cut along one line and make semi-circles with a saw file. Fix the pieces in place (**N**).

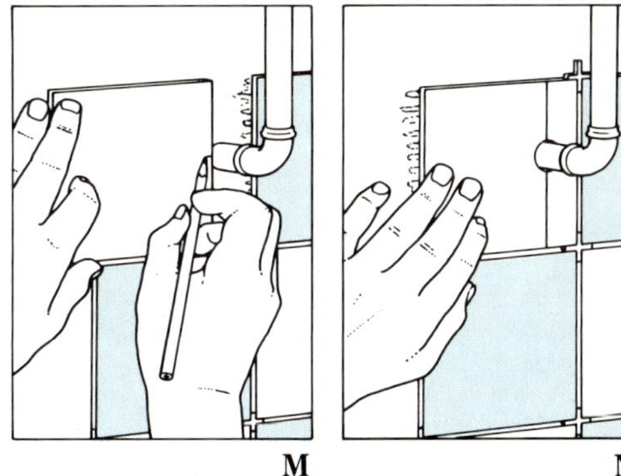

M N

12 To cut tiles to fit around curves and other awkward shapes, it is best to make a cardboard template of the obstacle, and transfer the outline to the tile (**O**). Cut with a saw file in a coping saw frame.

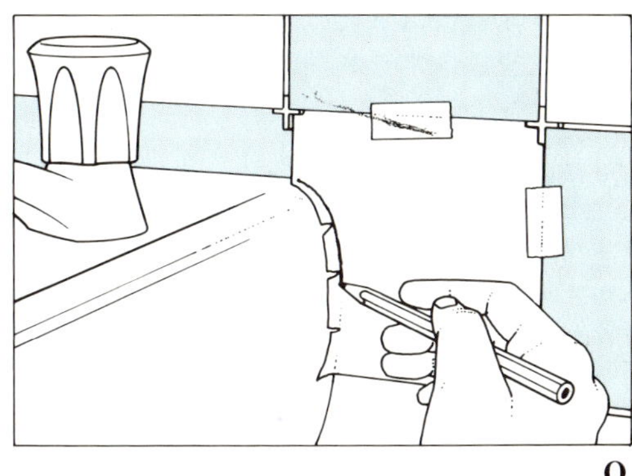

O

13 When you have fitted all the tiles and the adhesive is dry, you can start grouting. Spread the grouting over the face of the tiles with a spreader, working it into the joints (**P**). Wipe off the surplus grout with a damp sponge before it has a chance to set. To get a neat finish to the grouting, run along the joints with a piece of dowelling or the end of a pencil (**Q**). Whatever you do, don't use your finger tips – grouting is abrasive and will literally wear holes in your skin. After a couple of hours, rub off any powdery residue with a duster and polish the tile surface with a clean dry cloth.

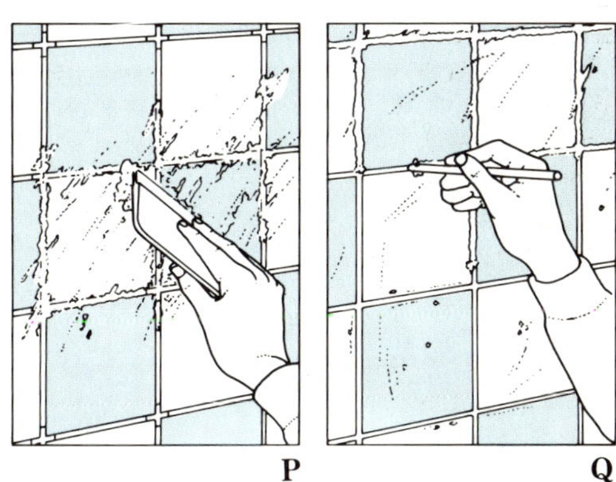

P Q

14 If you have tiled up to the edge of a bath or sink, seal the joins with caulking; this is usually sold in syringe-type plastic bottles. Cut the nozzle to suit the thickness you require, and, as you press the plunger, move the nozzle along the gap. If necessary, run a wet finger over the join to smooth it; it should dry with a slight sheen.

PAPERING A CEILING

A safe and comfortable work station is vital when you paper a ceiling. Working with your hands above your head is awkward and tiring and invariably the lengths of paper you have to work with on ceilings are longer than those on walls, and so are heavier and more cumbersome. Work with a partner if possible so that one of you can support the paper while the other applies it.

The only sensible way to paper a ceiling is to work from a simple scaffolding of two stepladders supporting a plank at just the right height for comfort when working (see page 57). Make sure this is firm and steady each time you move it.

Always paper a ceiling before you paper the walls. Ideally, lengths of paper should run parallel to the main source of light to prevent seams from showing, but it is easier, if you are doing this job for the first time, to paper across the width of the ceiling so that you will have shorter strips to handle. These two may not necessarily coincide so you will have to decide yourself which suggestion to follow.

Embossed paper and woodchip can be decorative used on a ceiling. They can also be repainted and easily cover any flaws in an imperfect ceiling. If you want a complete change of decoration, textured paper is also easier to remove when you come to redecorate than textured paint.

Trim textured papers to fit exactly to the junction with the walls whether you are papering the walls as well or not. With other wallcoverings, allow an overlap of about $\frac{3}{4}$ in (2 cm) if you are going to paper the walls as well. When using the same pattern on ceiling and walls it is impossible to match it up by papering one wall, across the ceiling and down the other side – as on the opposite wall the paper would be on upside down!

Prepare your work surface as described on pages 54-7; see page 74 for how to calculate your paper quantities.

Attractive and unusual windows were the starting point for this bathroom's decoration. The geometric device of the panes is picked up by the trellis wallpaper, which covers the ceiling, too. For a neat finish, the join between wall and ceiling is covered by a co-ordinating border, and a mixture of modern and Victorian tiles, in neutral shades of cream, brown and green, complete the scheme and provide a practical, wipe-clean surface.

You will need:
Paper
Dust sheets
Size or wallpaper adhesive
Pasting brush
Paperhanger's brush
Large, long bladed and small sharp scissors
Length of string and chalk
Drawing pins (thumbtacks)
Steel tape measure
Soft pencil
Seam roller
Sponge
Stepladders and plank
Either, if you need to paste the paper, a pasting bucket and pasting table
Or, if you are using a ready-pasted paper, a water trough

STARTING WORK

1 Having prepared the ceiling, size it well a couple of days before you want to paper.

2 In the same way as when papering a wall, you need a straight line from which to work with your first length of paper. Parallel to the window, measure out from the edge of the ceiling a roll width minus ¾ in (2 cm) (**A**). Mark this at each end, coat the string with chalk and attach it to the ceiling on your marks with drawing pins (thumbtacks). Pluck the string so that it marks a straight line. Remove the string.

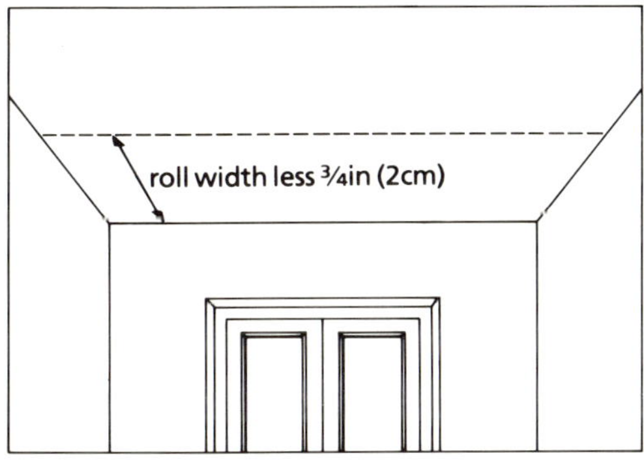

A

3 Measure the length of paper needed. Check in two or three places across the room as measurements may vary, then take the longest measurement. Add 2 in (5 cm) to this to allow for overlaps.

4 Mix up the adhesive, and cut and paste the lengths following the instructions on pages 76-7. This time fold the lengths concertina fashion so that the pasted side is on the inside of each fold (**B**).

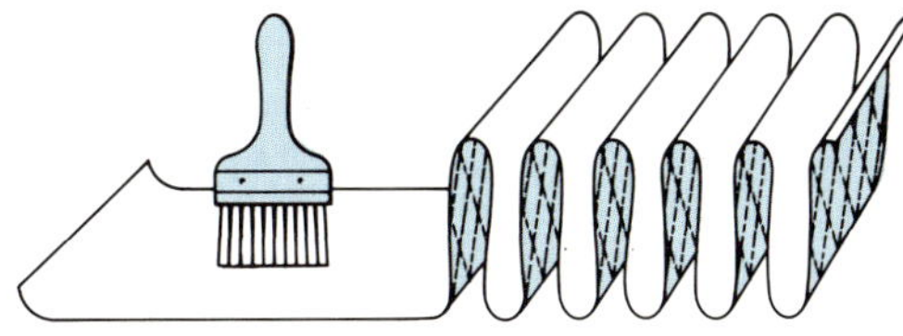

B

5 As you are about to start, brush a little adhesive on to the ceiling at the starting point to give extra adhesion. Then align the paper with the chalk line so that the far edge overlaps on to the wall. Support the length of paper with a spare roll (especially important if you are working on your own) (**C**). Allow 1 in (2.5 cm) overlap at the end. Apply the paper, progressively brushing down the centre while you – or if possible a second person – gradually unfold the strip.

Check that you are perfectly in line with your chalk line, then brush the covering out towards the sides.

C

6 Trim the overlaps (see page 78) if you are papering just the ceiling. Otherwise allow ½ in (13 mm) overlap all round after trimming. Cut out a triangle at each corner so the paper sits neatly (**D**).

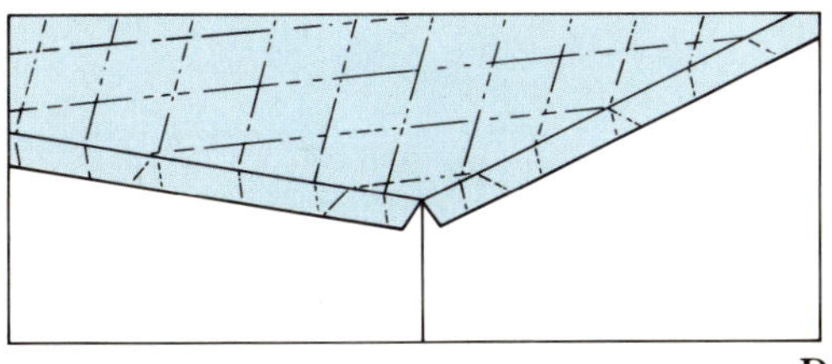

D

7 Apply the second length in the same way, butting up against the first as tightly as you can and taking care to match any pattern. Leave for about 20 to 30 minutes then run the roller down the seams to secure.

CEILING ROSE (OUTLET)

Turn off the electricity before starting work. When you come to put up the length which surrounds the ceiling rose, position the paper and lightly press it down over the rose to mark where it falls. Then, using small scissors, cut a hole in the paper at the centre point and pull the flex (cord) through (**E**). Make cuts from this centre point to make a star shape and to reveal the rose. Press the paper down over the rose to form creases around the outside; trim back just inside this circle (**F**). Unscrew the rose and loosen the screws in the fitting so that you can brush the paper well down under it; screw up again and replace the cover. Turn the electricity back on. *If you are using a foil covering cut this to fit around the outside edge of the rose.* Because foil is a conductor of electricity it must *not* be tucked inside where it might come into contact with the working parts of the light fitment.

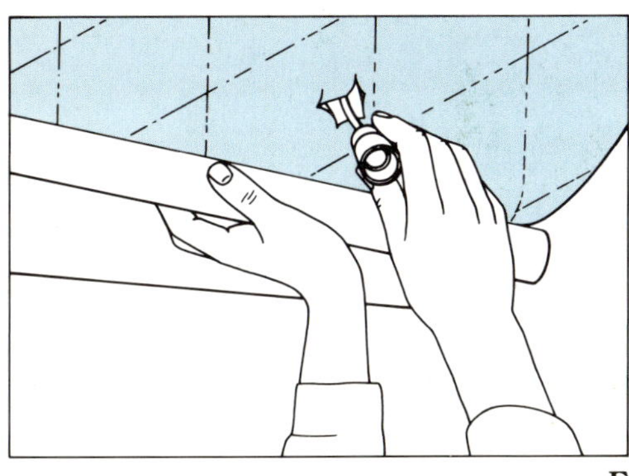

E

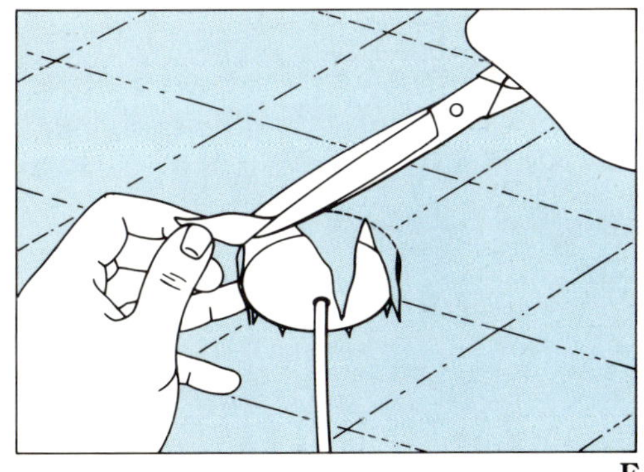

F

FITTING COVING

Fitting coving (cove moulding) is the perfect way to finish off a room; it rounds off the corners and covers any unsightly cracks where the walls meet the ceiling. It looks good where walls and ceiling are decorated in contrasting ways.

Today coving can be bought ready-made in pre-cut lengths and is commonly made out of one of two materials: polystyrene or plaster. Which you choose will probably depend on your room scheme. Polystyrene is cheaper than plaster.

POLYSTYRENE COVING

Polystyrene coving is made to match polystyrene ceiling tiles. It is usually quite narrow, about 2 in (5 cm) wide and should be put up *before* you put up the ceiling tiles – that way you can butt the tiles up against the coving, which is the same thickness. Polystyrene coving is easily shaped with a sharp trimming knife and is fixed with special adhesive which is sold in tubs. Angle pieces are available to fit around internal and external corners which simplify the job.

PLASTER COVING

This is made rather like plasterboard – it has a core of plaster covered with thick paper. It is available in a variety of lengths and with widths of 5 in (12.5 cm) and 4 in (10 cm). Plaster coving is put up before the ceilings and walls are papered or painted. Most manufacturers provide paper templates to help you cut the mitres for corners and you can buy decorative pieces to cover internal and external corner joins. Plaster coving is also secured with adhesive.

CALCULATING QUANTITIES

It is best to try to avoid joining lengths of coving end to end, although this may be necessary with very long walls. Measure up each wall separately and jot down the lengths. At the same time, make a note of the number of internal and external corners.

When you buy the coving, match lengths of wall with lengths of coving. Obviously, one long length of coving may be cut into two or more pieces to cover more than one wall. If in doubt, always overestimate. If you want corner pieces, buy these at the same time to avoid matching problems later.

Ready-mixed adhesive is easier to use than the powdered type and it saves you the messy job of mixing. Instructions on tubs of adhesive state the length of coving that the contents can fix.

FIXING POLYSTYRENE COVING

You will need:
Coving
Sharp trimming knife
Felt-tip pen
Adhesive and spreader
Damp rag

STARTING WORK

1 Before fitting the coving, check that the wall and ceiling are stable, clean and dry, so that the coving will adhere properly.

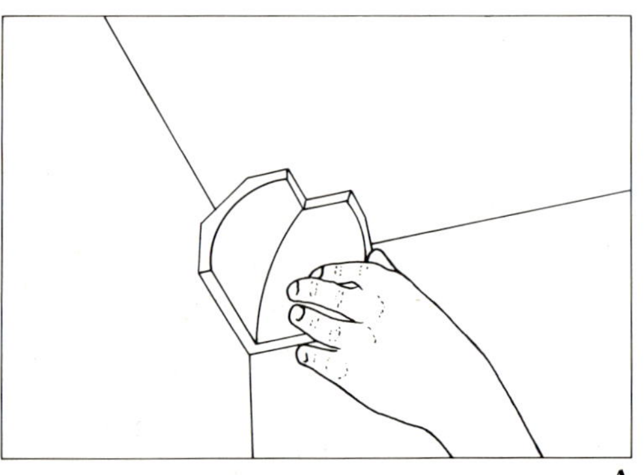

A

B

2 Fit the corner pieces first. Simply spread adhesive on to the backs of the angled sections and push them gently but firmly into place so that they fit snugly into or around the corners (**A**).

3 Measure up lengths of coving to fit between the corner pieces and cut them to size with a trimming knife (**B**).

4 Smear adhesive on to the backs of the coving lengths and smooth them into place (**C**). Wipe off excess adhesive with a damp rag before it has time to set. (The adhesive will also serve to fill any tiny gaps between coving and wall or ceiling.)

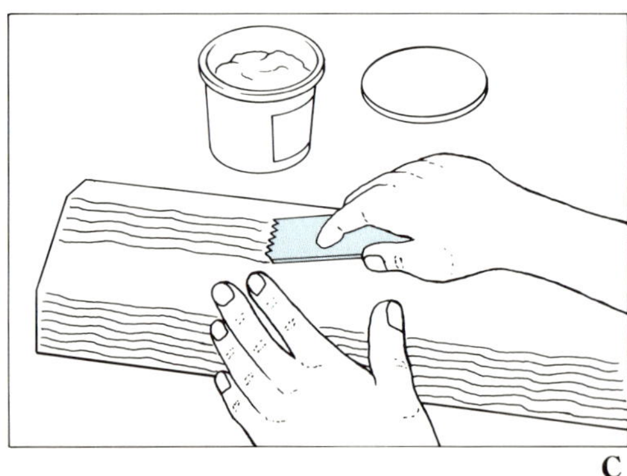

C

POLYSTYRENE CEILING TILES

Use polystyrene tiles to add texture and warmth to a ceiling. Prepare the ceiling as for papering (pages 54-7) and lay out and trim tiles as for floor tiles (pages 100-2) – use a sharp knife to cut them from their face side. Apply adhesive evenly to the back of the tile, allow to set slightly and press gently into place.

You can paint over polystyrene tiles with emulsion (latex) paint but never with gloss as these two elements combined can create a potential fire hazard.

FIXING PLASTER COVING

You will need:
Coving
Filling knife
Scraper
Fine-toothed (universal) saw
Pencil
Tape measure
Old paintbrush
Templates
Recommended adhesive
Adhesive spreader

STARTING WORK

1 Prepare the walls and ceiling by stripping away any loose paint or paper (see pages 54-7). Check that the plaster or plasterboard underneath is stable. You need a clean, dry and firm surface to work on.

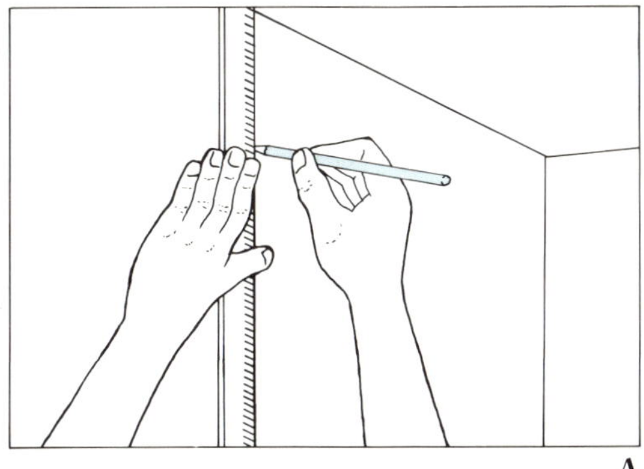

A

2 Pencil parallel guide lines around the perimeter of the room. The easiest way of doing this is to measure the height and depth of the coving and to transfer these measurements to the walls and ceiling (**A**).

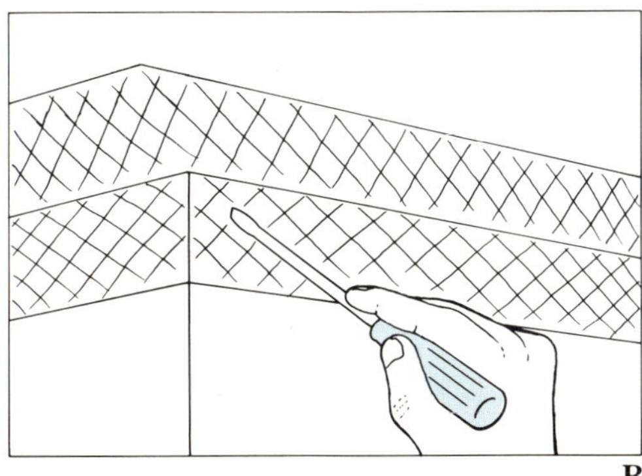

B

3 Score scratch lines on the surfaces within your guide lines using the edge of a scraper or screwdriver. These scratches provide a key for the adhesive (**B**).

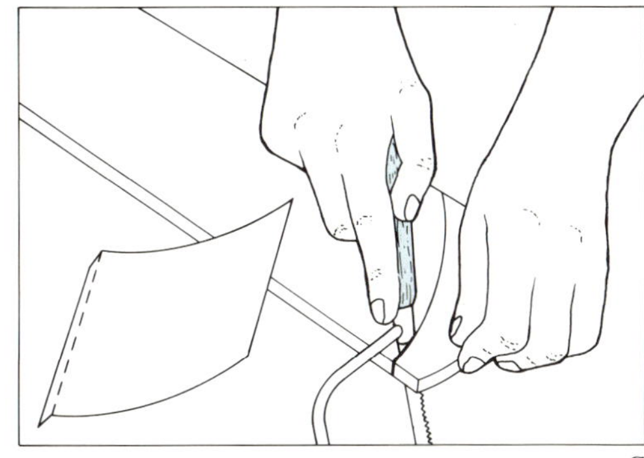

C

4 Measure up lengths of coving to fit, not forgetting to allow for the overlap necessary at external corners. Cut the pieces to size, using your mitre-shaped templates as guides (**C**). It's best to use a fine-toothed saw which won't be blunted by the plaster.

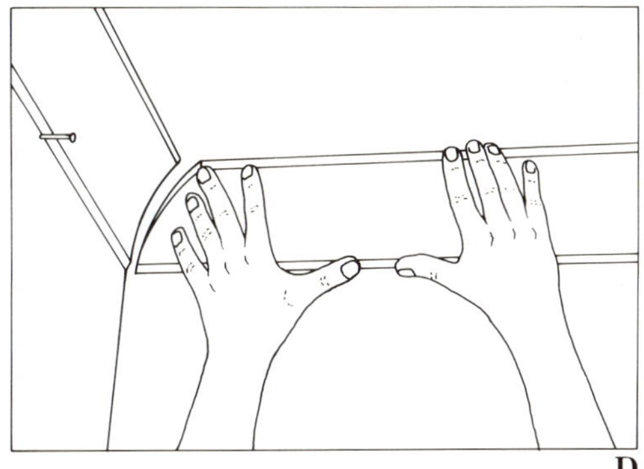

D

5 Dampen the ceiling and walls between your pencil lines with an old paintbrush and water. Coat the backs of the coving with adhesive and push each length into place between your guide lines (**D**). Wipe away excess adhesive with a damp cloth. A nail gives support while the adhesive dries.

6 If your walls aren't quite square or if you discover gaps at the corners, fill with adhesive, applying it with a filling knife.

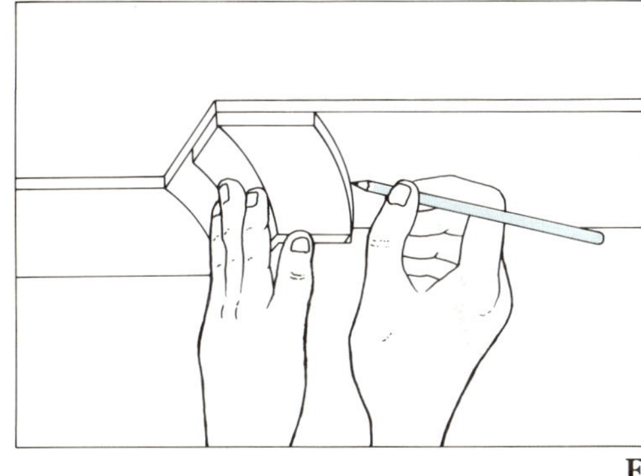

E

7 Adding decorative corner pieces is straightforward. Hold each section in position and pencil its outline on to the coving (**E**). Key the surface within your pencilled lines, smear adhesive on to the back of the corner piece and then press it into place.

8 When the adhesive has set hard, prime the coving ready for painting.

Decorative corner pieces have been added to this plaster coving for the finishing touch.

BORDERS

If flat-painted walls are too plain for you, and patterned paper coverings too busy, then a border makes a very effective compromise. Wallpaper borders are cheaper to use and quicker and simpler to put up than wallpaper. Many manufacturers now have a number of borders in their ranges, from animal and personality borders for children's rooms to sophisticated geometric and full-blown flower borders. Borders can also be painted on – in simple stripes or by means of paint sprayed or brushed through a stencil to form a decorative repeat pattern. A border can also look effective used with a sponged wall (see pages 69-70).

Some small patterned wallpapers look attractive with a superimposed border, also of wallpaper, and you can buy these in coordinating designs to suit almost every taste and style.

POSITIONING A BORDER

The traditional positions for a border are around the top of the wall, about 12 in (30 cm) below the ceiling at the old picture rail height, or at dado level, about 3 ft (90 cm) from the floor. You can also place a border around the room just above a skirting (baseboard) or around a door or fireplace – even around items of furniture to highlight them. Dado level borders or stripes are very effective and useful in a hallway and up the stairs if you paint the wall below the border a practical deep colour and the wall above, which is less likely to become damaged, in a softer or lighter tone.

PREPARATION

Walls should be prepared in the same way as for painting (see pages 54-7), then papered or painted with a water-based paint if you want a plain paint background.

This restful living room has been given definition by painted borders at picture rail and dado levels. Against a background of lavender-grey walls, borders in dark lilac and turquoise run around the room, and echo the material used for cushion covers and blinds. They pull together a scheme in which colours have been carefully chosen to blend in a harmonious whole. A little flair has made essentially simple ideas successful.

CALCULATING QUANTITIES

For a wallpaper border, simply measure around the room the area you want to be covered with the border to obtain the border length. For a striped border that is painted around the room in a wide band, say 12 in (30 cm) of one colour with a narrow darker stripe on top of this, you will need about 2½ US pints (1 litre) of paint for the wide band and a minimal amount for the narrow one. The quantity of spray paint needed to do a stencil will obviously depend on the size and design of your stencil; one can of spray paint will probably complete one wall so calculate accordingly.

PUTTING UP A WALLPAPER BORDER

The most important thing is to get your border straight and to do this you will first need to have a line on the wall to follow. Make a mark with chalk at the height you want at each end of all walls and then at about 2 ft (60 cm) intervals along the wall at exactly the same height. Join up your marks to form a line around the room and butt your paper up to this. To put up the border follow the instructions for pasting paper (see page 76) and putting up lining paper (page 75). Overlap at the corners as described for wallpaper on page 79.

PAINTING A BORDER

Mark the position for the border by using the method described left. To paint stripes use two strips of masking tape, pressing the tape down firmly so that the paint cannot seep under it. Paint the stripe using long, even strokes and when the paint is touch dry pull the tape away from the line and touch up any small drips. If you want to paint more adjacent lines allow the first stripe to dry hard (for about three days) then mask and paint the second in the same way.

You can also sponge a border around a plain wall. In this case pencil in the position of the border edges and sponge following the instructions on page 70. Mask the plain wall with cardboard. When it is dry, paint a plain stripe above and below the sponging to give some definition.

A SPRAYED STENCIL BORDER

Mark the position for the border as left. Practise spraying through the stencil on to some sheets of paper first until you can achieve a clean outline. The trick is to hold the stencil tightly up to the surface you are spraying and to use several thin coats rather than one thick one which could run.

When you are ready to start, further mask the edges of your stencil with about 12 in (30 cm) of paper all around. Mark a line along both stencil and mask where the edges of the border will be so that you can line this up with the chalk line along the wall. Position the stencil on the wall and tape it in place.

Wear rubber gloves and if possible work with a partner who can hold the stencil tightly against the wall with a length of wood. Spray through the stencil, holding the can parallel to the wall. When the paint is dry – spray paint takes only minutes – remove the stencil and move it to the next position.

Stencils are available to suit all tastes – rabbits and cars complement a child's bedroom, and a floral motif graces a country kitchen.

A border creates a neat and decorative edge where paint and paper meet. Here, a border at dado height prevents the stripes from making the walls appear tall and narrow. The horizontal line is neatly positioned at bed and furniture height and smartly separates plain and patterned surfaces.

CHAPTER 5

Flooring

Are you planning to invest in a brand new floor covering or forced for the moment to make do with what you've got? Carpet is hard to beat for a feeling of luxury and warmth. Wooden floors add richness to both traditional and modern interiors – perhaps your existing boards are in good enough condition to be sanded, stained and sealed? Tiles now come in a wide range of materials and styles; and sheet floorings are tough and practical. If you need a temporary measure, paint a concrete floor and add rugs for warmth. Whatever your taste and situation, don't neglect the decorative potential a floor can have.

PREPARATION OF SURFACES

Whether you intend to make the most of your existing floor and simply paint or varnish it, or whether you intend to cover it with tiles or sheet flooring, you must ensure that the floor surface is firm, dry and even, or the time, effort and money you put into the new – or refurbished – floor will be wasted. A floor that is not properly prepared will neither look good nor wear well. The preparation work required will depend on the floor that is already down.

DEALING WITH DAMP

Problems with damp are less likely if you are working with a wooden floor base than if you have a solid floor – concrete, quarry tiles or stone. Whatever your floor you must deal with any damp before you lay a new floor. Check by taping a small drinking glass to the floor somewhere it won't be in the way. Leave it there for two or three days and then look to see if any damp has collected inside. If the glass has become misted and wet inside then damp is rising from the floor and it will need to be treated. Damp on the outside of the glass shows that there is condensation in the room. Unfortunately, treating damp properly means lifting the old floor and laying a new one over a bituminous, liquid membrane or over heavy-duty plastic sheeting. Make sure the waterproof layer reaches at least 6 in (15 cm) up the walls to form a seal. You may need to get a specialist contractor for this job.

WOOD FLOORS

First of all hammer down or remove and replace any protruding nails (**A**). Use a nail punch to hammer nails down to avoid damaging the boards as you work. Remove any tacks that may remain in the floor from old coverings and nail down any loose boards. The boards should be flat and even; use a plane or rasp to smooth down any uneven edges. Check the spaces between the boards: wide gaps should be filled in with wedge-shaped wooden laths hammered into place. For narrow spaces use a wood filler, pushing it into the cracks with a flexible filler knife. Fill proud of the surrounding floor surface and then sand back.

If you are going to lay new tiles or sheet flooring you should really cover all the existing floor with sheets of hardboard for an even surface, unless it is in really good condition. Prepare the hardboard the day before it is going to be laid to prevent buckling later. To do this, wet the rough side of the hardboard with a sponge and a bucket of cold water, dampening it well and evenly all over (**B**). Leave it on a flat surface to dry overnight. Then, starting in the centre of the room, lay one sheet, rough side up, across the line of the floorboards. Hold it in position by hammering hardboard panel pins (brads) around the edge at 6 in (15 cm) intervals. Then hammer in panel pins all over the board about the same distance apart. Butt more sheets of hardboard up to this but stagger the joins and nail the boards in position in the same way. Cover the whole area with hardboard.

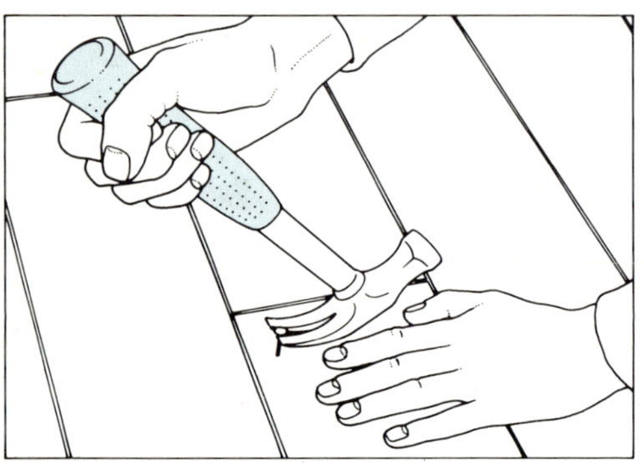

A

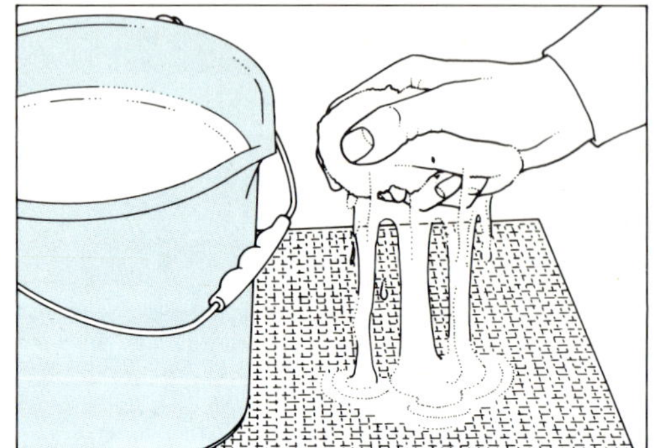

B

CONCRETE FLOORS

Sweep well, then wash down. Fill any cracks or holes with a cellulose filler and remove any lumps with an old scraper. If the floor is very dusty, paint it with a diluted PVA bonding agent, following the manufacturer's instructions, and allow it to dry.

If the concrete is uneven it is best to level it by spreading on a self-levelling compound. Wash the floor well then dampen it down with a wide decorator's brush and cold water. Mix the levelling compound, following the instructions supplied with it, until the consistency is creamy. Then, starting from the side of the room farthest from the door, pour the mixture evenly over the floor area using a flat tool (a plasterer's float is best) to smooth one area lightly into another (**A**). Then leave the compound to find its own level and to dry out.

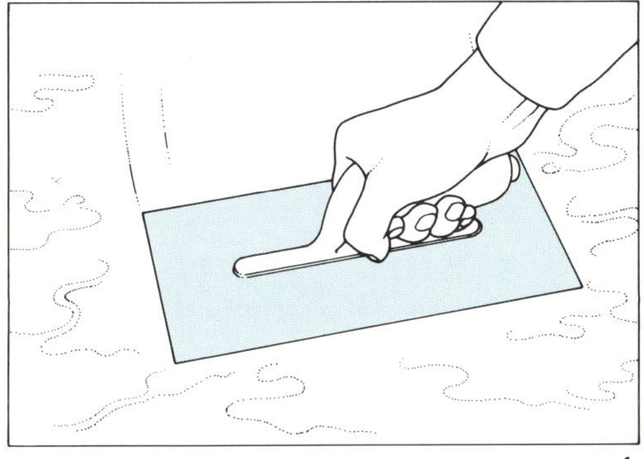

A

VINYL AND CORK TILES

It is advisable to remove these before you lay new sheet flooring or tiles. Do this by holding a warm iron over each tile in turn (**A**). The heat will loosen the adhesive so that the tiles can be prized up. Use white (mineral) spirit and wire wool to remove any remaining adhesive.

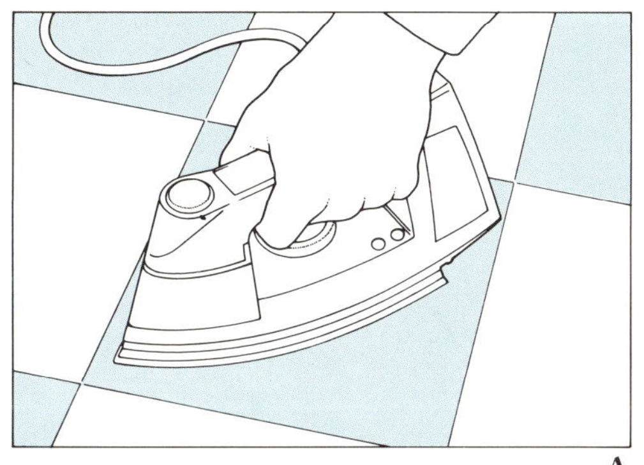

A

SHEET VINYL

Removing sheet vinyl is usually easier than removing tiles as it is normally stuck down only in doorways, along seams and around heavy equipment, such as cookers (ranges) and washing machines, that is moved back and forth occasionally. Use a warm iron on these areas as with vinyl tiles and, again, clean off any remaining adhesive with white (mineral) spirit and wire wool. (Make sure you don't allow the iron actually to touch the vinyl or it may melt on to the iron.)

QUARRY TILES

If the floor is dry, smooth, level and secure then vinyl tiles or sheet flooring can be laid on top of quarry tiles. Fill any spaces between tiles with an acrylic filler and if the surface is uneven level it with a self-levelling compound (see Concrete floors). Wash the tiles well with detergent first. They should be clean and grease-free before you begin.

MAKING THE MOST OF WHAT YOU'VE GOT

Whether as a stop-gap or a more permanent measure, existing wood or concrete floors can be treated for a fraction of the cost of a new floor covering and still look good.

As a temporary measure you can paint a concrete floor with floor paint. This comes in only a limited range of colours, but it will help to prevent the problem of concrete dusting. Or if you have old floorboards that are in good condition, they can be sanded and sealed to form a subtle natural background for furniture and rugs. You can use a wax emulsion for a deeper sheen. This type of floor may be vacuumed or swept, then washed with warm soapy water.

A concrete floor can be painted as a temporary measure until you have the time and money to select and lay a more permanent type of flooring.

If your wood floor is in good condition it is a pity to cover it up; sand and seal it instead, for a gleaming surface which can form an ideal background for rugs, too.

PAINTING A CONCRETE FLOOR

You may not feel that you want to live long-term with a plain concrete floor but it makes a good temporary measure, perhaps while you save up for those marble tiles!

The concrete should be clean, dry and free from grease (see page 93). Seal or prime the floor according to the manufacturer's instructions – some floor paints need to be put on to a sealed floor whereas an initial primer of thinned-down solution of the paint to be used is adequate for others. Work in a well-ventilated room, starting near the wall farthest from the door and working towards the door. Leave to dry thoroughly before the next coat – you will probably need a minimum of three.

USING A HEAVY-DUTY SANDER

Here again, preparation work is vital for a good result as projecting nails or floorboards not only will spoil the finished effect but will rip the sandpaper off the sander as you work and cause it to grind into the wood unevenly. (See page 92 for how to prepare the floor.)

The type of heavy-duty sander that makes sanding a floor a feasible proposition for the amateur can be hired quite easily. It comes with a dust bag and a supply of sheets of coarse, medium and fine abrasive paper. Hiring an edging sander too is recommended, although you can use an orbital or belt sander instead. The heavy duty sander will not cover the 4 to 5 in (10 to 12 cm) nearest to the skirting (baseboard). If you hire the equipment over a weekend you can do a number of floors or share the hire cost with a friend who wants to do some sanding.

In spite of the dust bag, sanding a floor throws up a lot of very fine dust. Protect your eyes with goggles, wear earplugs and a mask over your nose and mouth, and hang a sheet outside the door, covering the whole door and frame so that the dust cannot creep between any cracks or the sides of the door into the rest of the house.

You will need to empty the room completely before you start work.

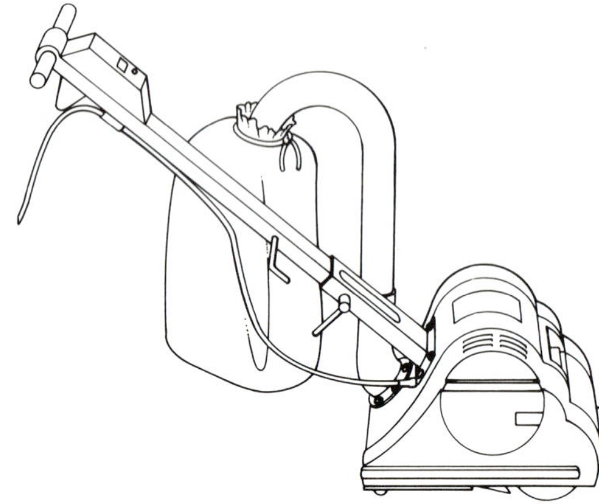

A heavy-duty sander for sanding floorboards.

SANDING AND SEALING BOARDS

You will need:
Sanders and paper
Protective clothing and mask
Goggles and ear plugs
Covering for your hair
Vacuum cleaner or brush

STARTING WORK

1 Using the edging sander and coarse sanding sheets sand the edges of the room to a width of about 6 in (15 cm) until the old surface is completely removed (**A**).

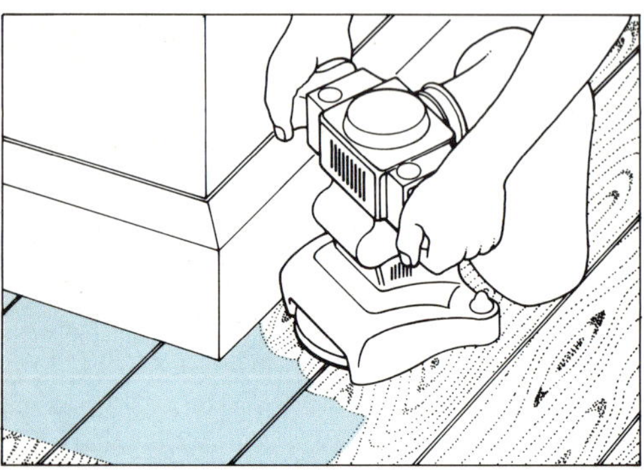

A

2 Again with coarse sanding sheets, use the large sander and work at a 45 degree angle to the boards (**B**). Always overlap work by about 3 in (7.5 cm).

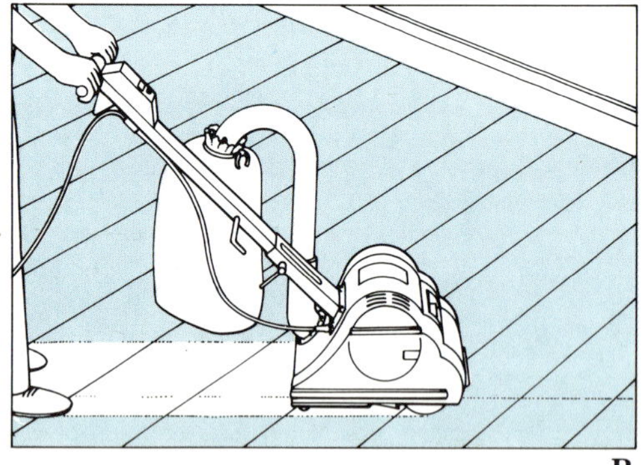

B

3 Using medium then fine sheets, sand the edges of the floor, this time working with the grain of the floorboards.

4 Working with the large sander, sand along the floorboards with the grain, using medium then fine sanding sheets. Overlap the strips by about 3 in (7.5 cm) as before. When you have finished all the boards should feel smooth to the touch – and you will probably be thrilled by the transformation, especially if they are old boards.

5 Vacuum or sweep up dust (**C**) then leave the work for a day. Clean again as more dust will have settled. Do this as often as seems to be necessary. The room must be absolutely dust-free when you start to varnish the floor or the dust will spoil it.

C

Safety tip: The fine sawdust produced by the sander is highly inflammable and may flare up dangerously if burned.

Finishing the floor

Wet the floor in one small area to get an idea what the colour of the finished floor will be if you use a clear varnish finish. If you want a darker colour you can stain the boards before varnishing or use a varnish stain.

APPLYING THE VARNISH

Use a gloss-finish polyurethane varnish as this will give the toughest result. Do not stir as this causes bubbles.

1 Dilute the first priming coat according to the instructions on the tin. Use a large brush and, starting in the area farthest from the door, brush on the varnish across the grain of the wood, working with quick, even strokes (**A**).

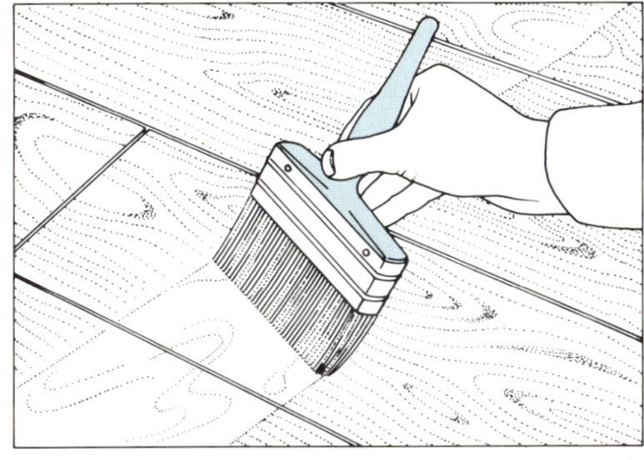

A

2 Brush out the varnish at right angles to this and then finish by lightly drawing the brush along the boards. Allow to dry.

3 Use at least two more coats of neat varnish. Sand lightly with sandpaper between coats then wipe over with white (mineral) spirit to remove dust before revarnishing (**B**).

B

Alternatively you could use an oleo-resinous seal instead of polyurethane varnish, although the finish is not as tough. This sort of seal sinks into the wood and gives a scratch-resistant satin finish to the floor. To apply, follow the manufacturer's instructions as supplied with the seal.

COLOURING FLOOR BOARDS

Before sealing, bleach or colour the floor if required. Use stain, which comes in different colours or wood shades, or a tinted varnish.

This beautiful stripped and sanded floor is mirrored by a ceiling of tongue and groove panelling. Wooden shelves and supports continue the natural theme, and the room provides a very pleasant working and eating environment.

SHEET FLOORING

Sheet flooring is usually cut and laid from one piece. This gives it a smooth, tough seam-free finish that is particularly suited to areas of hard wear such as kitchens and bathrooms. If extra strips do have to be cut they are best sited under tables or in recesses where they are less vulnerable to daily wear and tear.

There are three main types of sheet flooring: vinyl, rubber and linoleum. All are easy to care for, needing only a sweep or vacuum, followed by a wash with warm, soapy water. Vinyl can be polished with an emulsion polish if it loses its shine, but an oil-based wax polish makes it slippery.

VINYL

Now the most popular sheet flooring for domestic use, vinyl is fairly tough and is impervious to most kitchen stains, even to most household chemicals, although it will burn and can be cut, too, if knives and other sharp things are dropped on it.

Vinyl flooring comes in a wide range of colours and designs, and differs in quality and price. Most designs imitate natural materials such as brick or wood, and marble or ceramic tiles.

RUBBER

Modern rubber flooring is made from a mixture of natural and synthetic rubber and is most popular with people who prefer a high-tech or 'minimal' look. The range of colours available is small and patterning usually consists of embossed studs, ribs or squares.

Rubber is particularly hardwearing and is also quiet and waterproof. However, it is not as easy to lay as vinyl and the surface tends to mark more easily.

LINOLEUM

In the home this has almost completely been replaced by vinyl, but it is still used extensively in hospitals, public buildings and factories because when laid it makes a very tough floor. Linoleum is made from a mixture of drying oils, resins, ground wood, cork, whiting and pigments. It is more brittle than vinyl and therefore likely to suffer more damage in transit; it is also more difficult to lay because of this. Industrial-grade linoleum can be bought for the home.

CUSHION FLOORING

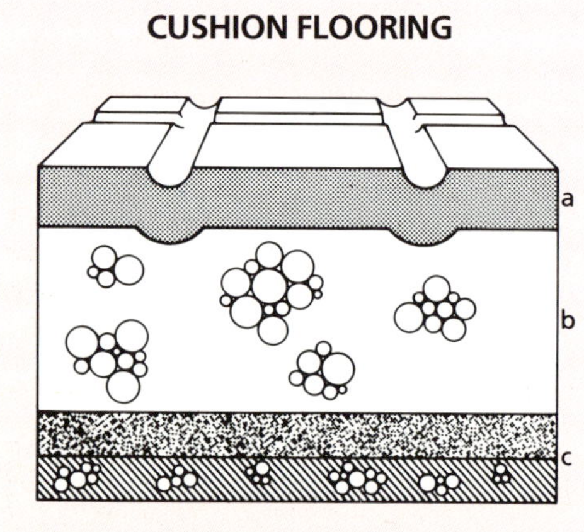

Cushioned vinyl usually has a textured finish which gives the pattern an attractive three-dimensional appearance (**a**). It is quiet and very comfortable, thanks to the layer of foam 'bubbles' (**b**) which is sandwiched between the outer layers. A glass fibre-reinforced backing keeps the flooring flat (**c**).

Sheet vinyl can successfully imitate a tiled surface. Here it gives the appearance of cool marble with diamond-shaped insets.

LAYING SHEET VINYL

Vinyl sheet flooring is not difficult to lay and usually only needs sticking at doorways, joins and points where heavy equipment may need to be pulled out. It should be laid on a dry base that is flat, sound, smooth and free from dirt and grease (see pages 92-3 for preparation of the floor).

When you bring the roll of flooring home leave it loosely rolled in a warm room for 24 hours to allow it to become supple.

CALCULATING QUANTITIES

Make a floor plan of your room and mark on it the width and length at the widest points, taking into account any recesses and measuring into the doorway to join up with any adjacent floor coverings. Ideally you want a sheet 4 in (10 cm) longer and wider than your room measurements. The most common widths are 2, 3 and 4 m in the UK, 6, 9 and 12 ft in the US. Take your floor plan with you when you go to buy the flooring so that the retailer can help you decide what will be the most economic way to lay the flooring and the best width to buy.

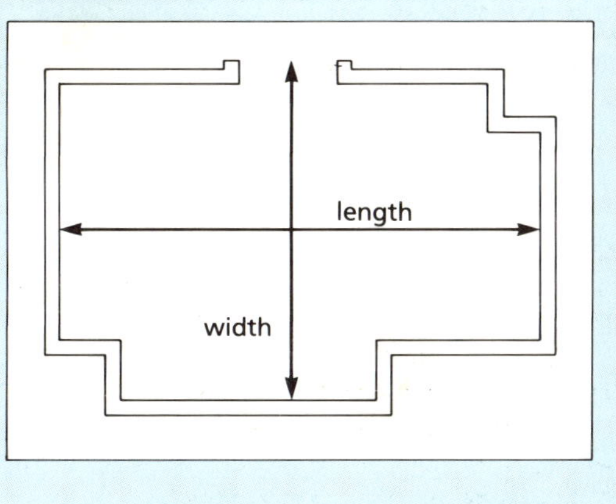

You will need:
Flooring
Recommended flooring adhesive
Soft broom
Large general purpose scissors and a heavy-duty craft knife
Block of wood
Paint scraper
Chalk
Metal straight edge
Duster

STARTING WORK

1 To make sure that any pattern in the flooring design runs parallel to the door wall, mark two points on the floor equally distant from this wall. Draw a line between these two with chalk, continuing it up the skirtings (baseboard) so you will still be able to see the marks when the flooring is in place (**A**).

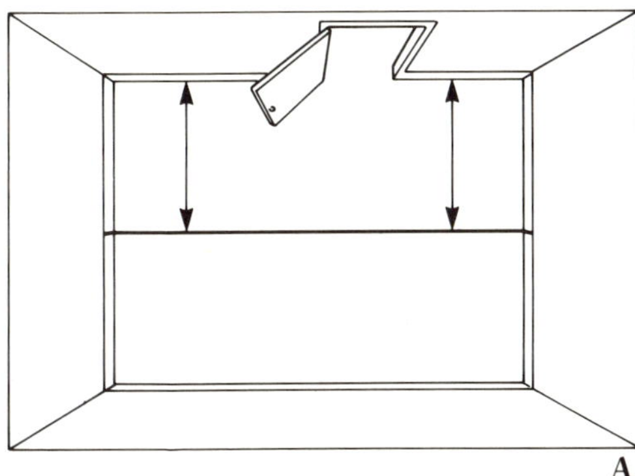

A

2 Take the roll of flooring into the room and place it on the floor diagonally, then unroll it, gradually drawing it round to its final position.

3 Lay the flooring so that it laps each wall by about 2 in (5 cm) and will fit right into doorways and any alcoves. Use the soft brush to smooth it out (**B**). Check that any lines in the design match up with your marks on the skirting (baseboard) and appear straight from the doorway.

B

C

4 Use the block of wood to press the sheeting against the base of the skirting (baseboard) and thus form a sharp crease at the point where the floor meets the skirting (**C**). You may need to make vertical release cuts into the 2 in (5 cm) flap.

5 Use the paint scraper to hold the flooring hard against the floor where it meets the skirting (baseboard) and at this point cut the vinyl with the craft knife. Move the scraper along the floor, cutting with the craft knife along its edge as you go (**D**).

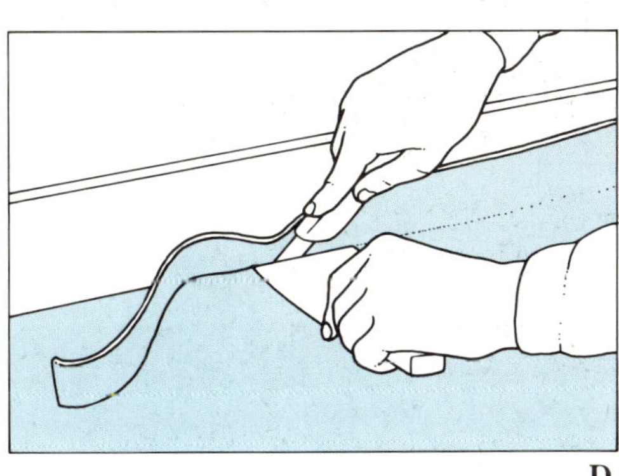

D

Around the door

1 See **A** on page 98. Make two vertical 2 in (5 cm) cuts in the vinyl at the projecting points of the door frame, from the top of the vinyl down to where it touches the floor (**ab** and **cd**). This allows the flooring to lie flat on the floor so you can trim it accurately.

Next make diagonal cuts to the same two points (**eb** and **fd**). Brush the flooring so no air is trapped beneath. Make another vertical cut around the frame (**gh**) and cut diagonally (**ih**).

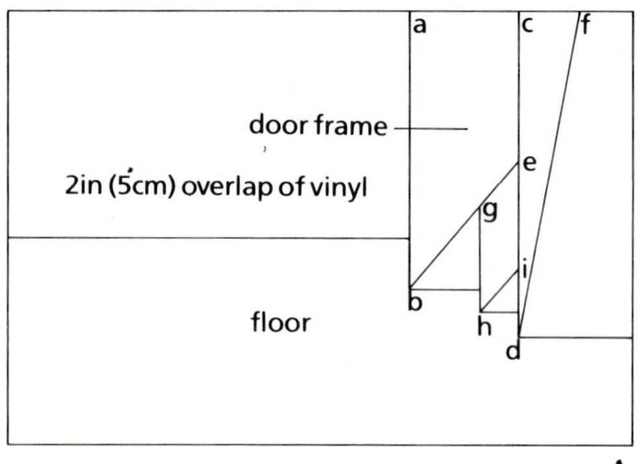

A

2 Trim the flooring so that it fits accurately around the frame, trim into the doorway and across the opening to butt up to adjacent floorings (**B**).

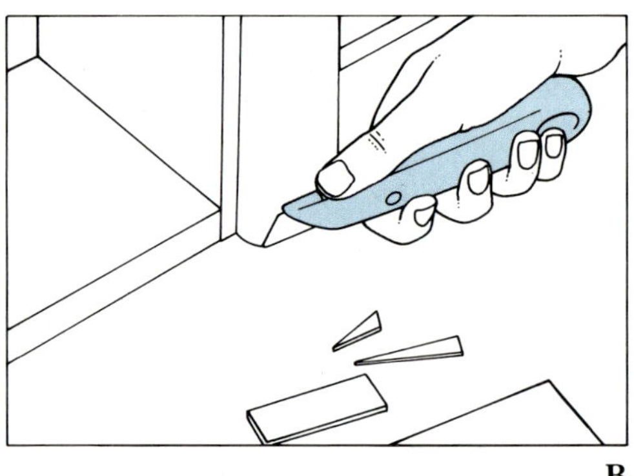

B

Inside corners

Mark two points 2 in (5 cm) each side of a corner and draw a line from these points down to the corner (**A**). Cut out this square so that the vinyl will fit snugly (**B**).

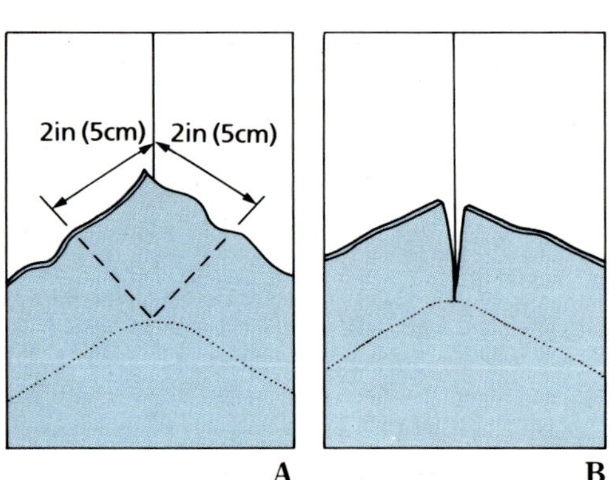

A B

Outside corners

Cut out a triangular shape from the flooring at the corner. To do this, measure 2 in (5 cm) each side of the corner and make a diagonal cut from each side to the corner point at floor level (**A**). Make further vertical cuts at 12 in (30 cm) intervals along the skirting (baseboard) or kitchen unit bases, making sure that the cuts go just to the point where the skirting (baseboard) meets the floor. This makes trimming the final sections easier. Brush to make sure that the flooring sits neatly on the floor, then remove the overlap as described in step 5 on page 97.

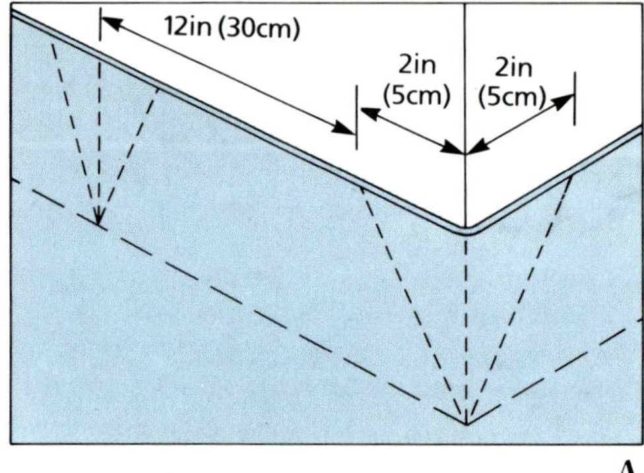

A

Around a wash basin or toilet

So that the flooring fits neatly around the shape of a wash basin pedestal or a toilet you will need to make a template of the shape. Roughly cut out the shape from tracing paper then position the paper on the floor around the pedestal and butting up to the skirting (baseboard). Make release cuts on the curved edge of the tracing paper so that it fits snugly around the shape. Draw the outline of the shape on to the paper (**A**); remove it and cut out the pedestal shape following your drawn curve. Draw the outline on to the flooring in the position of the obstacle. Cut the shape out roughly just inside your drawn curve, make release cuts, then position. Check and cut.

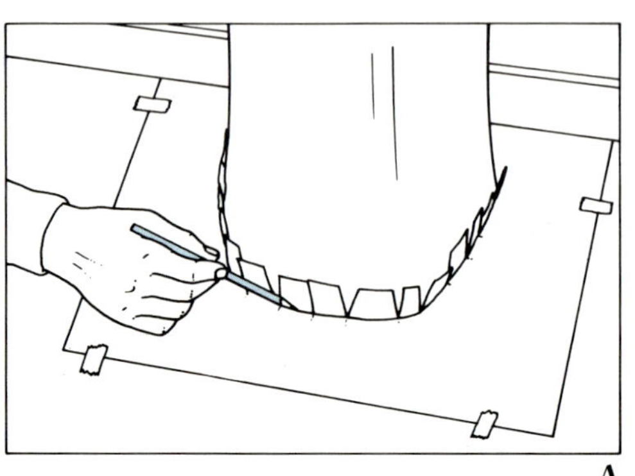

A

Joins

When one sheet is fitted around the edge, position the second sheet to overlap the first. Make sure that both sheets are running in the same direction and, starting from the centre of the second, adjust it where necessary so that the pattern exactly matches the underneath, already-fitted sheet. Cut through both layers at the overlap, remove trimmings and butt edges (**A**). Trim the second sheet at the edges and fit in the same way as the first.

Cut and fit all the flooring in a room before you attempt to stick any down.

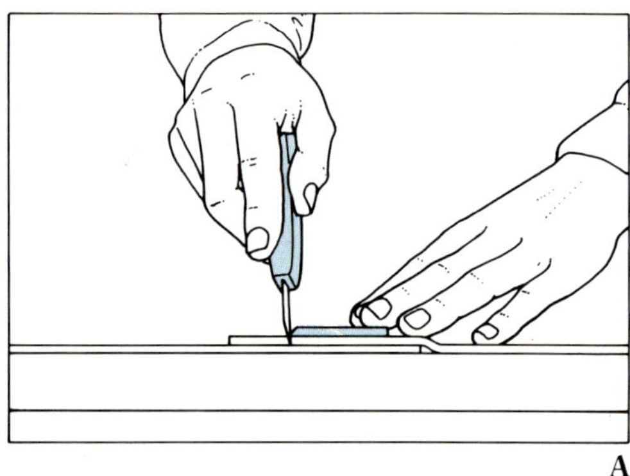

A

Sticking down

When the flooring is fitted spread the recommended adhesive on the floor in the doorway, in a 6 in (15 cm) band at any joins and at any point where equipment may need to be pulled out. Rub with a damp cloth to flatten the flooring on to the adhesive and remove any excess immediately (**A**). If there is more than one join in the flooring it should be stuck down all over the floor.

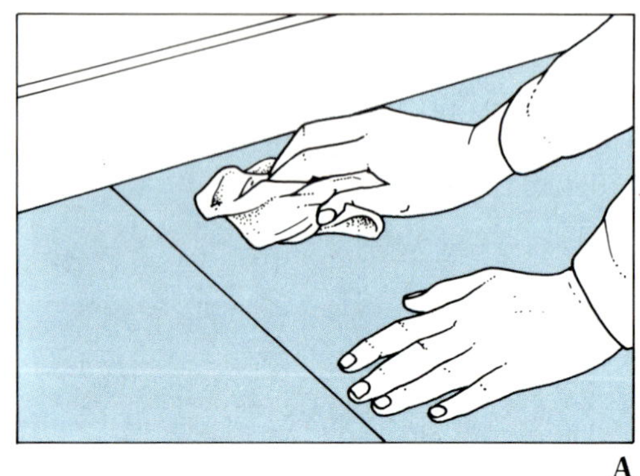

A

FLOOR TILES

You can buy floor tiles to suit every taste and pocket, from cheapest self-adhesive vinyl or unsealed cork to traditional quarry tiles and luxurious – but hard and cold – marble. Whatever your requirement you should be able to find something to suit.

VINYL

Vinyl tiles, usually 12 in (30 cm) square, are generally tough, comfortable to stand or walk on and easy to lay – particularly if they are self-adhesive. They come in a range of plain or marbled colours and a number of patterns which often imitate natural materials such as stone, brick, marble and ceramic. Some have a smooth finish, which can become slippery when wet, while others are made of the softer, warmer, cushioned vinyl. Those tiles which are not self-adhesive are laid on a bed of special adhesive.

CORK

This attractive natural material makes a warm, comfortable floor. It is not as durable as some of the other choices although you can buy cork tiles with a tough vinyl coating. Ordinary pre-sealed tiles are also available but the cheaper cork tiles have to be sealed with polyurethane varnish after you have laid them.

Cork tiles are laid in the same way as vinyl tiles, using a special adhesive.

RUBBER

Popular with those who want a high-tech look, rubber tiles are hardwearing, quiet and comfortable but expensive. Some of the sharp-edged designs are difficult to clean. They are available in a limited range of plain colours and designs.

QUARRY TILES

The slightly uneven finish and wonderful earthy colours make quarry tiles attractive to those who like a country or farmhouse style. They are less expensive than ceramic tiles and come in a range of interesting shapes – hexagonal, provençal and fleur de lys as well as square. The disadvantages are that quarry tiles are hard – any dropped plates are likely to break – and cold.

Quarry tiles should be laid in a bed of mortar. They are available either glazed or unglazed. The latter must be sealed after laying and then polished, and are best left to the professional.

CERAMIC TILES

To be suitable for laying on a floor, ceramic tiles need to be thicker than standard wall tiles and should have been fired at a higher temperature so that they will not break. A shiny finish can be slippery when wet but non-slip finishes are also available. Like quarry tiles, ceramic tiles are also laid in a bed of mortar (not dealt with here). They are expensive and it is probably worthwhile getting them laid professionally.

MARBLE AND SLATE

These two materials are extremely durable and produce luxurious, expensive – and cold – floorings. Slate may be polished or unpolished. Both should be laid by an expert.

a
b
c
d
e
f
g
h
i
j
k
l

(a) *and* **(b)** *marble;* **(c)** *rubber;* **(d)** *sealed cork;* **(e)** *unsealed cork;* **(f)** *vinyl;* **(g)** *natural polished slate;* **(h)** *quarry;* **(i), (j)** *and* **(k)** *ceramic;* **(l)** *natural unpolished slate.*

LAYING VINYL, CORK OR RUBBER TILES

Laying vinyl, cork or rubber tiles is not difficult. The instructions below are for laying tiles on adhesive. You can also buy self-adhesive tiles. Apart from the fact that they need no extra adhesive they should be laid in the same way. Simply peel the protective backing off the tile to expose the adhesive as you put it down. See page 100 for instructions on how to lay. If you are not using self-adhesive tiles make sure that you buy the correct adhesive for the material. Unsealed cork tiles will need to be sealed after laying with wax or with polyurethane varnish (it means extra work but the varnish layer will prevent water seeping between the tiles).

Prepare your sub-floor: it must be dry, clean, grease-free and smooth before you lay the tiles, otherwise they will not stick down properly (see pages 92-3).

CALCULATING QUANTITIES

Most cork and vinyl floor tiles are around 12 in (30 cm) square, although some may be 9 in (23 cm) square. Boxes of tiles usually state the area the contents will cover which makes calculating easier. All you have to do is measure the length and width of the room at the *widest* points, taking measurements into alcoves and into doorways to butt up to other floorings. Then multiply length by width to find out how many square feet or metres you have. Divide this figure by the box contents to see how many boxes you require.

To work out the exact number of tiles, if you need to, multiply the length of one tile by its width to find its square area and then divide the area of the room by the area of this one tile to find the total number of tiles needed to cover the floor.

If you want to create your own patterns from different-coloured plain tiles, or to add a border of patterned tiles around a central square of plain, you will have to work this out on graph paper. Draw the dimensions of the room on the paper and colour in your floor design. You can then work out from this how many tiles in each colour or pattern you need.

Add 5 per cent to any total to allow for mistakes or incorrect cutting.

You will need:
- Tiles
- Recommended adhesive and notched spreader
- Steel measuring tape
- String, chalk (stick or powdered) and drawing pins (thumbtacks)
- Steel straight edge
- Heavy-duty craft knife
- General purpose scissors
- Pencil
- Profile gauge (this gives more accurate cutting around curves)
- Tracing paper
- Soft cloth

STARTING WORK

1 The first step is to find the centre of the room, as this is the point from which all the tiles should be laid. Measure and mark the centre of two opposite walls, then stretch string, covered in chalk, from one mark to the other. Hold with a drawing pin (thumbtack) at each end then snap the string so that a chalk line is formed on the floor. Do the same from the other two opposite walls (**A**). Where the lines cross is the centre point.

A

Dry lay the tiles along the edge of the lines in each direction to check for fit (**B**). If the gap between the last tile and the wall in either direction is less than 2½ in (6 cm) you will need to adjust the 'centre point' so that you can fit a wider edge piece.

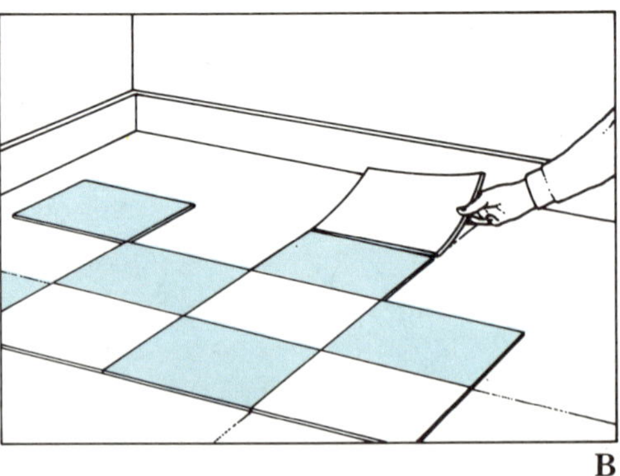

B

2 Spread adhesive over a centre area of about 1 square yard (metre). Spread it thinly, using a notched spreader to get a ridged keying surface (**C**). If the adhesive is spread too thickly it will squeeze out between the tiles when you press them into place, and a thin layer is more effective.

C

3 Place the first tile in position, aligning two sides with the meeting point of the lines (**D**). Continue positioning the tiles over the adhesive, pressing in place with a damp cloth to prevent air bubbles. Remove any adhesive that oozes out immediately.

D

4 Continue laying complete tiles in this way, working from the centre of the room out towards each wall, and laying about nine tiles in a square at a time.

LAYING SELF-ADHESIVE TILES

Many vinyl tiles are self-adhesive and very easy to lay. Prepare the floor so that it is clean, smooth and grease-free. Mark out the floor as described above, and cut any tiles which require trimming to fit around walls, obstacles and corners. Don't peel the protective backing away until you are ready to start fixing the tiles in place. Peel away the backing and stick the tile in position in line with your guides.

Vinyl tiles produce a hardwearing and easy-to-clean flooring especially suited to kitchens and bathrooms.

Fitting edge tiles

Place the tile to be laid at the edge exactly on top of the last laid full tile (**A**). Put another tile on top of this, butted up to the skirting (baseboard) and draw a line across the first tile along the edge of the second tile (**B**). Using scissors or craft knife and the straight edge, cut the tile along this line (**C**). Cut on top of a spare tile to prevent damage to your floor.

Spread the cut tile with adhesive and position with the cut edge next to the skirting (baseboard). Align the corners with the previously laid tile and press in place. Fit all edging tiles in this way.

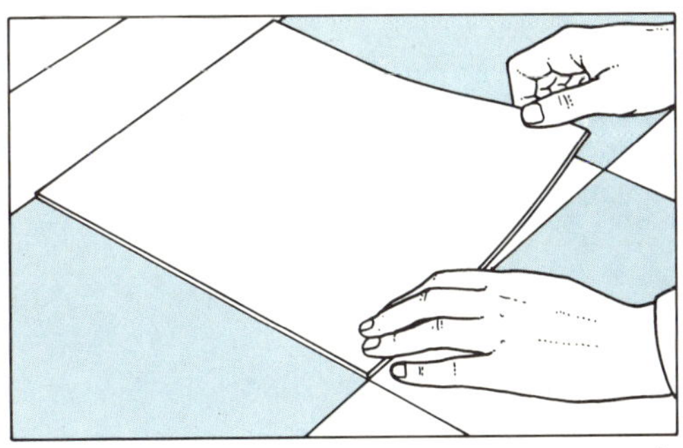

A

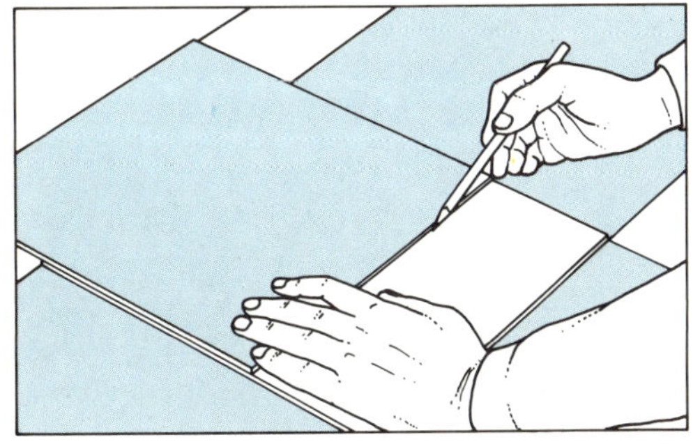

B

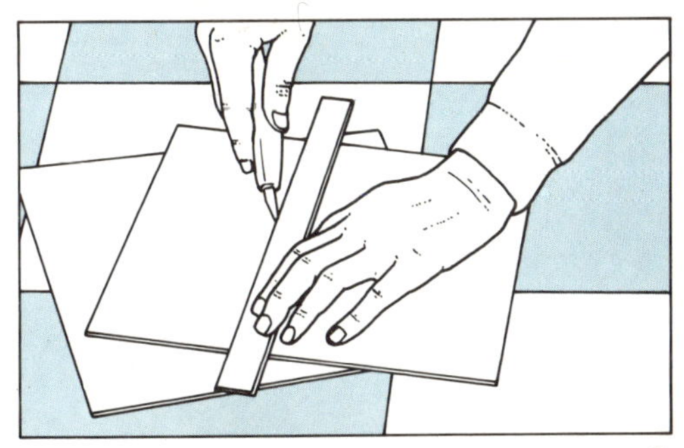

C

Around doorways and pipes
Use the profile gauge to form an accurate curved edge around the door frame. Push the profile gauge against the frame to follow its exact shape, then place the pushed-out edge in the correct position on top of the tile to be laid and trace its outline with a pencil (**A**). Cut out the shape and continue cutting the line along the tile to fit skirting (baseboard) edge (**B**). Check for fit, spread with adhesive and put in position. Use the profile gauge in the same way to fit tiles around pipes or decorative mouldings.

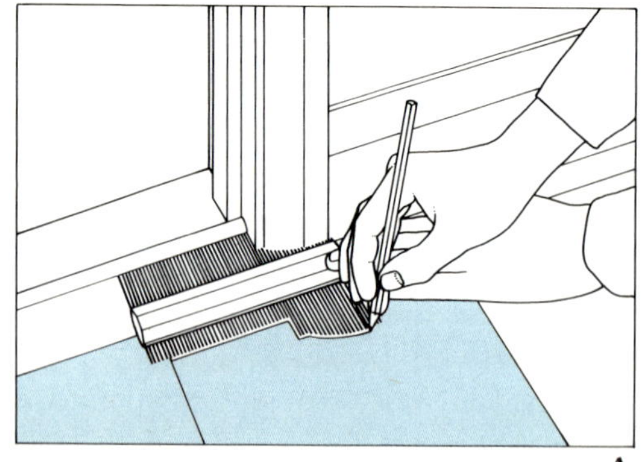
A

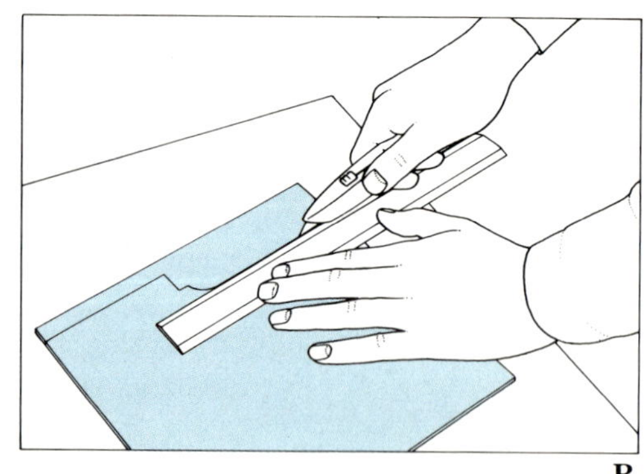
B

External corners
If an L-shaped tile is needed on an external corner, position the tile to be laid there on top of the last-laid full tile, place another tile on top to use as a template and make a light pencil mark where the cutting edge should be for the first wall (**A**) (see Fitting edge tiles). Then, *without twisting them*, move the top two tiles round the corner and mark the edge position from this side, at right angles to your first line, in the same way (**B**). Cut out the inner section to leave an L-shaped tile. Check for fit, spread adhesive over the back and position, aligning with adjoining tiles (**C**).

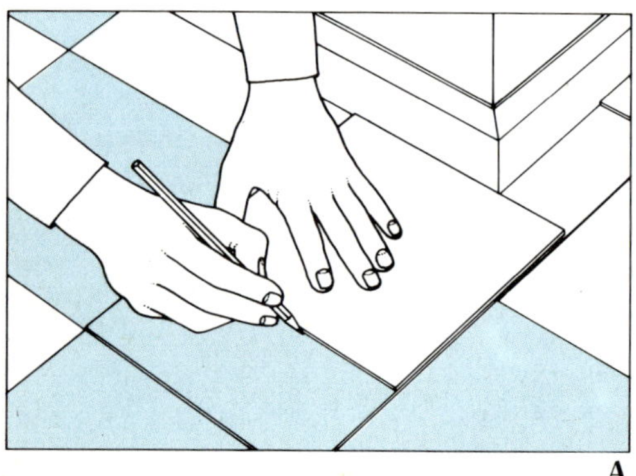
A

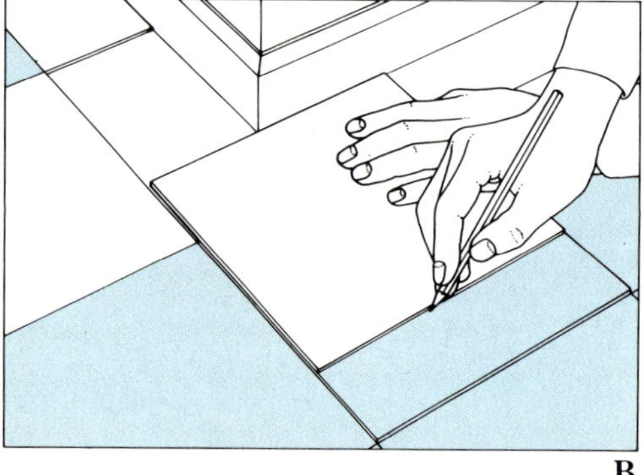
B

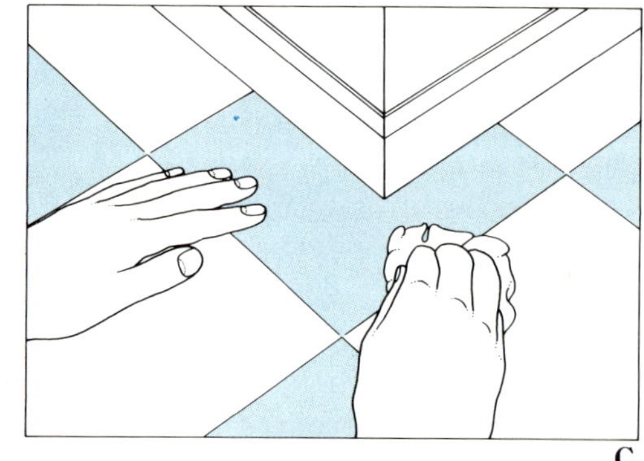
C

Around a wash basin or toilet
To ensure that tiles sit neatly around an obstacle such as a wash basin or lavatory, you will probably have to make a template.

Take a sheet of tracing paper and roughly cut out the shape of the obstacle. Place the tracing paper on the floor around the foot of the basin or lavatory and butt it up against the skirting. So that it fits smoothly around the shape, make release cuts on the tracing paper. Draw the outline of the curve neatly on to the tracing paper and don't forget to mark the positions of the tiles you have already laid (**A**).

Remove the paper and cut out the curve accurately. Place the template on the tile which is to be laid around the obstacle, and line the edge marks up with the tile edges. Draw round the inside of the curve (**B**) and cut it out. Position the tile, check it for fit and make any adjustments necessary. Spread adhesive on the back of the tile and press it into place.

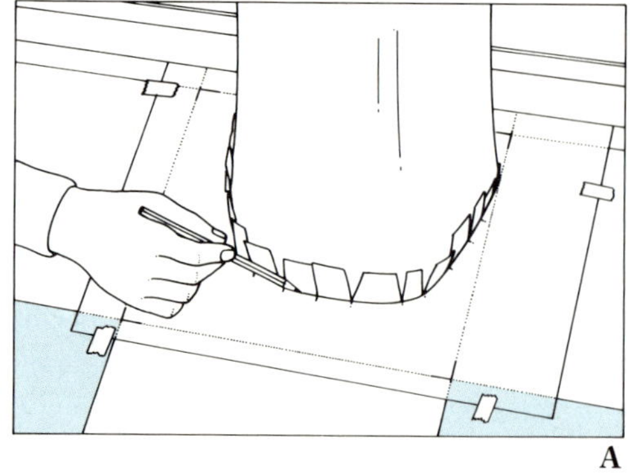
A

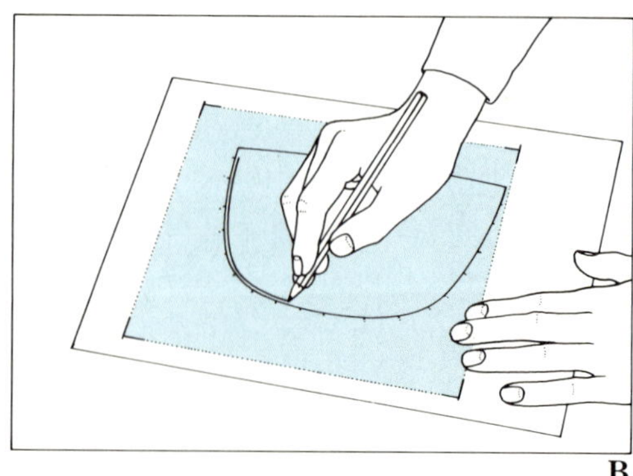
B

CARPET

Nothing beats carpet underfoot for a feeling of warmth and luxury, which is why it remains the most popular form of floor covering. Since this item accounts for a large portion of your budget when furnishing a home, it is important to make a considered choice – the wrong one could be a costly mistake you will just have to live with.

Your initial considerations undoubtedly will focus on the colour and design of your carpet – colour seems to be the most important decision and after that choosing between patterns and plains. There are, however, a number of other factors to bear in mind. For instance, it is useful to know a little about different carpet fibres, about the various methods of construction and the different types of pile. Knowing which carpet is most appropriate for different parts of the house is also an important factor to consider when making a purchase.

COLOUR AND DESIGN

The decoration and furnishings in the room, the size of the room and your personal preferences will all have to be borne in mind when you choose a new carpet. A small room will appear larger if carpeted with a light colour, and a small house or flat can be made to seem more spacious if the same neutral colour is used throughout. Neutral colours – beige, sand or grey, for instance – will also allow you to change colour schemes when redecorating without having to replace little-worn carpet to coordinate.

A patterned carpet need not necessarily make a room appear smaller; small patterns and some geometric designs can have the opposite effect but large bold designs and strong colours do tend generally to have a shrinking effect so save these for rooms that appear over-large and unfriendly.

WEAR

Information concerning the wearability of a carpet appears in coded form on most carpet labels. Domestic (residential) carpets are graded into one of the categories below:

- **Light domestic use (grade 1)**
Normally considered suitable only for bedrooms and areas of little traffic.
- **Medium domestic (grade 2)**
Suitable for the above, for bathrooms and lavatories, if the fibre is suitable, and for other secondary areas.
- **General domestic (grade 3)**
For any of the above, plus dining rooms and living rooms for those without children or pets.
- **Heavy domestic (grade 4)**
Suitable for the areas of the house which get the most wear, such as halls, stairs and landings and well-used living rooms.
- **Luxury use (grade 5)**
A long pile carpet of better quality than grade 3 but not suitable for heavy traffic.

These categories will help you decide what carpet is suitable for the area you wish to cover, bearing in mind that a bedroom used as a playroom will obviously get more wear than one used only for sleeping.

When examining carpet bend the sample back on itself; in a thick, good-quality carpet you will not be able to see the backing. Tug at a couple of tufts to make sure they don't come away too easily.

A plain, light-coloured carpet will increase the spacious look of a room and if used throughout the house will produce a light, integrated effect.

Simply decorated, traditional rooms often benefit from the use of a patterned carpet, as do large rooms.

Far left: Synthetic carpets can be very hard-wearing. Man-made fibres are often mixed with wool to improve a carpet's durability.

Left: Pure wool carpets may be expensive, but can't be bettered for luxury, warmth and sheer good looks.

PILE

Carpet pile has various finishes: some may be looped, such as cords and many Berbers. The most common is cut pile, in which the loops are cut to produce a velvet plush, shag or hard twist pile. (In hard twist a kink is built into the pile.) The third type of pile is either a mixture of cut and looped pile or a mixture of two lengths of cut pile resulting in a sculptured pattern.

Looped pile

Cut pile

Cut and looped pile

Sculptured pile

FIBRES

Wool is the traditional carpet fibre. It is warm, retains its body, resists dirt and is naturally fire-resistant, but pure wool carpets are expensive. Nylon is very hard-wearing but attracts dust and dirt, although the newest non-static nylon fibres, which are at present very expensive, do not do so. Acrylic fibres are the closest in feel and appearance to wool but flatten more easily while polyester, which is used mainly for cords, is a medium-wear fibre.

Mixing wool with man-made fibres gives the advantages of each and produces a less expensive carpet than one made of 100 per cent wool. A mix of 80 per cent wool, 20 per cent nylon produces a very hard-wearing carpet. A minimum of 20 per cent of a given fibre must be present in order for it to affect the quality of the carpet.

CONSTRUCTION

Carpets are either woven, tufted or bonded. The traditional method of carpet-making is to interweave the fibres with the backing. Axminster and Wilton carpets are made this way. The names refer to the loom type and the way the fibre is woven through the backing. Axminster carpets can contain many colours, but the Wilton construction of interwoven pile and backing allows for a maximum of five colours to be used. Where a colour does not appear in the pile it is woven into the backing, producing an extra-thick, strong carpet.

The fibres in tufted carpets are inserted into a pre-woven backing, held in place with a latex adhesive, and a second backing is added for strength.

Bonded carpets are different again. They have pile that is bonded – often heat-fused – on to pre-made backing and, as a result, they are relatively inexpensive.

SIZES

Carpet can be bought in many sizes and shapes: broadloom comes in wide rolls of up to 6 yds (5.5 m); body carpet (carpet runner) in narrow strips of 26½ in (68 cm) wide (3 ft or 92 cm wide in the US). Broadloom is most suited for use in main rooms (signs of wear appear first at any seams), while body carpet is usually the sensible choice for halls, stairs, landings and other small, awkwardly shaped areas. It can also be added as a strip down the side of matching broadloom if slightly more width is needed.

You can also buy carpet squares and rugs to lay on wood floors or plain carpet. Carpet tiles are another option.

Left: Carpets may be either bonded (left), tufted (centre), or woven (right). Woven carpets include Axminster or Wilton types, named after the loom on which they are made.

UNDERLAY

Carpet wear is greatly enhanced by providing a protective layer underneath. Underlay also provides extra insulation and soundproofing while making the carpet feel thicker and more luxurious. Use felt or rubber, depending on the carpet you are laying.

Felt underlay is available (**A**) and should be used if you have an underfloor heating system. If you choose a felt that contains a percentage of hair, the underlay is much less likely to flatten with time. The most widely used underlay is rubber with a hessian (burlap) or paper backing (**B**); it is very hardwearing and won't flatten.

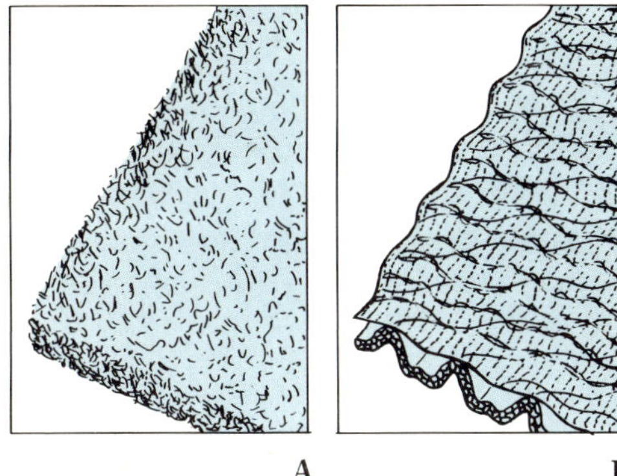

Although foam-backed carpets do not need underlay, they should not be put straight on to a floor, since the foam will stick to the surface and can disintegrate if not protected. Instead, lay the carpet on a felt paper lining available from some carpet suppliers. This paper lining should also be used with underlay where there are gaps between the floorboards. If the gaps are very large it would be wise to lay hardboard before laying the carpet (see page 92).

SPECIAL CARPET-LAYING EQUIPMENT

• Grippers

Grippers are strips of ply, usually available in 30 in (75 cm), 47 in (120 cm) and 59 in (150 cm) lengths, which hold carpet in place along the skirtings (baseboard). They are easy to cut to length at corners, in alcoves and around door frames using garden secateurs (shears) and come with nails already fixed in position – ordinary nails for fixing to timber floors or masonry nails for use on concrete floors. Use angled grippers on stairways.

• Threshold strips

These come in aluminium or brass finish and are used at door openings. There are two main types of threshold strip: one joins two carpets in adjoining rooms, while the other kind acts as a tough border for one carpet. They can be cut with a hacksaw. If you are using the same carpet on both sides of the door it looks better if the carpet is sewn or stuck at the seam.

• Carpet stretcher (knee kicker)

When laying a hessian (burlap) backed carpet, use a carpet stretcher for a much more professional result. The head is placed on the carpet so that the pins in the head just connect with the backing without tearing the pile. You then 'kick' the pad using the muscle just *above* your knee. (Don't use your knee cap, you could damage it.) As you tension the carpet with the stretcher, smooth it with your free hand. Carpet stretchers can be hired quite easily.

• Carpet bolster (tucking tool)

This is used to push the carpet into the space behind the grippers and to force it firmly into the grippers. A clean, rust-free paint scraper or a wide-bladed brick-laying bolster can be used instead.

• Carpet tape and latex adhesive

If you have to join two pieces of carpet together carpet tape and latex adhesive are necessary tools. Make sure the pile runs the same way before you join the two pieces.

You will also need a staple gun, craft knife, hammer and metal straight edge.

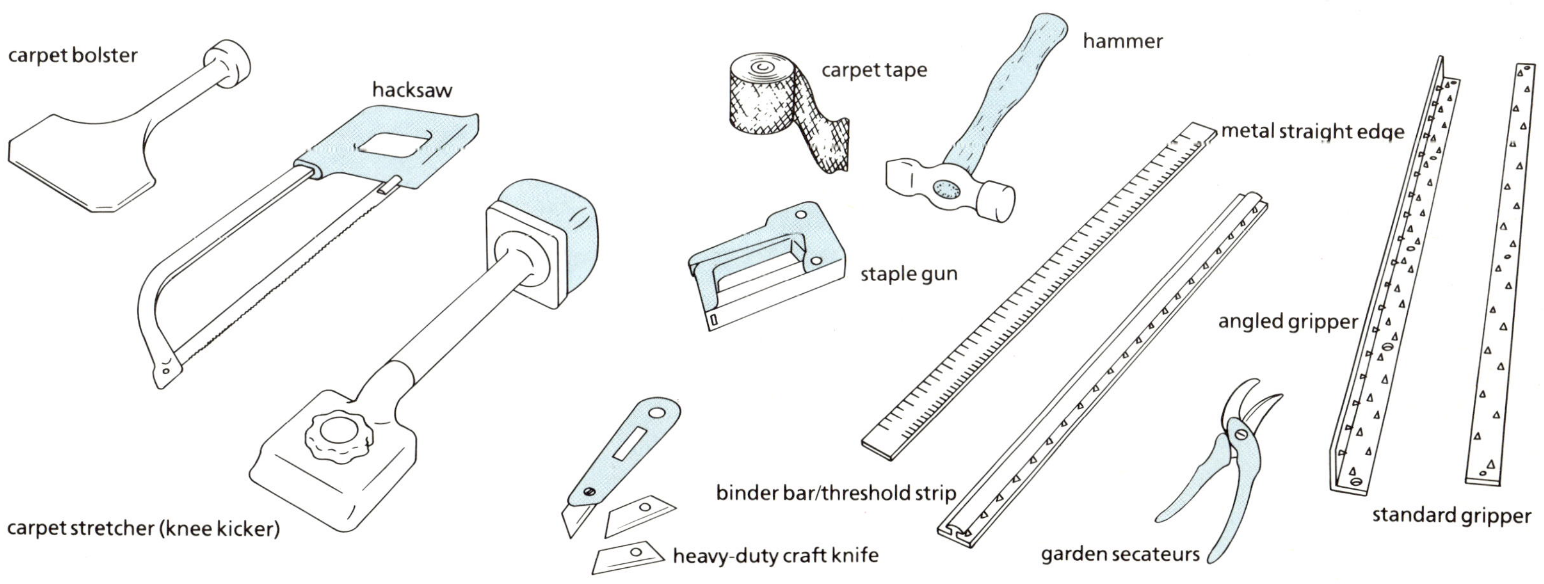

LAYING CARPET

Carpet is not difficult to lay in an empty room, but laying carpet in a hall, up the stairs and on the landing is a skilled job. If you are buying a new carpet for these areas I would strongly recommend that you pay the extra and have it laid professionally. Estimating the quantity of carpet needed for such a complicated shape, making sure you use the most economical width and ensuring that the pile all runs in the same direction require the expertise and knowledge of a specialist.

PREPARATION

Remove any furniture from the room for it is very difficult to get a good result if you are working around heavy items, and remove any doors that open into the room. For preparation of the floor see pages 92-3. The carpet should be laid on a damp-free, smooth floor and, wherever possible, laid with the pile running away from the light to avoid shading.

CALCULATING QUANTITIES

For fitted carpet make a floor plan of your room and mark on it the width and the length at the widest points, taking into account any recesses and measuring into the doorways, to a point where the new carpet will butt up to any adjacent flooring. Add 4 in (10 cm) to each measurement to allow for a 2 in (5 cm) overlap on all sides. Take this floor plan with you when you go to buy the carpet so that the retailer can help you decide what will be the most economic width to buy and the best way to lay the carpet.

For underlay you will need a finished piece the size of your room without overlap. You will not need underlay if using foam-backed carpet, but you will need carpet liner to the size of the room.

To work out the length of grippers you need, measure all round the room, into the alcoves and around all door frames, then add on 5 per cent.

LAYING HESSIAN (BURLAP)-BACKED CARPET

You will need:
- Carpet
- Rubber underlay
- Grippers
- Threshold strips
- Heavy-duty craft knife with new heavy-duty blades
- Metal straight edge
- Clean, rust-free paint scraper or clean bricklayer's bolster
- Staple gun (you can use nails instead)
- A few ¾ in (20 mm) nails (for neatening corners if necessary)
- Carpet stretcher (also called knee kicker)
- Hammer
- Secateurs (garden shears)
- Hacksaw

STARTING WORK

1 Nail the grippers to the floor along the skirting (baseboard) edge all round the room (**A**). The spikes should face towards the skirting, and the gap between the grippers and skirting edge should be about ¼ in (6 mm) to allow for the carpet edge to crease under. If the floor is concrete use hardened pins or a recommended adhesive.

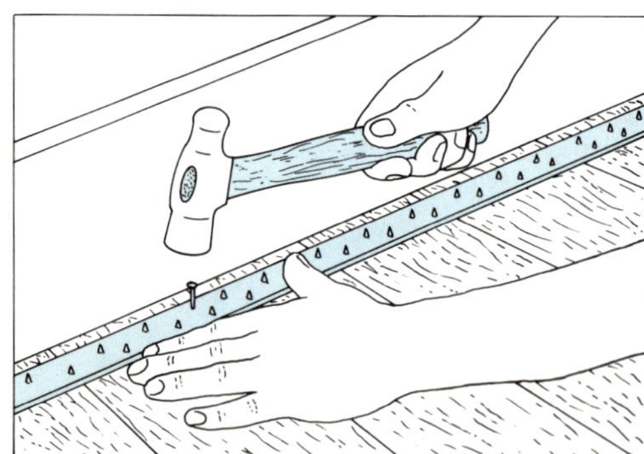

A

2 Around the door architraves cut short lengths of gripper and nail to follow the curves around the base of the frame.

3 Cut any threshold strips to size with a hacksaw and nail in place between the jambs. The strip should be hidden by the door when it is closed.

4 Lay out the underlay and carpet at the same time. Place underlay rubber side down. Fold the carpet back leaving the underlay exposed on one side of the room. Make sure that it is smooth but not stretched and there are no ripples. Tack down at about 12 in (30 cm) intervals just inside the gripper strips using tacks or staples. Replace the carpet. Fold back the second half of the carpet and do the same on the rest of the underlay. On a solid floor use blobs of adhesive to anchor it. Cut to shape so that the underlay just butts up to the inside edge of the grippers. If you need to use two widths of underlay, overlap them at the join, then using the metal straight edge and craft knife, cut through both thicknesses. Fix down the butted edges with tacks, a stapler or adhesive (**B**).

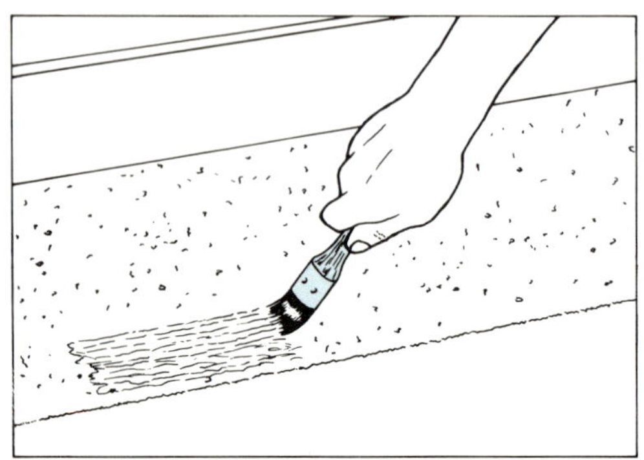

B

5 Start fixing the carpet over the gripper in one corner. Line the carpet up at the corner so that it overlaps each wall by about 1 in (2.5 cm). Push down from the corner about 12 in (30 cm) on each side so that the carpet is hooked on to the grippers (**C**), and then run the hammer over this (**D**).

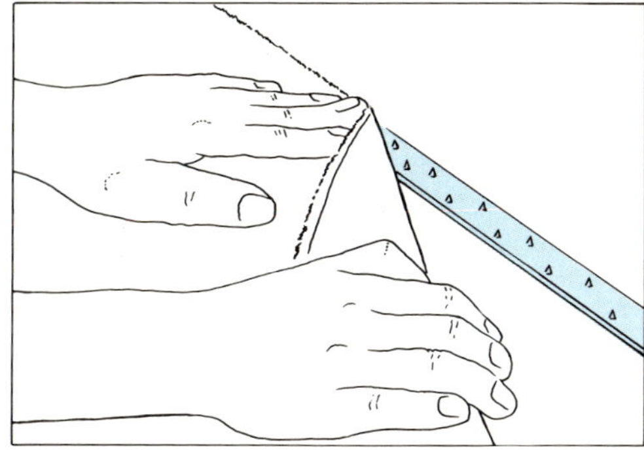

C

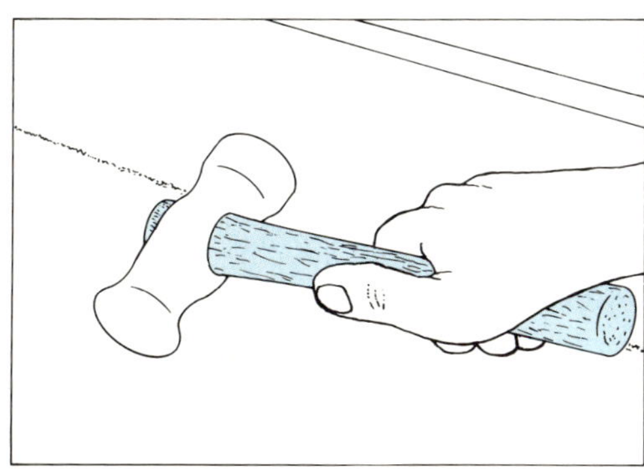

D

6 Stretch the carpet across the room to an adjacent corner that is along a wall with no interruptions, and hook it over the grippers here. Use the carpet stretcher (knee kicker) to ensure a taut fit (**E**) (see page 105). Smooth the carpet down with your free hand as you work.

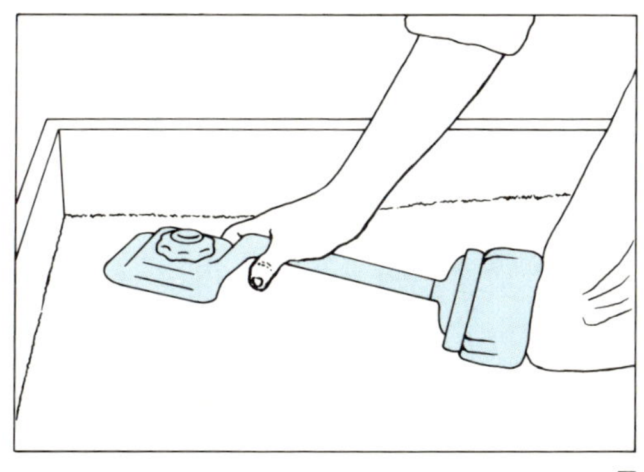

E

7 Use the carpet stretcher to hook the carpet over the grippers along the second wall. Use the muscle above your knee, not your knee cap.

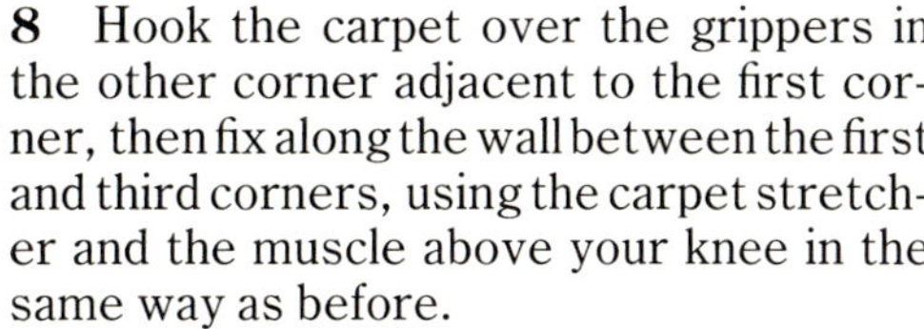

8 Hook the carpet over the grippers in the other corner adjacent to the first corner, then fix along the wall between the first and third corners, using the carpet stretcher and the muscle above your knee in the same way as before.

9 Complete the final corner and the remaining two walls in the same way, making sure that the carpet is stretched completely taut and wrinkle-free in all directions, with no bumps.

10 To trim the carpet, crease it back into the skirting (baseboard) and mark a cutting line. Fold the carpet back and cut along the line using a straight edge and craft knife. Protect the carpet underneath with a cutting board (**F**). Push the carpet edge well down into the grippers with the scraper, so that the carpet is tucked under around the skirting (**G**).

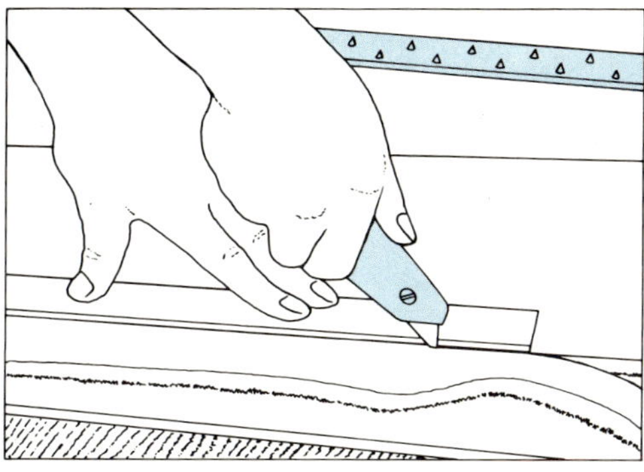

F

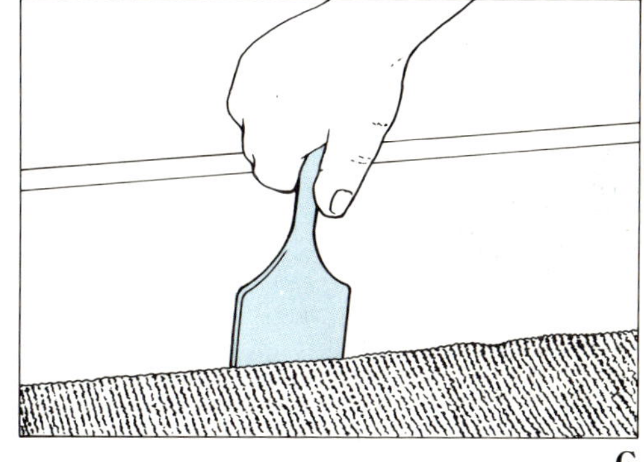

G

Joining carpet

If you can't avoid a join in your carpet use 2 in (5 cm) wide carpet tape and latex adhesive suitable for carpet to join the two pieces.

Cut the carpet tape to length, then brush the adhesive along one half of it and along the underside of the first carpet edge in a matching 1 in (2.5 cm) wide strip (**A**). Allow the adhesive to dry slightly then press the glued carpet edge on to the glued tape edge.

Coat the remaining half of the tape and the 1 in (2.5 cm) strip along the second carpet edge, leave till almost dry and then align the glued carpet edge to butt closely against the first piece of carpet, holding the pile back and pressing the carpet down firmly on to the tape (**B**).

Note: Before joining two pieces of carpet, place the widths of carpet face to face to make sure that you have matched any pattern and to check that the lie of the pile is the same on each of them. Otherwise, the join will be very obvious.

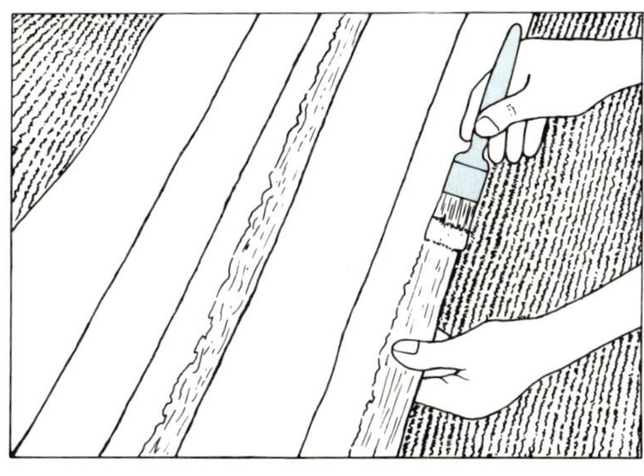

A

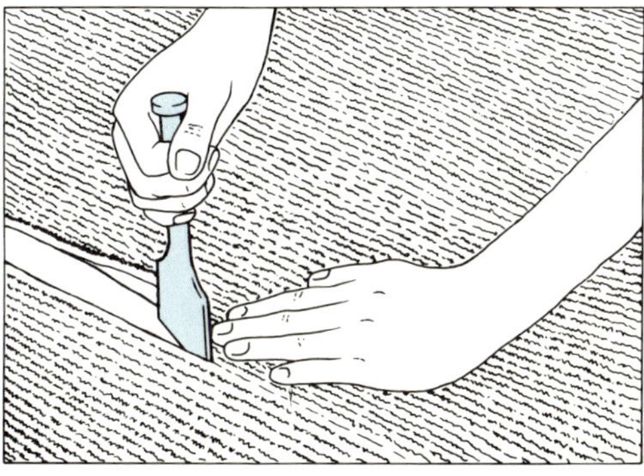

B

Around door frames and alcoves

Make V-shaped release cuts in the carpet overlap as for trimming sheet vinyl around frames and corners (**A**) (see pages 97-8). Cut away the overlap allowing ½ in (13 mm) to turn under at the edge (**B**).

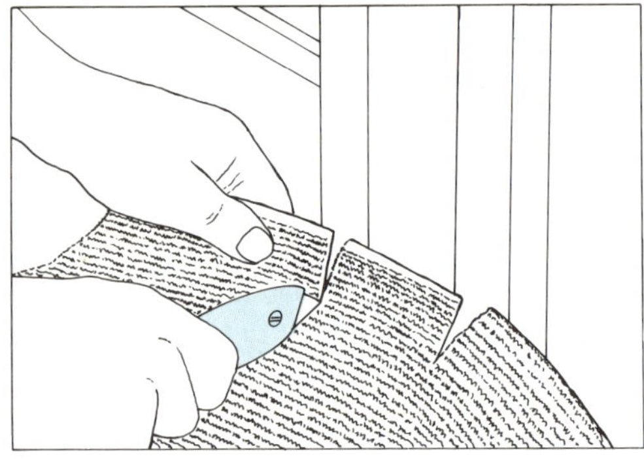

A

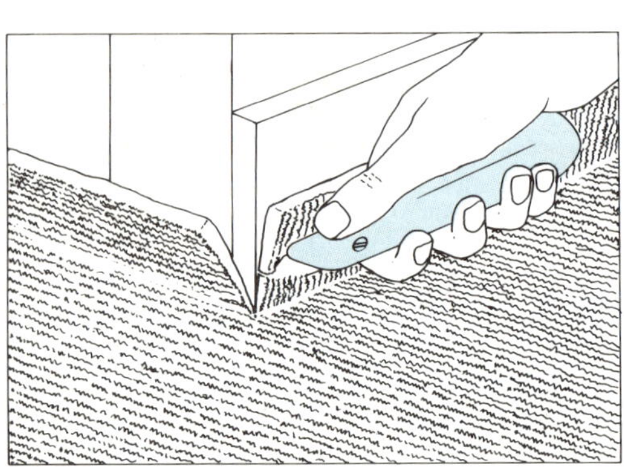

B

In doorways

Use the carpet stretcher to fix the carpet over the grippers on the threshold strip then trim the carpet to fit inside the lip of the threshold strip, push the carpet edge into position with the bolster or scraper (**A**) and lightly tap down the strip top using a hammer and a block of wood.

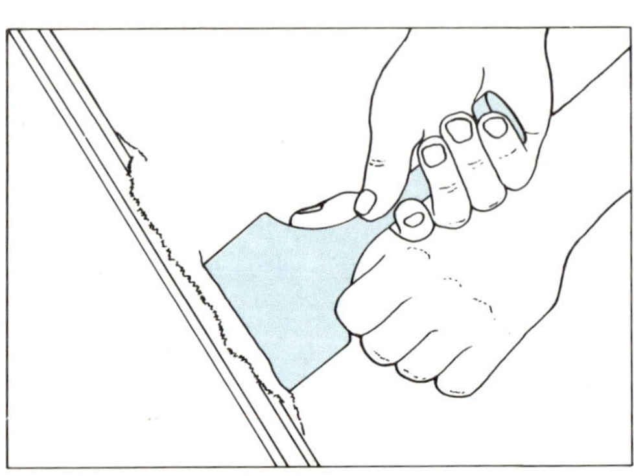

A

Foam-backed carpet needs to be laid on a well-prepared surface and special felt liner.

LAYING FOAM-BACKED CARPET ON CARPET LINER

You will need:
- Carpet and liner
- Double-sided adhesive tape or tacks and hammer for securing edges
- Heavy-duty adhesive tape for joining widths of liner
- Staple gun or adhesive for attaching liner to floor
- Heavy-duty craft knife and new heavy-duty blades
- Clean, rust-free paint scraper

STARTING WORK

1 To lay the liner, join cut strips of felt paper with heavy-duty adhesive tape to fit room size (**A**), then attach the liner to the floor with a staple gun on a wood floor, adhesive on a concrete floor.

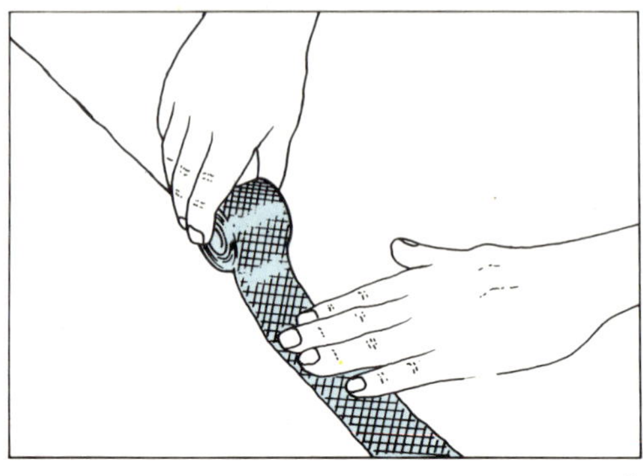

A

2 To lay the carpet, position two edges of it against two adjacent walls, flush to the skirtings. If the walls are not true you may need to overlap in places and then do some trimming. Fit it along these two walls using tacks positioned at 12 in (30 cm) intervals or attach it with double-sided adhesive tape. Trim the other two sides to fit and secure them in the same way. When trimming along the edge, mark a cutting line on the underside, fold the carpet back and cut using a straight edge and craft knife (**B**). Using a sharp blade will ensure a clean cut.

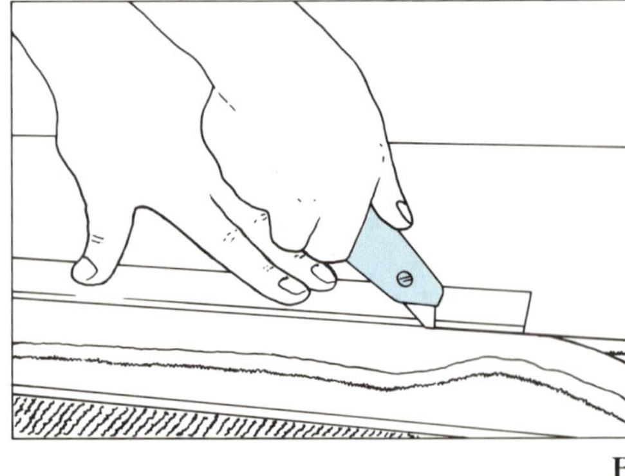

B

3 To join the carpet, follow the instructions for joining two pieces of hessian-backed carpet (see page 107).

4 To fit in doorways follow the instructions for hessian-backed carpet (see left).

5 To fit around door frames and in alcoves, trim to fit following the instructions for sheet vinyl (see pages 97-8).

LAYING A NEW HARDWOOD FLOOR

Hardwood flooring is coming back into fashion as an alternative to fitted carpets – hardly surprising, considering how elegant and hardwearing it is.

It is a misconception to believe that a hardwood floor has to be laid professionally. It is true that special skills are required to lay a traditional parquet floor because all the blocks have to be interlocked, but two modern alternatives – mosaic panels and hardwood strips – are straightforward to put down on any type of well-prepared floor.

Both mosaic panels and strips are available in a wide variety of woods. The commonest in Britain are iroko, which is initially yellowish in colour but darkens to a deep brown; maple, which has a pale cream colour; and oak, which can vary from light to dark brown and has an intriguing texture. Mahogany is a beautiful reddish-brown.

Once a floor has been sanded and sealed, it should remain in good condition for many months. However, you may find it necessary to apply a fresh coat of sealer every so often to maintain the lustre of the wood. If you do this, clear the room of all furniture and vacuum up the dust before you start work. Complete the floor in one session or else you may end up with 'tidemarks'.

Some people apply a wax polish to flooring. There is no denying that it gives a superb finish but it does then need regular applications of polish to retain the finish.

MOSAIC PANELS

These are made up of narrow 'fingers' of wood glued together in a basketweave pattern. In the US they come in various sizes, from 6 to 19 in (15 to 48 cm); in Britain they are usually 18 in (45 cm) square.

Most panels are fixed to a bitumen-impregnated backing which prevents damp from rising up into the wood and are stuck down on to either a concrete or wooden floor with special adhesive. Manufacturers invariably sand down their panels before they package them – this saves you the bother of having to do the job yourself later on and simplifies the laying process.

HARDWOOD STRIPS

These are either sawn from solid timber or constructed from veneered plywood. Once they have been laid and sealed, they give a more uniform look than mosaic panels. Strips are sold in various lengths and may be ⅜ in (1 cm) or ¾ in (2 cm) thick and 3 to 7 in (7.5 to 18 cm) wide.

Hardwood strips are tongued-and-grooved and, in many cases, they are 'secretly' nailed to a wooden sub-floor (see page 111). However, if you want to lay the strips over a concrete floor, it is possible just to glue the joints together, leaving the floor to 'float'.

TIMBER-FACED CORK TILES

These are essentially ordinary cork tiles, faced with a thin hardwood veneer. They feel softer under foot than the other options and are often put down on cold concrete floors because the cork provides insulation. If you want to use timber-faced cork, see the section on laying vinyl and cork tiles (pages 99-102) for instructions.

Left: Mosaic wood makes a gleaming hallway.

Below: Wood strip provides a perfect background for rugs and furniture in earth tones.

CALCULATING QUANTITIES

Obviously the first thing to do when buying hardwood flooring is to measure the floor area of the room you are decorating. When you do this, take into account any alcoves and bays which will be covered by the flooring. After you have measured up the room and calculated the area, add on an extra 5 per cent to allow for cutting and wastage.

It's always a good idea to draw up an accurate scale plan of the room. This enables you to work out how best to lay the flooring so that you can minimize cutting.

Once you have worked out the total area of the room, you should be able to calculate how much flooring you need.

In addition to the flooring itself, you will almost certainly have to buy threshold strips to protect the wood from getting scuffed in doorways. There are many different kinds of threshold strip but most are nailed or screwed to the floor. When you buy them, make certain that they match the thickness of the flooring material – if anything get them slightly thinner as you can always pack them out if they don't match up perfectly.

You may also need to buy a floor sealer, especially if you go for strip flooring. There is a choice between a polyurethane varnish and a resin-based sealer – polyurethane is tougher but resin sealers give a more natural finish. To complete a floor, you will have to buy in quantity bearing in mind that you should apply at least three coats of whichever you choose.

PREPARING THE SUB-FLOOR

Preparing the sub-floor is all-important – if you lay the new flooring any old how on an uneven or damp floor, it is bound to crack or warp later on. Preparing sub-floors is covered in more detail on pages 92-3 but there are some specific tasks to carry out before laying a hardwood floor.

When it is laid, your new flooring is likely to expand and contract with changes in the climate, even if it is nailed or glued to the floor. It is impossible to see this movement with the naked eye but if you don't leave a ½ in (13 mm) expansion gap around the edges, the flooring will buckle and twist. The neatest way of hiding this expansion gap is to conceal it underneath the bottom edges of the skirtings (baseboards) which means that they have to be levered off at the preparation stage with a stout screwdriver.

A

If you are reluctant to go to the trouble of taking off all the skirting, the gaps can be bridged at the end of the job with lengths of quadrant beading (**A**).

If you have any doors that open into the room, you may have to take a fraction off the bottom to allow for the thickness of the flooring. Coping with this problem is covered in detail on page 122.

LAYING MOSAIC PANELS

You will need:
Mosaic panels
Recommended adhesive
Rag and white (mineral) spirit
Tape measure
Serrated adhesive spreader
Tenon saw
Trimming knife
Hammer and nail punch
String
Sharp pencil
Plus optional materials such as quadrant beading, ¾ in (19 mm) panel pins (brads) and sealer

STARTING WORK

1 Start laying the panels in the centre of the room and work towards the edges. Measure up two opposing walls of the room and mark the mid-points. Stretch string between the two mid-points and then repeat the process with the other two walls to get two strings which cross at the centre of the room (**A**). 'Dry lay' rows of panels along these strings (**B**) and adjust so that equal amounts of panel have to be cut at each end. If necessary, reposition the strings.

A

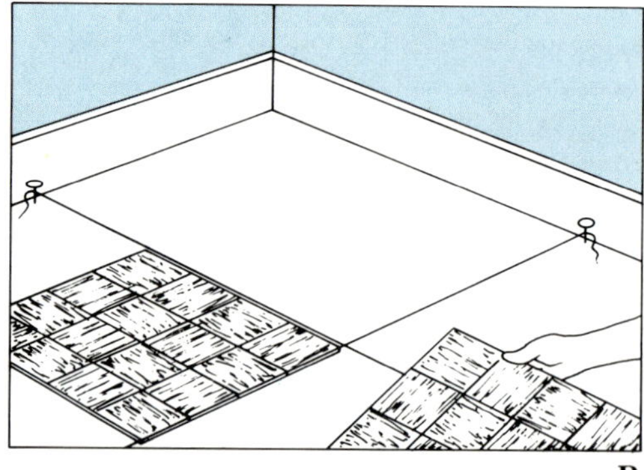

B

2 Where the strings cross, spread sufficient adhesive on to the sub-floor for the first panel (**C**). Try to keep the layer of adhesive thin and even – remember that a thick layer of adhesive doesn't necessarily mean that the bond will be stronger.

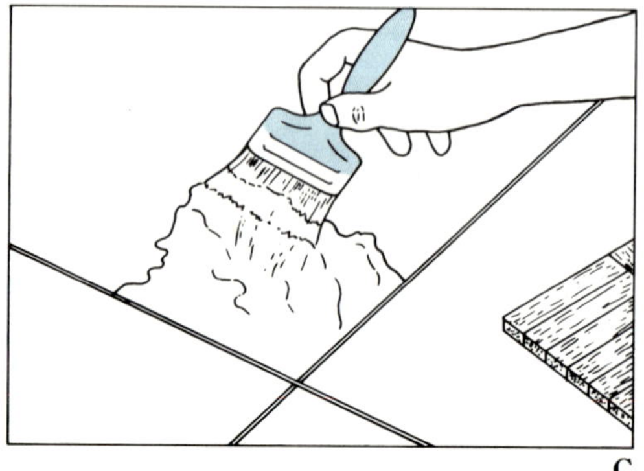

C

3 Bed the first panel on the adhesive, aligning it with your guides (**D**), and firm it into place with a soft cloth. If you get adhesive on the panel, wipe it off with a rag dipped in white (mineral) spirit.

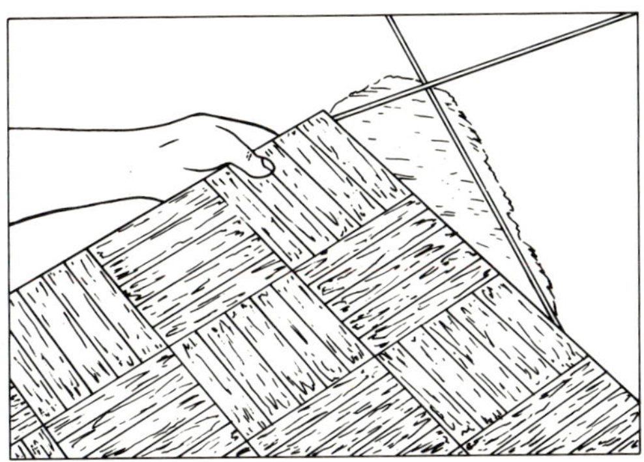

D

4 Add more panels, butting them together, until only the border around the edge has to be filled with cut sections.

5 To mark an edge panel for cutting, position it accurately over the last whole panel in its row and lay a spare panel on top with one edge ½in (13mm) from the wall. Pencil in the cutting line using the other edge of the top panel as a ruler (**E**). (Instead of measuring up the expansion gap at each wall use a scrap of timber as a spacer.)

E

6 Cut the edging panels to size with a tenon saw, try them for fit, and then bed them in place in the usual way. To complete the job, see page 112.

LAYING HARDWOOD STRIPS

You will need:
Hardwood strips or planks
Chalk line
Tape measure
Panel (hand) and tenon saws
Try square
Hammer and nail punch
1 in (25 mm) oval nails
PVA woodworking adhesive

STARTING WORK

1 Start by marking the expansion gap all around the perimeter of the room. The easiest way of doing this is to snap a chalk line on to the floor. If you haven't got a purpose-made chalk line you can improvise your own by rubbing chalk along a length of string. Anchor each end of the taut chalk line ½ in (13 mm) away from a wall, lift it up and then let it snap back into place – it will leave a line of chalk on the floor (**A**). Follow this procedure for each wall in turn.

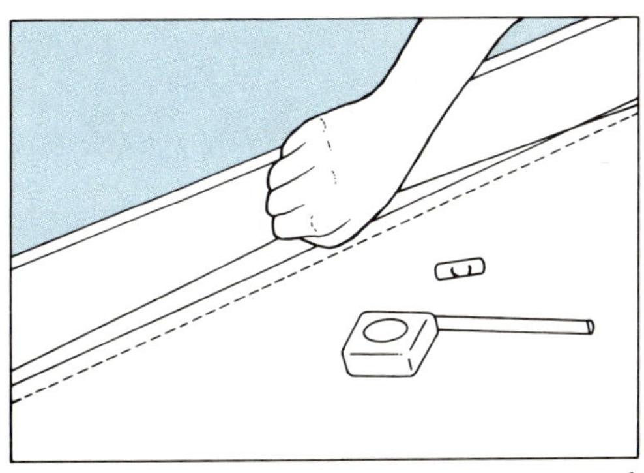

A

2 Ideally, the strips should be laid at right angles to the floorboards and parallel to the longest wall. Position the first row of strips along your chalked line with the tongues facing into the room (**B**). You will inevitably have to cut a piece off one length so that the row fits – do this with a tenon saw, not forgetting to allow for the expansion gap at the end. Fix the strips by nailing them at 45 degrees through their tongues (**C**). This is called 'secret' nailing. Use 1 in (25 mm) oval nails at 6 in (15 cm) intervals. Sink the nail heads below the surface of the wood with a nail punch and hammer so that they will be obscured by the next row.

B

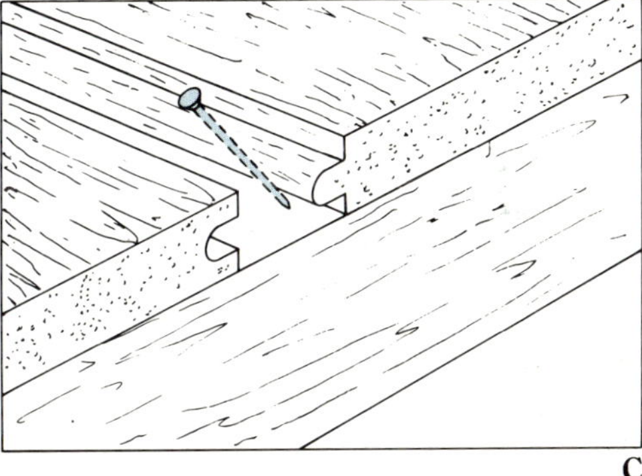

C

3 Before adding the next row of strips, smear PVA adhesive over the exposed tongues (**D**) – this will prevent the strips from creaking when you walk on them. Position the second row against the first, making sure that the joints are staggered. When you are satisfied, nail in place (**E**).

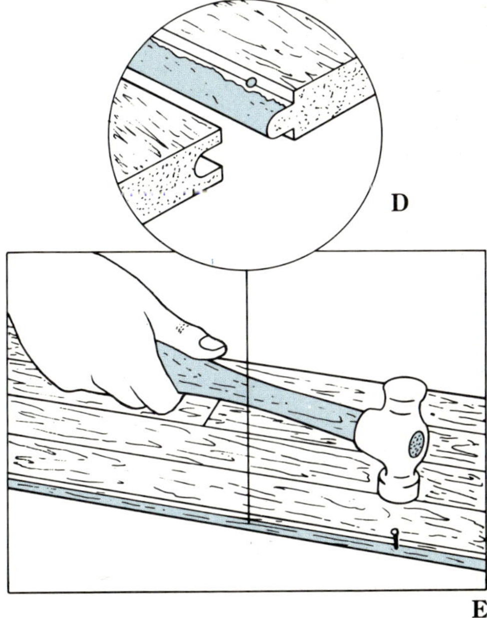

D

E

4 As you add more rows, you will probably find that you have to cut a few strips lengthwise to fit into alcoves and bays. Mark the strip accurately with a cutting line first, make sure that it is well supported and use a panel (hand) saw (**F**).

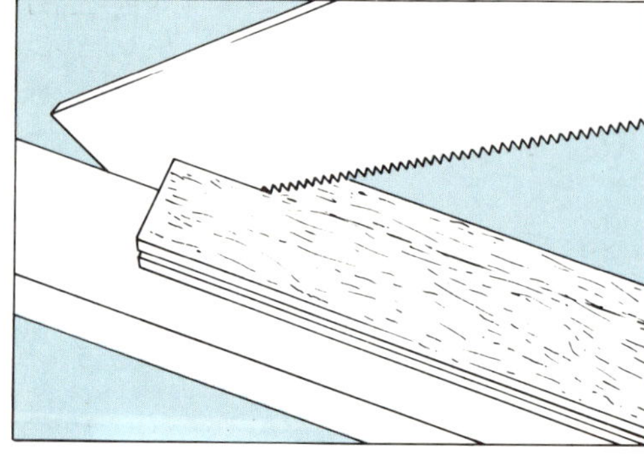

F

5 You won't be able to 'secret' nail the last row, so fix it in place with nails driven through the top surface. Punch the nail heads home so that they aren't exposed.

FINISHING A HARDWOOD FLOOR

You will need:
Threshold strips
White (mineral) spirit
Sealer
1 in (2.5 cm) quadrant beading
¾ in (19 mm) panel pins (brads)
Paint
Hammer
Nail punch
Screwdriver and junior hacksaw
To seal the floor:
Floor sander (which you can hire)
Wide 6 in (15 cm) paintbrush
1 in (2.5 cm) paintbrush

STARTING WORK

1 Refit the skirtings (baseboards), copying the original fixing method. If you left the skirting in place, cover the expansion gaps with lengths of quadrant beading. Paint the beading to match the skirting before you pin it to the skirting using ¾ in (19 mm) panel pins (brads), spaced at 12 in (30 cm) intervals. Don't pin it to the flooring. Alternatively, fill the expansion gap with ½ in (13 mm) strips from a roll of cork (**A**).

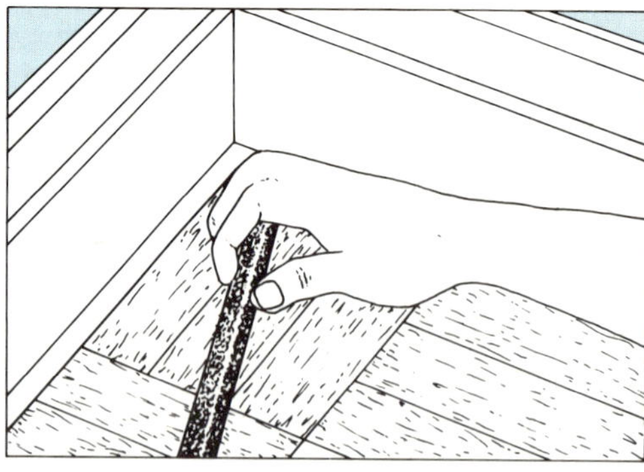

A

2 Fit threshold strips in doorways to protect the exposed edges of the flooring (**B**). There are many different kinds of threshold strip and most are nailed or screwed in place – it's best to follow the manufacturer's instructions. If necessary, pack out a threshold strip with lengths of ⅛ in (3 mm) hardboard to keep it level.

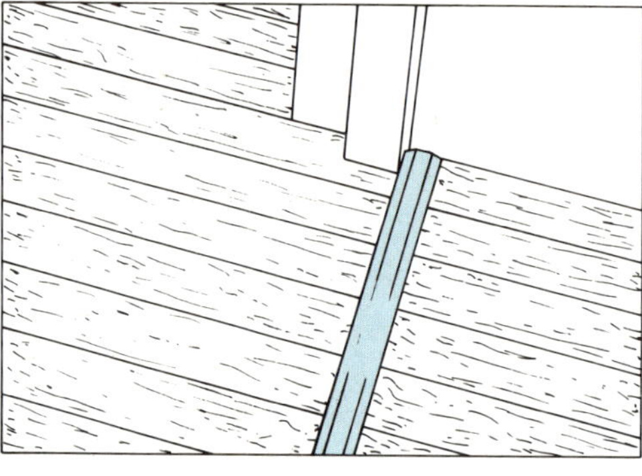

B

3 Some hardwood strips are not pre-sanded, in which case they will need sanding now to make them uniformly level and smooth. The best way to do this is to hire a floor sander as it makes the job much quicker and easier. Use a fine grade – 120 gauge – paper and don't be tempted to oversand the floor. Sand diagonally across the floor first and then follow the direction of the strips (**C**).

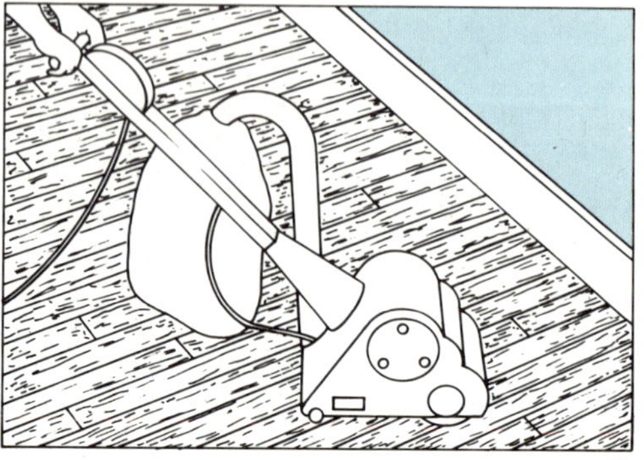

C

Vacuum after sanding and wipe the floor with a cloth dipped in white (mineral) spirit.

4 If you have had to sand down your new floor, you will also have to seal it, either with a polyurethane varnish (**D**) or with a resin-based sealer. Apply the required number of coats and sand down each one, following the manufacturer's instructions.

D

WOOD FOR HARD FLOORS

Oak
This type of wood is light brown in colour and generally has a medium to coarse texture.

Iroko
Iroko is also called African teak. Its colour starts out quite a light yellow, but it generally tends to darken with age.

Mahogany
This wood is a lovely reddish brown in colour and has a fine to medium texture.

Maple
Maple is a pale cream or reddish colour with slightly darker veining. It generally has a fine texture.

CHAPTER 6

Finishing off

So you've transformed your room with a coat of fresh paint, hung a beautiful wall covering and treated the floor to a new look? What next? Before you replace the furniture and add those vital finishing touches, there comes an intermediate stage. Perhaps those smart new mosaic tiles mean that you can no longer open or close the door? And those worn curtains or drapes just don't look right with your new decor? Reluctant to throw all your books and treasures in any old how, when they really should be gracing good-looking shelves? This chapter shows you how to solve this sort of problem at one fell swoop, with the least amount of fuss.

PUTTING UP CURTAINS AND BLINDS

Whether you make your own or buy them, the array of curtain, drapery, blind and shade styles is confusingly wide. An unwise choice could ruin the effect of your new room scheme.

You might opt for slim Venetian blinds to suit a high-tech interior or volumes of lace or muslin to drape softly round a picture window but, whatever your style or how much money you have to spend, windows always tend to repay imaginative treatments.

Although there are no hard and fast rules about which should go where, the information listed below may help you choose a style to fit your requirements and your budget.

Make a splash with curtains from the same range as your upholstery fabric to finish off a living room stylishly.

A roller blind with delicate tulips against a fine red stripe shows that primaries don't have to make a bold statement – they can be subtle, too.

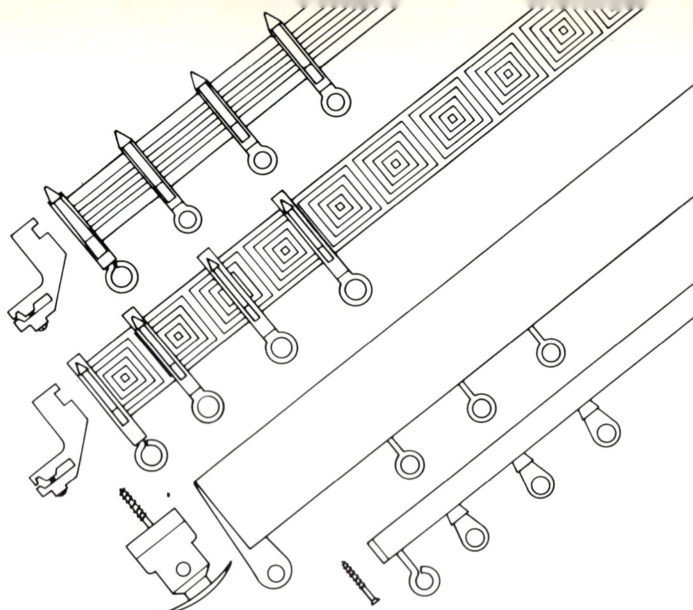

Curtain (drapery) tracks come in a variety of designs. They are usually made of plastic, but metal tracks are also available. Some are even purpose-made to be painted or papered to coordinate with a room scheme, but most are concealed once the curtains (draperies) are hung from them.

Usually, tracks are sold complete with fixings, screws and end stops. Choose curtain hooks that are compatible if you find you have to buy them separately.

CURTAINS AND DRAPERIES

Curtains and draperies show off beautiful fabrics to best advantage and are particularly suited to large windows where they can be used full length. They are excellent insulators; in Britain they are often lined with an aluminium-backed lining fabric or interlined. Curtains can be dressed up with frills, tie backs, valances or pelmets (flat valances) and can be installed on either a curtain track (rod) or a pole.

Although curtains and draperies can be used at most windows they are sometimes not practical behind a sink or top of a cooker (range) where hems may get in the way. Similarly, there are more practical treatments for bathrooms and for sloping and attic windows.

Net (glass) and lace curtains can be used to soften an unattractive view while still allowing light in. Café curtains screen the bottom half of the window, allowing a view but still affording some privacy.

CURTAIN TRACKS AND RODS

Now usually made of plastic, tracks are reasonably cheap, pliable to bend round bays and quiet in use. Standard track is suitable for most curtains but a sturdier plastic track is available for large windows and heavy curtains (draperies). Plastic tracks should be fixed every 12 in (30 cm). Most plastic tracks are white but some can be painted or even papered to match the surrounding decor. Others have a gold-pattern finish. There are also strong metal tracks in silver- or gold-finish aluminium that need fixing only every 24 in (60 cm).

Tracks are usually sold complete with all the necessary hardware including fixings and screws, end stops and in some cases special curtain hooks that clip over the track.

In the United States curtains (draperies) designed to open and close are normally hung from a traverse rod, which is equipped with sliders operated by cords. In Britain, special cords, called a 'cording set', can be purchased for use with some tracks. In either country tracks can be bought or adapted to project from the wall at various depths, to accommodate two pairs of curtains and/or a valance.

Where to use

Most tracks are designed to be invisible – to let the curtains be the focus. Short-length curtains usually look best hung from a track (conventional rod), as does a 'wall' of curtains hung across a large picture window. Curtains used on a number of different-sized windows in the same room are also shown off to advantage by using the same kind of track and curtain or drapery style on each. This provides a unifying visual link between them and gives the room better balance.

How to fix

If you want to enjoy maximum light extend your track by 12 to 24 in (30 to 60 cm) on each side of the window to allow the curtains to be pulled well back during the day.

Some tracks (rods) can be screwed into either the wall or the ceiling. Most tracks come with clear fixing instructions but see also pages 119-20.

CURTAIN (DRAPERY) POLES

There are two different types of pole. The first is a real pole, made of either wood or brass. Wooden poles are available in different stains and natural finishes, white and other colours and can also be bought to paint or stain yourself. There are also a number of different diameters available for use with different-sized windows and curtains (draperies). As a set with the pole or sold separately, you can also buy brackets for fixing the pole to the wall, big rings with screw eyes inserted in them to take a curtain (drapery) hook, and decorative pole ends, called finials. Recess brackets are available which attach to the side walls in a recess and the pole ends slot into them. In Britain you can now buy a cording set for use with wooden poles.

The second type of curtain pole looks like a real pole from the front, but in fact has a space at the back where a track is fitted. It does not use ordinary curtain rings but instead has small rings which hang from the track and the curtains are attached to these. In the US this kind of pole is constructed as a traverse rod.

Where to use

Unlike curtain (drapery) track, poles are designed to be used as a decorative feature, not to remain hidden. They can now be used at most windows, but they are particularly suited to long, fairly narrow shapes like traditional French windows (doors). There are even designs to fit bay windows. They look good used with curtains at two identical windows in the same room. Use a narrow pole on short-length curtains; a thick one will look top-heavy.

How to fix

Mark the positions for the brackets to ensure that the pole will be held far enough above and extend just beyond the side of the window so that the curtain heading will cover all the window top. If you need an extra-long pole you can improvise by fixing two poles together using wood glue and then positioning a third bracket centrally to hide the join from view.

Put poles up following the manufacturer's instructions which come with them. See pages 119-20 for information on fixing brackets to different types of wall.

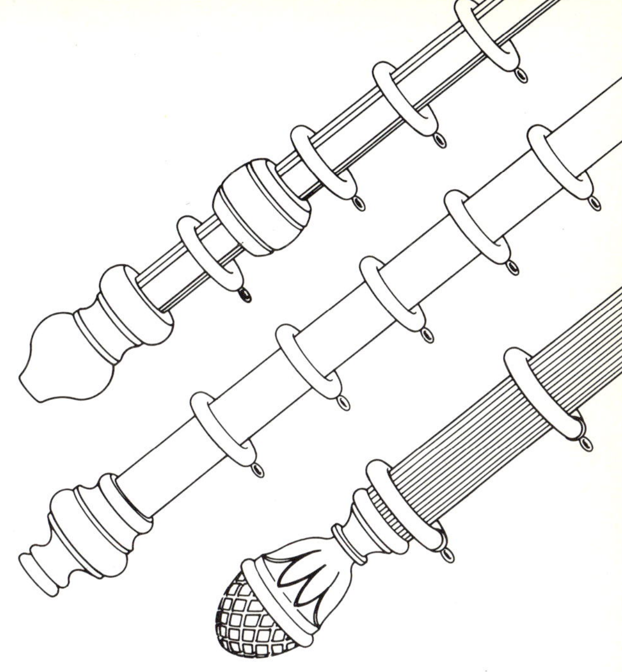

Above: Curtain (drapery) poles are sold in a variety of designs, and finishes include brass and natural wood, which may be stained or painted if you like.

Left: Wooden curtain (drapery) poles may be left bare, or painted to co-ordinate with a room's dominant colours, as here.

ROLLER BLINDS (SHADES)

These are made from a length of flat, stiffened fabric which is attached to a roller containing a spring. Special brackets hold the roller in position at the top of the window and when the blind is tugged, ratchets release the roller and the spring rolls the blind up. Similarly, when the blind is pulled down the ratchets hold it in varying positions down the window.

You can buy ready-made roller blinds (shades), have them made to measure for your window, or make your own from stiffened fabric and a roller-blind kit.

Where to use

Roller blinds (shades) are particularly suited to kitchen and bathroom windows, as they roll up neatly out of the way when not in use. The stiffened finish is spongeable so marks are easily removed. They are also good on sloping windows where hooks in the frame will hold the blind in a number of positions. They work best on medium, narrow or small windows. A wide blind is more difficult to manipulate and can lose its neat, flat appearance. Roller blinds do not mask out the light in the same way as lined curtains or draperies, nor are they good insulators.

How to fix

Fit brackets to the sides of window recesses with the round pin-hole bracket on your right. Trim the roller to fit.

The blind (shade) is attached to the roller with the wrong side uppermost. Place the fabric right side up and place the roller on top, with the spring mechanism to the left. Position the wrong side of the blind along the marked line of pole and fix with tacks or a staple gun at roughly 1 in (2.5 cm) intervals.

Roll the blind (shade) up and position it in the brackets. Pull it down, take it out and re-roll it to tension the spring. Refit.

Roller blinds (shades) can be made inexpensively, using a kit which contains instructions, together with all the elements you will need.

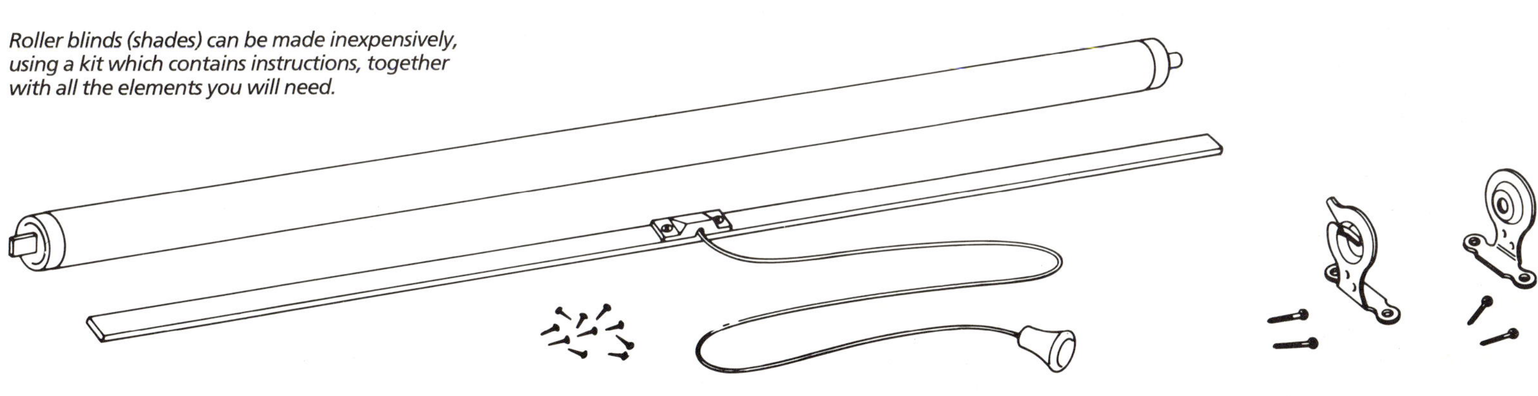

ROMAN BLINDS (SHADES)

Made from a rectangle of lined fabric, a Roman blind (shade) has lengths of vertical tapes with equally spaced loops (or rings) attached to the back. Cords threaded through the loops pull the blind up into neat horizontal pleats. If the spaces between the loops are altered so that small spaces at the top graduate to larger ones at the bottom the blind can be pulled up to form graduated pleats. You can buy Roman blinds, have them made or make your own.

Where to use

The neat, tailored appearance of a Roman blind (shade) makes it suitable for most rooms in the house. It can be used on a short, wide window but it is better suited to medium-sized longer windows. It can also be used to partner curtains in a fine, slightly see-through fabric.

How to fix

A Roman blind (shade) is attached to a batten (2 in × 1 in/5 cm × 2.5 cm is usually the best size) and in turn the batten is attached by brackets to the top of a window recess or just above the window. Because the batten is difficult to put up with the blind attached it is best to position the brackets and batten (having first painted the batten), then remove the brackets and batten to fit the blind. This way you only have to screw back into the ready-made holes.

The fabric should be attached to a wide side of the painted batten so that it covers this edge and the right side of the fabric is uppermost. Tack or staple the fabric in place. Then re-attach the brackets to the opposite side of the batten. Position screw eyes along this edge in front of the brackets and space them to match the top of each vertical tape on the back of the blind.

Thread the cords through the screw eye at the top of the tape then through any others on the batten until all are hanging together at one side of the blind (shade). Screw the batten back in position and screw the cleat in place on the same side of window as the cords. Tie the cords together, pull up the blind and wind the cord round the cleat to secure it.

A tailored Roman blind (shade) uses an inset panel of yellow fabric to great effect.

AUSTRIAN BLINDS (SHADES)

The traditional Austrian blind (shade) as used in the United States is gathered only vertically; the upper edge is smooth, apart from pleats on either side of the vertical tapes to give a slight fullness, and is either attached to a board or threaded over a simple curtain rod. The kind fashionable in Britain is also gathered horizontally, by means of a heading tape, and hung with hooks from a curtain track. Otherwise, both types are similar to a Roman blind in their basic construction.

Where to use

Because of their pretty, decorative effect Austrian blinds (shades) are most suited to bedrooms or living rooms. They are especially good for use on windows with a radiator underneath as this excludes the use of full-length curtains. Because they are unlined, they will not exclude light nor are they good insulators.

How to fix

If the blind (shade) is already corded through rings sewn to the top then you will only need to put up a curtain track following the instructions that come with the blind. To prepare the blind, pull the cords up in the heading tape until the gathers are even and the blind covers the required width, then tie the cords. (Don't cut them as you will need to release them for laundering.) Insert the curtain hooks at regular intervals, making sure there is one at the top of each vertical tape. Install the track and attach the blind to it, making sure that the hook at each end is placed through a fixed ring. Attach the cleat at a convenient height at the side of the window. Knot off the cords at this height. Draw up the blind and wrap the cords around the cleat to hold it securely in the position you prefer.

Alternatively screw the curtain track to the front narrow edge of a batten. Position screw eyes along the wide batten base to take the gathering cords in the same way as for a Roman blind (see above).

An Austrian blind (shade), gathered at the top like a curtain, pulls up in decorative flounces.

SHELVING SYSTEMS

For many people shelves simply serve a practical purpose: somewhere to stash pots and pans or store books and clothes. That's all very well but shelves can also be decorative in their own right and can be used to display ornaments and other prized possessions to great advantage.

Before investing in a shelving system, first consider what function you want it to serve and then look at the various options that are available. Start off by considering some of the following points.

- What will you be putting on the shelves? Books and stereo systems are heavy and consequently demand shelving that is robust; ornaments and photographs on the other hand are usually light and for these more delicate shelving is perfectly suitable.
- Will you want to alter the heights of the shelves at any time?
- Is an easy-clean surface on the shelves essential? Shelves in the kitchen and bathroom usually need to be wiped down frequently if ventilation is poor, because of cooking and condensation.
- Do you want especially good-looking shelves? The most sturdy types don't always look elegant.
- Should you be thinking about fixed shelving at all or would a freestanding system be more suited to your needs?

Having decided on what you require of the shelves, take a look at the options.

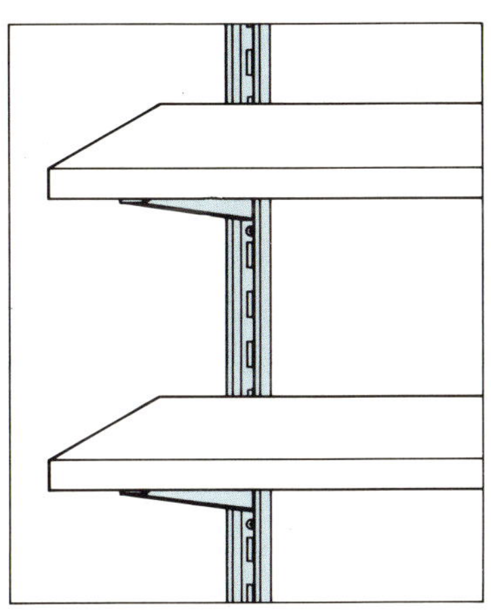

Adjustable shelving

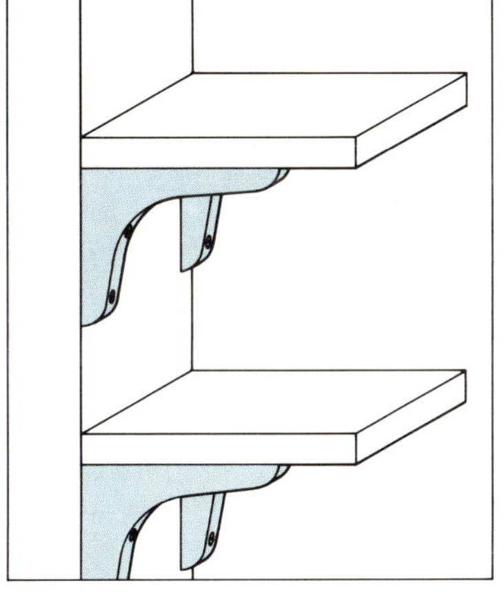

Fixed shelving

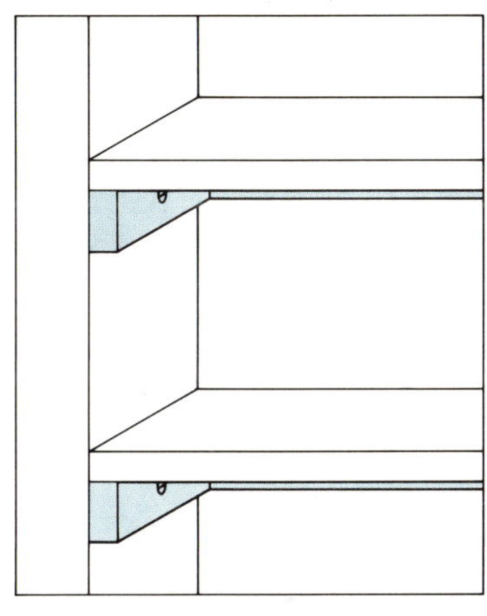

Battened shelving

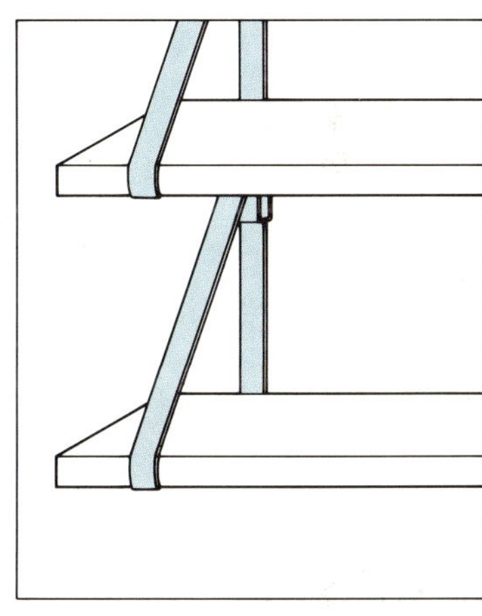

Slung systems

ADJUSTABLE SHELVING

This usually consists of a pair of uprights that are fixed vertically to the wall; brackets slot into the uprights and support the shelves which are laid on top. The more expensive types have continuous channels in the uprights which means that the brackets can be fixed anywhere. Slotted channels are more common and with these brackets are pushed into holes which are spaced at roughly 1 in (2.5 cm) intervals in the uprights. One of the great advantages of adjustable shelving is that the weight on the shelves is distributed down the whole length of the uprights; another is that any number of shelves, within reason, can be added.

Most adjustable systems are made out of aluminium and there is a good choice of colours including gold, red, silver and white. The uprights are sold in pairs in various lengths. Matching brackets are also sold in pairs and come in a number of widths so you shouldn't have any trouble finding a system to suit your needs exactly. In most instances you have to buy the actual wood for the shelves separately. If you are not sure what to get ask the shop where you buy the brackets to advise you (see also Shelving materials).

FIXED SHELVING

This is normally supported on L-brackets of which there are any number of designs, from scrolled metal to bent angle-iron. The brackets are screwed to the wall and the shelves are screwed to the brackets. Recently, however, manufacturers have been patenting designs to rival the L-bracket. One of these is similar to the 'knockdown' fittings that hold many kitchen units together and has the advantage of being less conspicuous when in place. If you decide on a fixed system, you will again have to buy the shelving material separately.

BATTENED SHELVING

This is usually tailor-made to fit an alcove and is supported on lengths of narrow-section timber which are screwed to the walls so that you end up with a truly 'fitted' system. Battened shelving can be made strong enough to cope with most things that you are likely to put on it and is straightforward to make yourself if you are prepared to cut all the components, including the 2 in by 1 in (5 cm × 2.5 cm) battens.

SLUNG SYSTEMS

These are comparatively new to the market. Although they are not particularly strong, they have a high-tech look which may be exactly what you are after. Two polyester slings are anchored to the wall and a shelf is slipped between them. The slings, which are available in many different colours, are adjustable so that you can alter the height of the shelf if you need to.

PLANNING AND CHOOSING SHELVES

PLANNING

Sagging is a potential problem with all shelving but there are two ways of preventing this from happening.

First make sure that the brackets you buy are big enough for the shelves themselves. All too often wide boards are placed on small brackets which just can't take the strain.

Second, if the span of a shelf is too great in relation to its thickness, it will sag in the middle. If you decide to support a shelf from the back using either brackets or an adjustable system, the supports must be sensibly spaced. For example, a 1 in (2.5 cm) thick timber shelf should be supported about every 3ft (90 cm); a similarly sized chipboard (particleboard) shelf will need support at least every 2ft 6in (75 cm), especially if bearing a heavy load, such as books. There are no hard and fast rules and manufacturers often give helpful advice on their packs. Use your common sense.

Another mistake people make is to buy too thin a shelf and this can also result in sagging. For heavy objects – perhaps books, which are often the most dense load put on a domestic shelf – you will need a minimum thickness of 1 in (2.5 cm).

This study has practical adjustable shelving, with sturdy, regularly spaced supports to take the books' weight – vital for safety and durability.

Natural wood

Sturdy glass

Plywood and blockboard

Laminated chipboard

SHELVING MATERIALS

Natural timber

This is the first option for many people, especially where you are going to support the shelves on battens or brackets. Suitable timber includes pine, Parana pine (which has few knots in it) and all kinds of (more expensive) hardwoods such as teak and mahogany. Although you can construct slatted shelves from timber battens, it is usually best to use planks which are available ready planed in a number of widths, lengths and thicknesses according to the type of wood. Pine is one of the most commonly used.

If you do decide on natural timber, seal it with a coat or two of varnish or lacquer to protect it and for ease of cleaning.

Laminated chipboard (particleboard)

This is extremely practical in that it can be wiped clean easily but on the other hand it is not as strong or as durable as natural timber. Laminated chipboard suits adjustable shelving systems and is available in a selection of widths and thicknesses. If you have to saw the chipboard to size, the exposed edges can be covered with strips of iron-on edging.

Plywood and blockboard

These are fairly strong and durable but they do have the drawback of ugly exposed edges. You can, however, cover these with strips of hardwood (such as ramin) or with matching iron-on (press-on) veneer.

Glass

This is a good choice for bathroom shelving provided it is at least ⅜ in (6 mm) thick. Have the glass cut to size by a glazier and ask for the edges to be ground smooth. Special clips will be needed to hold the glass to the support brackets – you can't just screw it on!

PUTTING UP SHELVES

There are two types of wall commonly found in houses, whether old or new, and it makes sense to know the difference between them so that you can use the right fixing for shelves or any other items so that the fixing won't fall out.

MASONRY WALLS

These are constructed from bricks or building blocks and are consequently very solid. The outside walls of most houses (timber-framed houses being the most obvious exception) are usually solid but block walls are often found as interior walls as well. Masonry walls are invariably rendered or plastered and the easiest way of detecting one is to tap it with the handle of a screwdriver: if it sounds solid then it probably is, but tap in several places just to make sure.

Ordinary screws (wood screws) by themselves won't hold in a masonry wall; the threads have nothing to grip on to and they fall out. However, if they are used in conjunction with wallplugs (anchors), they will stay firm. Wallplugs can be made out of either fibre or plastic but all depend on the friction of the wallplug against the masonry holding the screw in place.

There are many different types of wallplug – some are sold as strips which you cut to suit the length of screw you are using; others are individual plugs which are designed to fit a specific size of screw. Whichever type you decide to use, make sure that it is suitable for the screws you have. Screws vary not only in length but in diameter as well – the diameter is indicated by a number; for example, no. 8 screws are smaller than no. 10 screws. Most wallplug packs indicate what size screws fit them.

Whenever you wish to put up shelves or other fittings and have determined that you are working on a masonry wall, carefully follow the procedure outlined below.

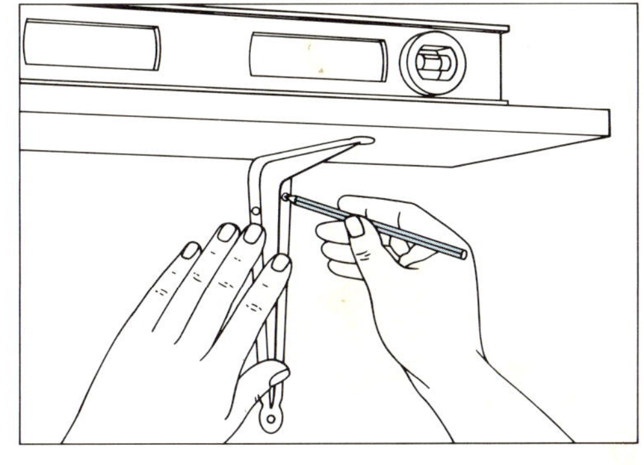

A

1 On the wall mark the position for the screws which will hold the shelf brackets in place (**A**). Check everything with a spirit level before you start drilling into the wall.

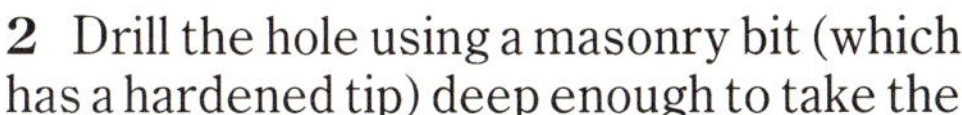

2 Drill the hole using a masonry bit (which has a hardened tip) deep enough to take the wallplug (**B**). Don't forget that the plug (anchor) must go right into the masonry and not just in the plaster and make sure that the bit matches the size of the wallplug.

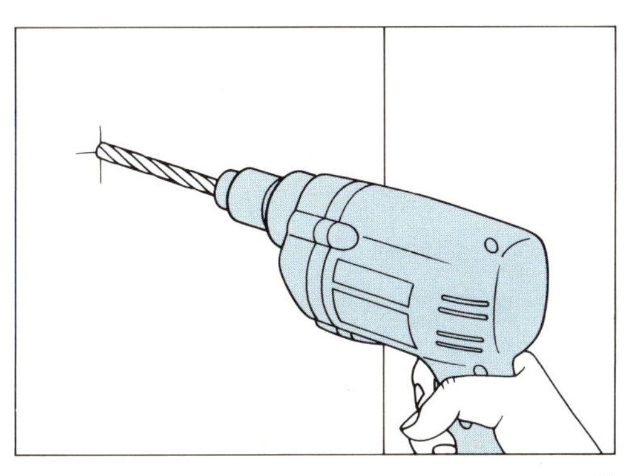

B

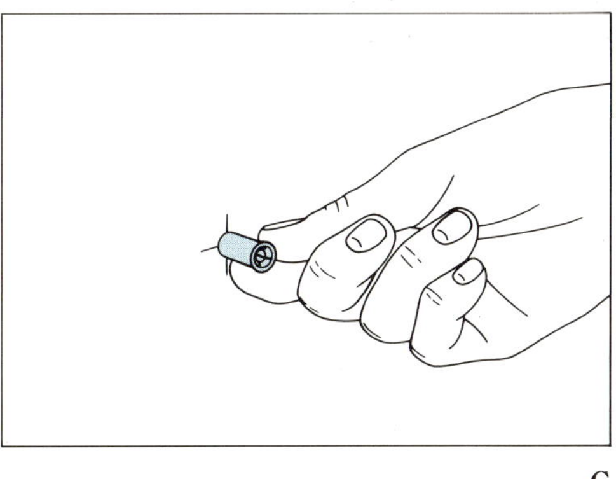

C

3 Insert the wallplug (anchor) so that it is flush with the face of the wall (**C**).

4 Add the screw to hold up whatever it is you are fixing. The important thing to watch out for here is that the screw tip engages the centre of the wallplug (**D**).

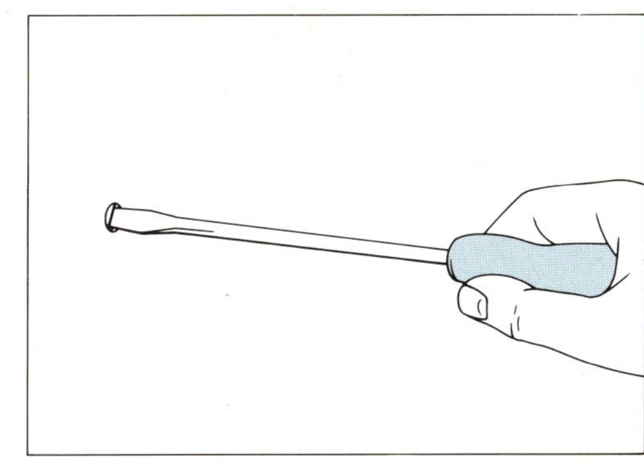

D

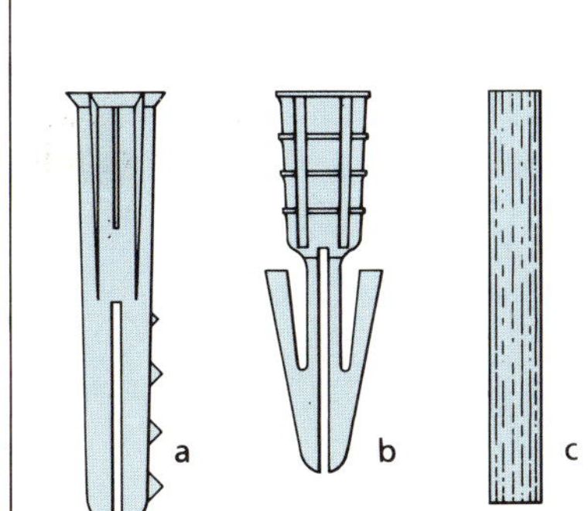

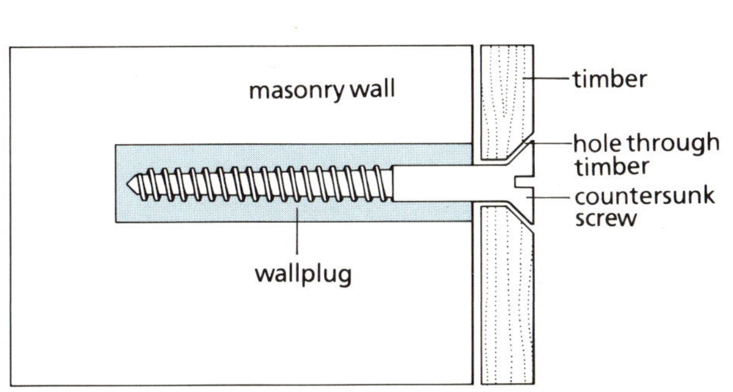

Wallplugs (anchors)

Wallplugs should be chosen to suit the type of wall you are working on. Plastic wallplugs are suitable for brick, concrete and masonry walls. Different types are available for solid walls (**a**) and for cavity walls (**b**). Fibre wallplugs (**c**) are suitable for use when fixing into brick, concrete and masonry walls also.

STUD WALLS

These are also called cavity, plasterboard or partition walls and are usually found only inside a house. They are made by nailing sheets of plasterboard to vertical (stud) timbers which stretch from the floor to the ceiling (with the occasional cross-timber). The plasterboard is 'skimmed' with plaster which is then papered or painted.

There are two ways of fixing into a stud wall and one method is decidedly better than the other. If at all possible it is best to screw directly into the studs themselves. This dispenses with the need for any wallplugs (anchors) and you can use ordinary wood screws provided they are long enough to penetrate the wood. All you have to do is:

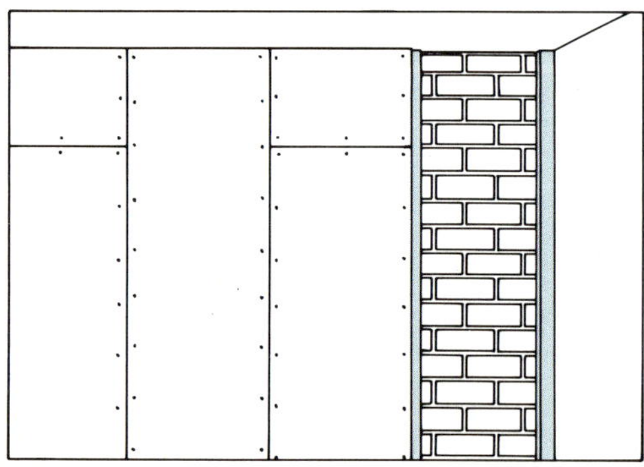

Plasterboard panels are affixed to vertical wooden struts called studs, leaving a cavity behind.

1 Locate the studs by tapping along the wall with something hard such as a screwdriver. When you hear a more solid thump, you know you have found a stud and you can confirm this by poking through the plasterboard with the point of a bradawl.

2 Drill a pilot hole (a hole smaller than the screw) into the stud and then insert the screw itself.

The second method of fixing to a stud wall involves using any one of a range of special plasterboard fixings. These usually combine a screw with an attached plug (anchor). A hole is drilled in the plasterboard, the screw and plug are inserted (**A**), and the screw tightened up. As the screw is tightened the plug grips the reverse side of the plasterboard (**B**). These fixings are adequate for lightweight objects but are not normally suitable for anything heavy.

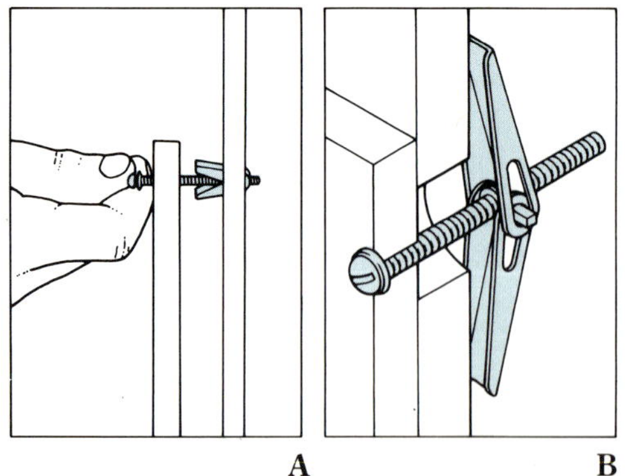

A B

FIXING ADJUSTABLE SHELVING

You will need:
Shelves, supports and brackets
Pencil and tape measure
Spirit level
Screwdriver
Try square
Panel (hand) saw
Electric drill and bits
2 in (50 mm) wood screws
Wallplugs (anchors) (for masonry walls)

STARTING WORK

1 Determine first which kind of wall you are dealing with. If your wall is the stud type, locate the studs and lightly pencil in their positions. Decide where you want to position the supports, bearing in mind the span of the shelves. If you are fixing to a stud wall, their position will be dictated to a certain extent by where the studs fall. Hold the first support in place and fix it, lightly at first, by its top screw only (**A**). This is so that you can check its position carefully.

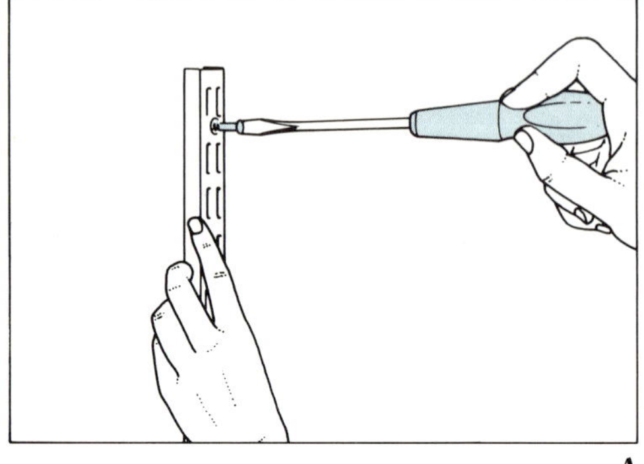

A

2 Let the support hang free and check that it is vertical with a spirit level. When you are satisfied, fix the other screws in place. If you discover that the wall you are working on is uneven, pack out behind the support with slivers of cardboard (**B**).

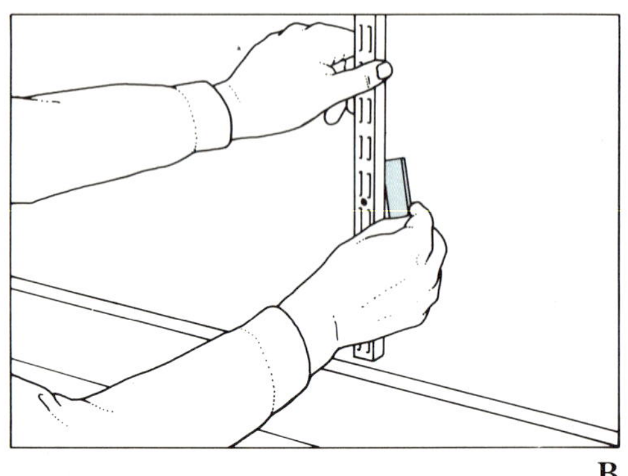

B

3 The second support must be both vertical and level with the first. Check that it is aligned by using a spirit level (**C**), mark its position and fix it to the wall as you did the first. Fix further supports, if necessary, in the same way.

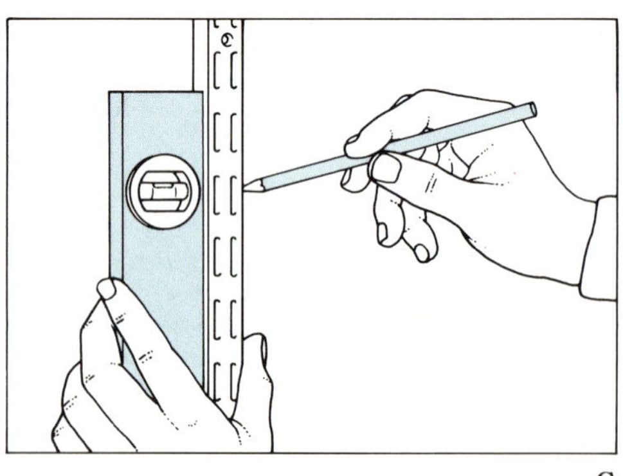

C

4 Tighten up all the screws and add the brackets. If you have to cut shelves to size, mark a cutting line first against a try square and then use a panel (hand) saw.

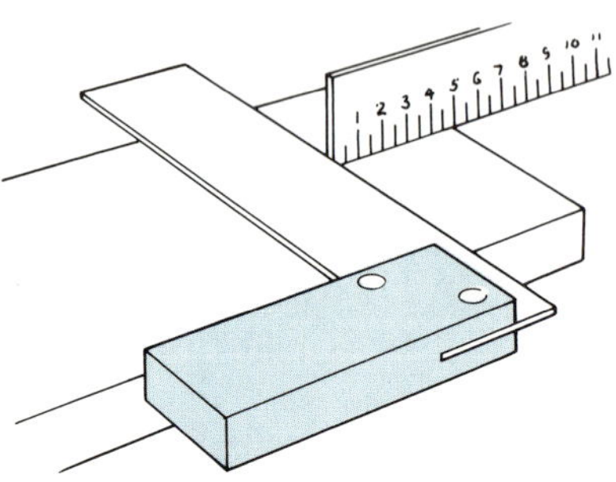

FIXING BRACKETS

You will need:
Shelves and brackets
Spirit level
Screwdriver
Electric drill and bits
Tape measure
Panel (hand) saw
2 in (50 mm) wood screws and wallplugs (anchors) (for masonry walls)

STARTING WORK

1 After finding out what sort of wall you are dealing with (see pages 119-20) pencil in where the brackets are to go, checking they are equally spaced, level and truly vertical.

2 Drill the fixing holes and attach the brackets to the wall (**A**).

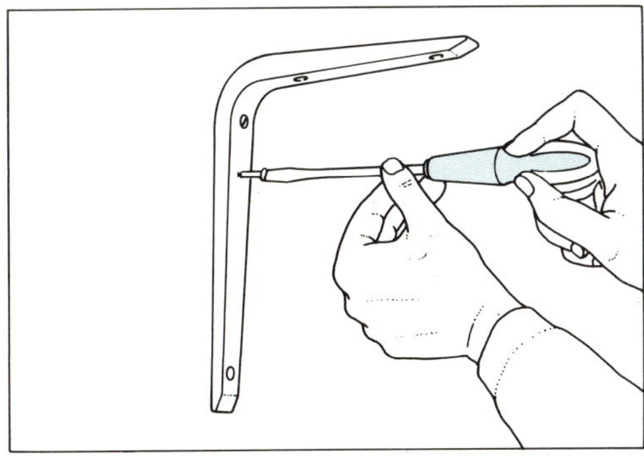

A

3 Add the shelves, fixing them with screws from underneath to provide extra security (**B**). This is particularly important if the shelves are to hold heavy objects.

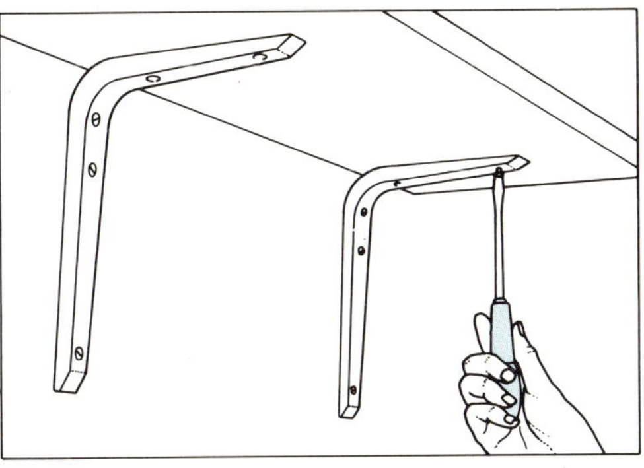

B

FIXING SUPPORT BATTENS

You will need:
Shelves
Tenon saw
Spirit level
Try square
Electric drill and bits
Countersink bit
Tape measure
2 × 1 in (5 × 2.5 cm) support battens
2 in (50 mm) countersunk wood screws
Wood stopping

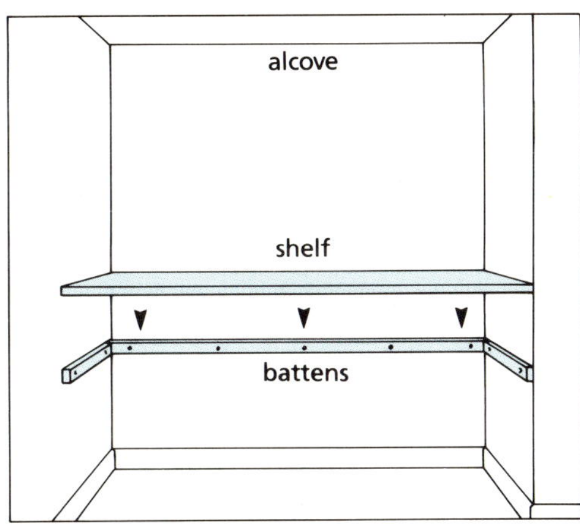

Cut the battens to size to support the shelf.

STARTING WORK

1 If you are supporting the shelves on three battens (one at the back and one at each side) cut the back batten to fit the alcove, using the tenon saw. Hold this in place and saw the side battens to size. If using two battens, cut to right depth.

2 If you are fixing into a masonry wall, drill clearance holes through the battens, spacing them at 12 in (30 cm) intervals. If you are fixing to a stud wall, find the positions of the studs and transfer them to the battens. Drill clearance holes at intervals (**A**).
Note: A clearance hole is one which allows the thread of a screw to pass through unimpeded; in other words it should match the diameter of the screw itself. Countersinking allows the head of a countersunk screw to lie below the surface of the wood.

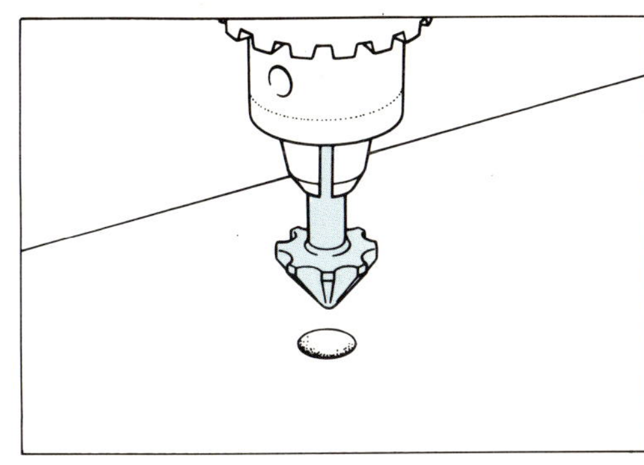

A

3 Hold the battens up to the wall, check that they are level, and mark the wall through the clearance holes. Drill the wall to take the screws.

4 Screw the battens to the wall and then position the shelf on top; trim to fit. If you want to screw the shelf on, drill countersunk clearance holes through the shelf, and pilot holes into the battens. Cover exposed screwheads with wood stopping.

FIXING SLING SHELVING

You will need:
Shelves and slings
Screwdriver
Spirit level
Electric drill and bits
2 in (50 mm) wood screws and wallplugs (anchors) (if appropriate)

STARTING WORK

1 Mark the position of the first sling and screw it in place through its fixing toggle.

2 Before adding the second sling, check that they are both level.

3 Slide in the shelf and adjust its height to suit your requirements.

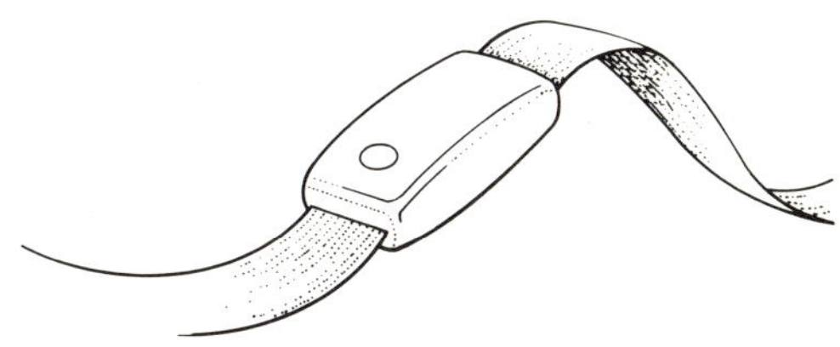

A fixing toggle for slung systems.

DOOR ALTERATIONS

Doors that stick on carpets can be impossibly frustrating and they don't do the carpet much good either. If you are putting down a new, thicker floor covering, it is well worthwhile removing and trimming any door that opens into the room so that it will not ruin the new carpet.

Similarly, if you are rearranging the furniture in a room and discover that a door inconveniently opens the wrong way, the problem is easily rectified by turning it round to open from the opposite side. Instructions are given on pages 123-4 for changing a door from left to right, or right to left, but not so that it opens inwards instead of out (or vice versa).

ADJUSTING THE HEIGHT

The secret behind shortening a door successfully lies in accurately marking up the amount to be removed – take away too little and the door will still stick, too much and draughts whistle underneath.

> **You will need:**
> Stout screwdriver
> Bench plane or planer file
> Home-made wooden wedges
> Panel (hand) saw, if necessary

STARTING WORK

1 Remove the old floor covering and slide an offcut (scrap) of the new floor covering and its underlay against the bottom edge of the door. Mark off the thickness of the two layers on the door (**A**) and repeat the process on the reverse side.

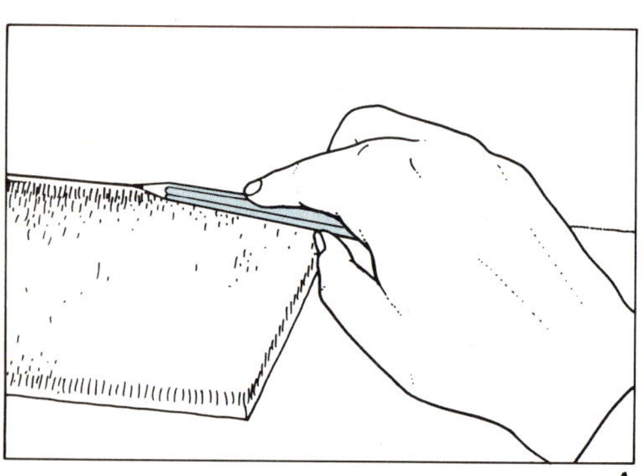

A

2 The next stage is to remove the door, a job which is made much easier if you push home-made wedges under the edge of the door to take the weight off the hinges. Loosen all the screws holding the door to the frame (**B**) but don't remove them all yet – leave one screw in each hinge for the time being. Hinge screws are invariably covered with paint and can be difficult to remove: try placing the tip of your screwdriver in the slot of a stuck screw and tapping the end with a hammer – the shock is often enough to chip the paint and loosen the screw threads. Alternatively, a dab of paint stripper will usually soften the paint sufficiently for you to remove the screw.

With the door wedged from underneath, remove the screws in each hinge, starting from the bottom and working up (**C**). When you have removed all the screws, knock away the wedges and the door will come away. Don't forget that doors can be extremely heavy, so have someone standing by to help. It is also helpful to have someone take the strain off the hinges while you unscrew (and later rescrew) them.

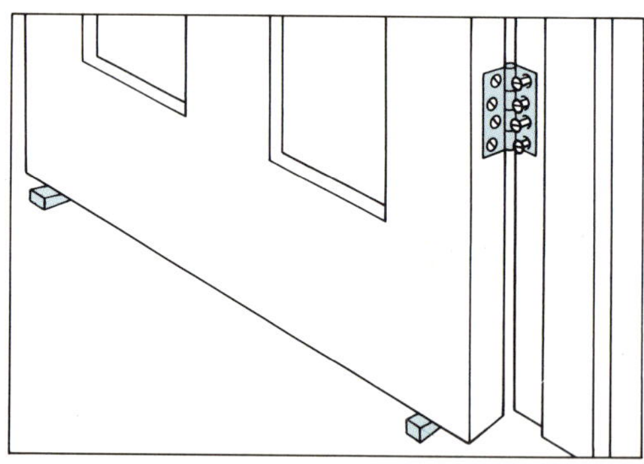

B

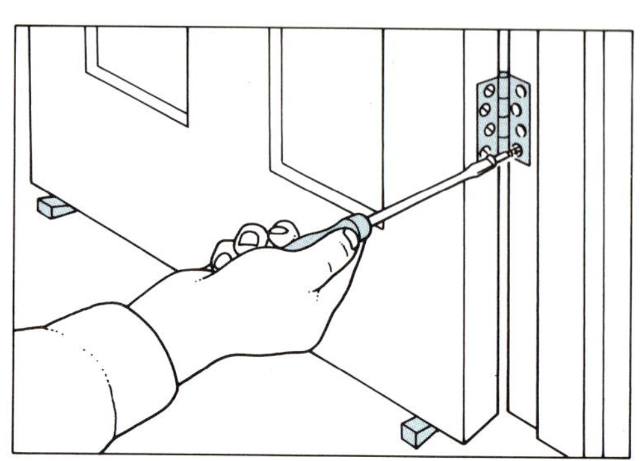

C

3 If you have only a little to remove from the bottom of the door, use a plane or planer file to remove the waste (**D**). The trick is to plane in from each end; never plane from the middle outwards for the timber will split at the corner. Most people find it easiest to plane a door down with it clasped between their knees. Keep removing waste until you reach your pencil lines.

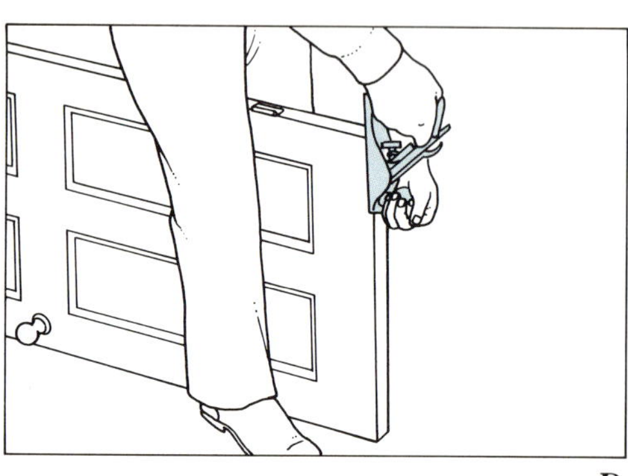

D

4 If you have ½ in (1 cm) or more to remove from the door, it is easier and quicker to cut it off with a panel saw. Make sure the door is well supported and then cut down, keeping the saw just to the outside of the cutting line (**E**) scored with a trimming knife. When you are about half-way through, turn the door over and start from the other end; if you saw right through, the wood will probably split at the end. Tidy up the saw cut with a plane or planer file.

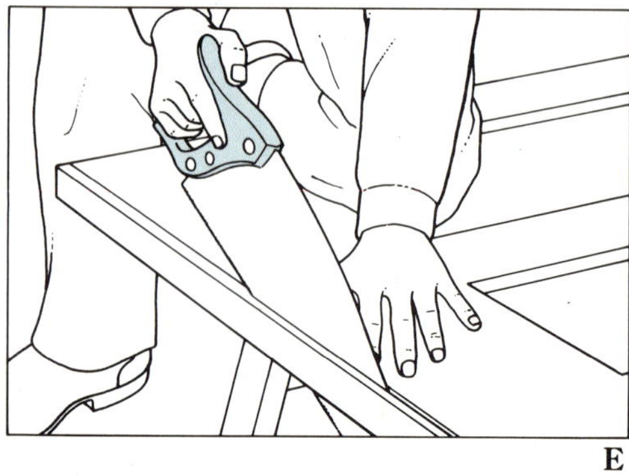

E

5 When you rehang the door, fix a screw in the top hinge first – in other words, reverse the process you followed when removing it.

CHANGING SIDES

The easiest way to change the opening direction of a door is to turn it around so that the two faces change places. You don't have to make any major alterations to the frame but you will have to resite the locks and hinges. The door will still open the same way into, or out of, the room but on a different side of the doorway (**A** and **B**).

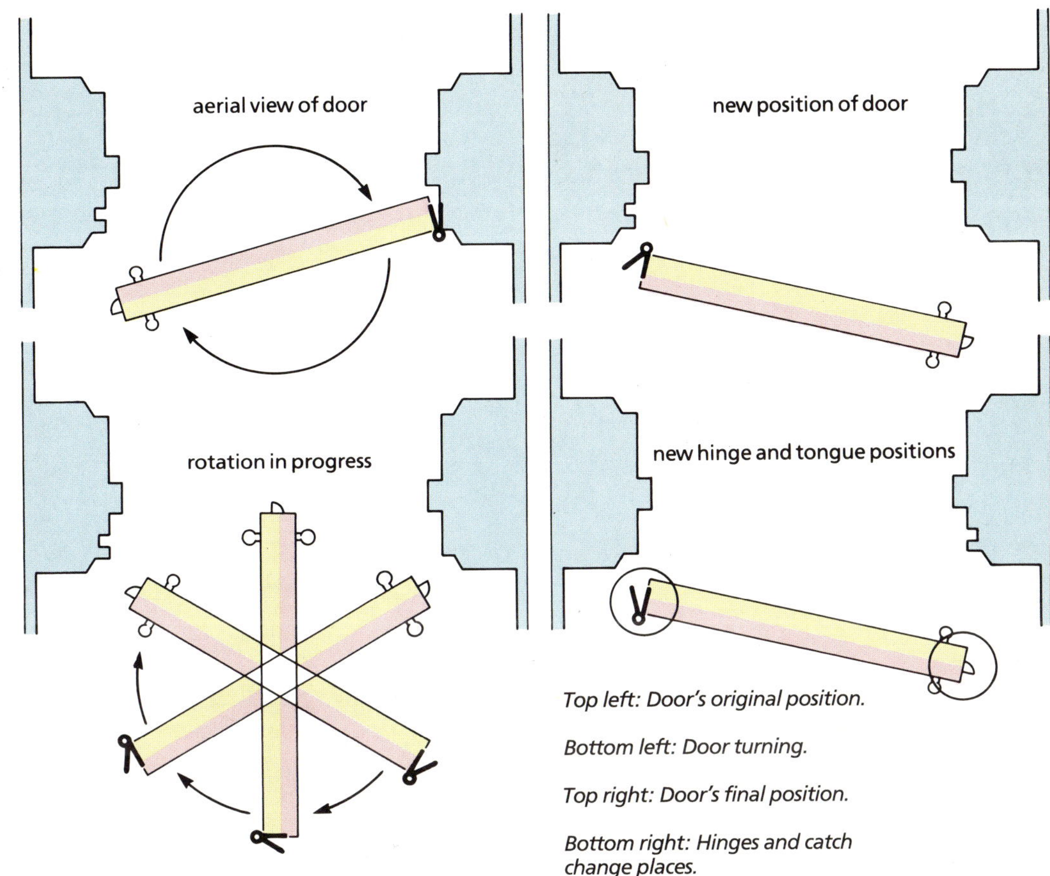

Top left: Door's original position.

Bottom left: Door turning.

Top right: Door's final position.

Bottom right: Hinges and catch change places.

You will need:
- Screwdrivers
- Filling knife
- Tape measure
- Sharp pencil
- 1 in (2.5 cm) and 1/4 in (6 mm) bevel-edged chisels
- Planer file
- Electric drill and bits
- Home-made wedges
- Wooden mallet
- 1 in (2.5 cm) paintbrush
- Try square
- Epoxy wood filler

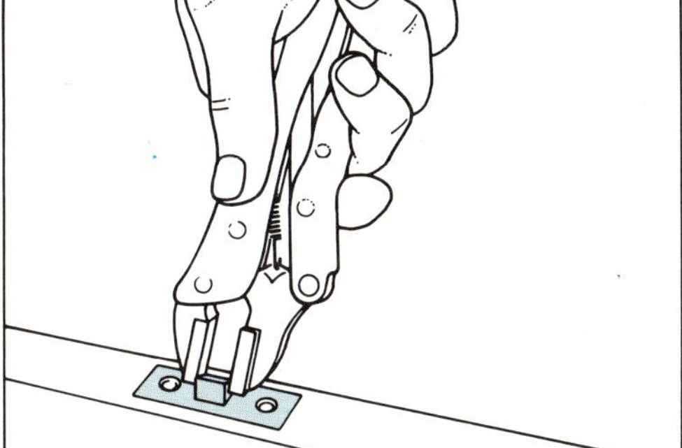

STARTING WORK

1 Prop the door up on wedges and remove the door and hinges from the frame (see above, page 122).

2 Unscrew the door handles and release the lock and catch which may be held in place with screws (**A**).

3 Hold the door up in its new position and try it for size. If it isn't square to the frame, plane down the edges to fit (see page 122).

4 Unscrew the striking plate from the door frame (**B**) and patch up the holes. The easiest way to do this is to use a two-part epoxy wood filler. Mix this up in the proportions recommended by the manufacturer and spread it over the holes. Leave the filler slightly proud of the holes and allow it to set. When the filler is hard, use a planer file to shape it flush with the surrounding wood. Sand down any marks on the filler before touching it up with paint.

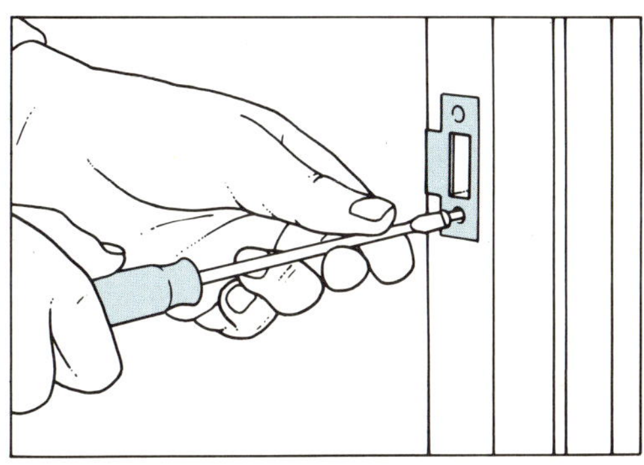

5 The hinges will have to face the opposite direction now that the door is in its new position so remove them from the door (**C**) and chisel away the back of the old hinge recesses, working inwards so that the wood doesn't split (**D**). This make the new area in which the hinges will fit.

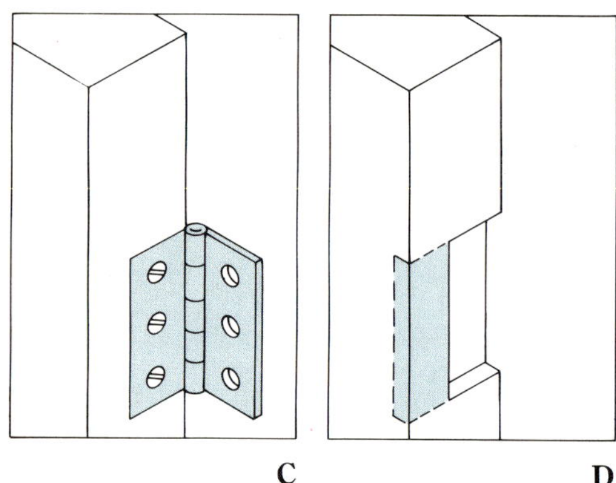

C **D**

6 Wedge the door in the opening and mark the hinge positions on door and frame (**E**). Chisel out the hinge recesses (**F**): pencil in the area and depth of the hinge. Using a sharp chisel, make a series of cuts along the pencilled outline of the recess. Follow this with another series of shallow cuts, *across* the grain of the wood, inside the marked area (**G**). The cuts must not go beneath the depth of the hinge. Pare out the waste timber, holding the chisel level with the edge of the frame or door (**H**). Test fit the hinge (**I**).

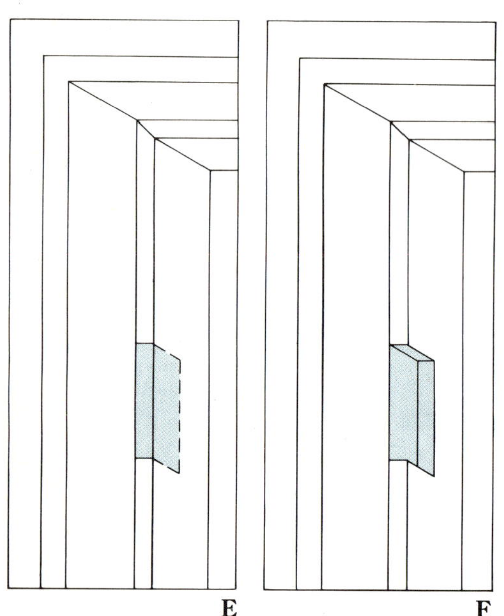

E **F**

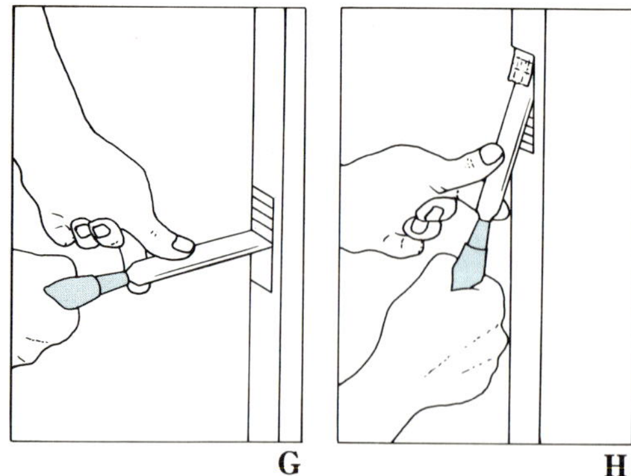

G **H**

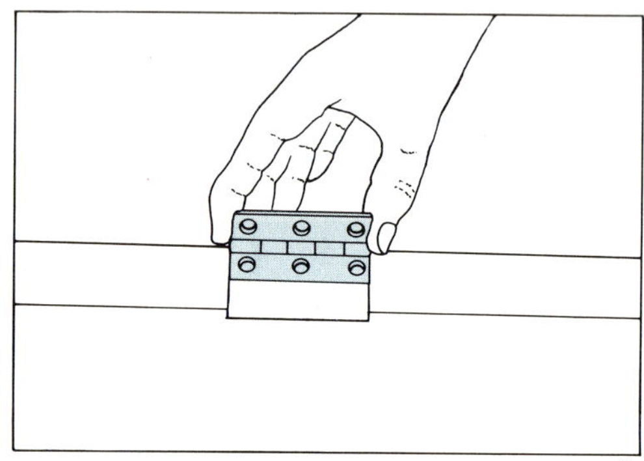

I

7 Screw the hinges on to the door (**J**) and fill behind them with epoxy filler. Again, fill slightly proud of the holes, allow the filler to set hard, then use a planer file to shape it flush with the surrounding wood. Hang the door in the frame, fixing a screw in the top of the top hinge first and working down.

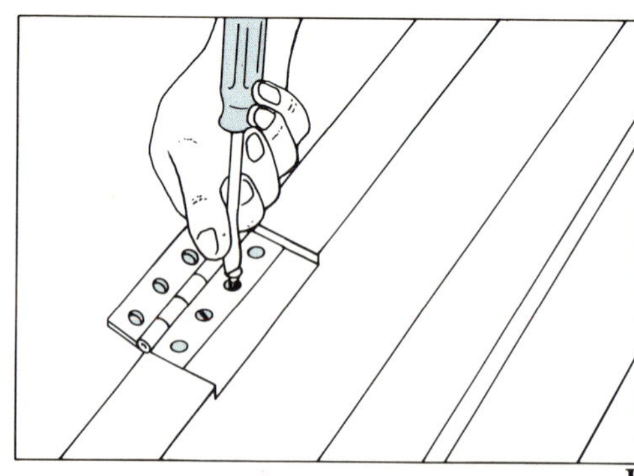

J

8 Refit the lock and insert the catch so that it faces the other way (**K**). If you can't remove the catch from the lock because the mechanism is old and stiff, you may have to buy and fit a new lock. The fixing method depends on the type of lock you fit, so follow the instructions that come with it.

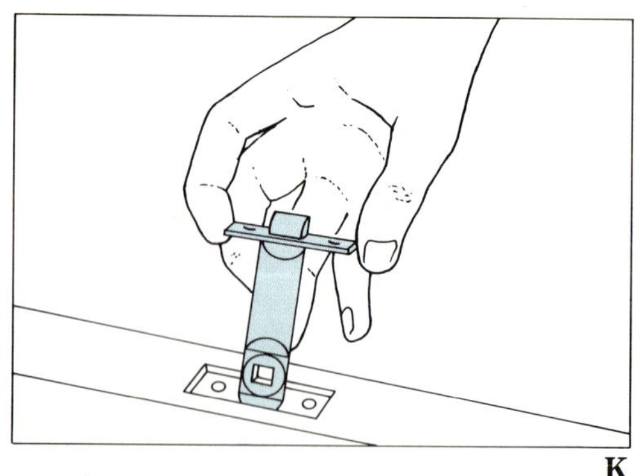

K

9 Close the door and turn the handle – the catch should make a mark on the side of the frame and this is where the striking plate must be fitted. It is important to mark the position accurately.

10 Hold the striking plate in position and mark carefully and accurately around it (**L**). Chisel out the wood inside your marks and screw the plate securely to the frame. Use a narrow chisel to gouge out a hole for the catch to fit into (**M**).

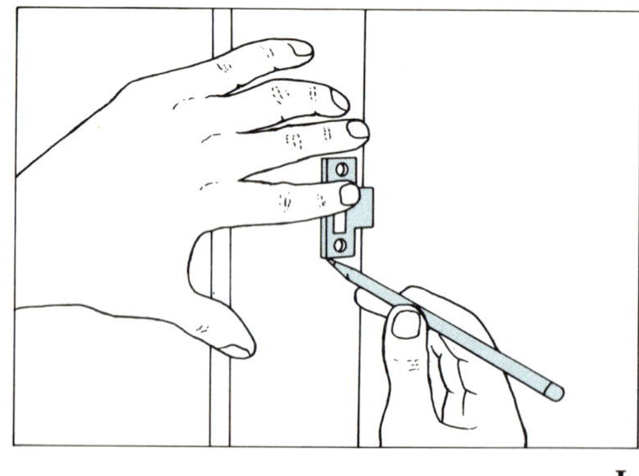

L

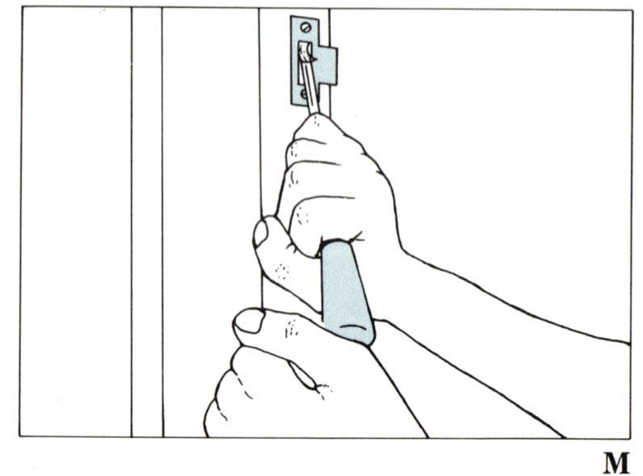

M

11 Test the door and make good any holes with epoxy filler before repainting.

Index

Page numbers shown in *italic* type indicate illustrations

A

accent lighting 26-7
  living room 36
accessories
  colour contrasts 15, 16, 17
  kitchen 38
  pattern 21
  texture 19
adhesive
  carpet 105
  coving 88
  sheet flooring 98
  tiles 82
  wallpaper 76
aerosol paint 64
alcoves
  accentuating 34
  carpeting into 108
  cupboards 48
  dining area 10
  lighting 27
  mirrored 12
  shelving 35, 117
alkyds 63
aluminium sealer 54
Anaglypta 18, 72
anchors *see* wallplugs
atmosphere with colour 15-16
attic conversion 10
Austrian blind 116
Axminster carpet 104

B

background lighting 26
  living room 36
bag graining 69, *70*, 71
baseboard *see* skirting
bathroom 43-5, *70*, *82*, *86*
  colours 15, 16, 43-4
  dado 28
  flooring 45, 96, *101*
  furniture 44-5
  laying flooring 98, 102
  lighting 24, 45
  paint 58
  plants 15, *28*
  shelving 118
  storage 12
  wallpaper 72
  window treatments 114, 115
bed 47
  child's 49
  curtained 47
  guest room 52
  sofa bed 47, *52*
  storage under 12
bedroom *17*, 46-8
  flooring 48
  furniture 47-8
  lighting 48
  mirrors 12
  multi-purpose 10
  storage 12, 48
  see also bed
beige colours 16, 17
black colour 14
bleach, wood 64
blinds (shades) 113
  Austrian 116
  bathroom 45, 115
  child's room 49
  roller 12, 39, 46, 115
  Roman 29, 116
blockboard shelving 118
blown vinyl 72-3
blowtorch 62
blue colours 14, 15, 16
body carpet (runner) 104
bonded carpet 104
borders 21, 28, 72, 90-1
  hall & stairs 30
  painted 91
  quantities 91
  sponged 91
  stencilled 91
  wallpaper 91
broadloom carpet 104
brushes
  cleaning 66
  paint 58
  paperhanging 75
  stippling 60

C

cane 12, 45
  painting 64
carpet 103-8
  Axminster 104
  bathroom 45
  bedroom 48
  child's room 50
  colour 12, 16, 35, 103
  construction 104
  fibres 104
  foam-backed 105, 108
  hall, stairs & landing 31-2
  living room 35-6
  patterned 21, 103
  pile 104
  sizes 104
  texture 18
  tiles 104
  underlay 105
  wear 103
  Wilton 104
  see also carpet-laying
carpet bolster 105
carpet-laying 105-8
  equipment 105, 106, 108
  foam-backed 108
  hessian-backed 106-7
  joins 107
  quantities 106
carpet stretcher 105
carpet tape 105, 107
casement window, painting 68
caulking 85
cavity wall 120
ceiling
  canopy 28
  coving 28, 34, 72, 88-9
  exposing joists 28
  fabric tent 28
  height effects 12, *15*, 16, 28, 58
  lights 24
  mouldings 28
  night-sky effect 51
  papering 72, 86-7
  polystyrene tiles 88
  preparation 54-7
  textured paint 58
cellar 10
ceramic tiles
  fixing 83-5
  floor 99
  wall 18, *82*, 83
character, adding 28-9
children
  beds 49
  furniture 22
  lead-free paint 64
  rooms for 49-50, 72, 90
  safety 32
  windows 68
chipboard (particleboard),
  laminated 118
cleaning
  equipment 66
  paint from glass 68
  see also maintenance; preparation
colour 14-17
  colour wheel 16
  creating space with 12
  monochromatic 16, 17, 18
  neutrals 16, 17, 103
  room dimensions 16
  schemes 16-17
concrete floor
  carpeting 106, 108
  laying hardwood floor on 109
  levelling 92-3
  painting 92
  preparation 92
condensation 56, 58, 73, 92
cool colours 15
coordinated ranges 17, *20*, 21, 72
cork tiles 83, 93, 99
  floor 44, 50
  insulation 109
  laying 99-102
  sealing 99
  timber-faced 109
  wall 18
cornice lights 26
country style 35
coving (cove moulding) 28, 72
  accentuating 34
  fitting 88-9
  quantities 88
curtains (drapery) 113-14
  living room 36
  patterned 20
  pelmet lighting 26
  poles 114, *115*
  quilted 20
  small window 29
  tracks & rods 114
'cutting in' 59

D

dado *15*, *18*, 28
  borders as 90
  hall & stairs 28, 30
damp 56
  floors 92

desk
improvised 52
lamps 26
dimmer switch 26, 36, 50
dining area 10
colours 15
furniture 35
hall 10, 31
kitchen *42*
lighting 25, 36, 41
display shelving 28-9
lighting 27
window 32
see also shelving
distemper, removing 57
doors
adjusting height 110, 122
carpeting round 108
changing sides 10, 123
glass panels 12, 29
laying floor tiles round 102
laying sheet flooring round 97-8
mirrored 12, 30, 48
murals 29
painting 67
papering round 79
storage 12
double glazing 48
downlighters 26
dragging (paint) 71
drapery *see* curtains
drawers, kitchen 39

E

electrical outlets
ceiling rose 87
papering round 79, 87
preparation for decorating 57
tiling round 85
embossed wallpaper 18, 72
hanging 72
pasting 72
emulsion (latex) paint 58
painting over 54
preparation 54–7
quantities 59
solid 58, 59, 60
using 59-60
vinyl silk 58, 59
equipment
adjusting doors 122, 123
carpet-laying 105, 106, 108
cleaning 66
decorative paint finishes 70-1
emulsion paint 59
fitting coving 88, 89
gloss paint 66, 67, 68
hardwood floor 110, 112
ladders 57
laying sheet vinyl 97
painting 58
pasting 75
sanding floors 94
shelving 120, 121
textured paint 61
tiling floors 100
tiling walls 83
wallpapering 75, 87
ethnic style 35

F

fabrics
covering ceiling 28
patterns 20
wall coverings 18-19, 29, 73
see also blinds; curtains
felt underlay 105
filler
plaster 56
wood 62, 123
flock wallpaper 73
floodlights 26, 36
floor
damp 92
laying hardwood floor 109-12
loft 10
painting 93, 94
parquet 109
preparation 92-3
sanding 93, 94
see also concrete floor; floorboards; hardwood floor
floor coverings
bathroom 45
bedroom 48
child's room 50
colour 16
hall, stairs & landing 31-2
kitchen 38, 42
living room 35-6
pattern 21
preparation for 92-3
textures 18
see also carpet; rugs; sheet flooring; tiles
floor lamps 26
floor paint 93, 94
floor tiles 93, 99-102
ceramic 99
cork 93, 99
equipment 100
laying 99-102
marble 99
quantities 100
quarry 93, 99
rubber 99
slate 99
vinyl 93, 99
floorboards 36, 46, 105
colouring 95
making good 92
preparation 92
sanding 93, 94
sealing 94
varnishing 95
fluorescent lighting 14, 26, 27
foam-backed carpet 105
laying 108
french windows 68
fungicidal grout 82
paint 56
paste 72, 73, 76, 77
furniture
arranging 22, 33
balancing 23
bathroom 44-5
bedroom 47-8
child's room 49
choosing 12, 22
guest room 52
hall & landing 30-1
kitchen 38-9
living room 35
painted 21, 23, 46, 69
space-saving 22-3
stripping 62
futon 35, 46

G

glass
door panels 12
painting on 29
removing paint 68
shelving 118
tables 12
gloss paint 63
doors 67
equipment 66, 67, 68
non-drip 63, 65
painting over 54
quantities 65
skirtings & radiators 66
using 65-8
windows 68
green colours 15
grey colours 16, 17
grippers 105
grout 82, 85
grouting paint 82
guest room 52

H

hall 30-2
colours 15, 16, 30
dado 28, 30
flooring 31-2
furniture 30
lighting 32
multi-purpose 10, 31
wallpaper 72
hanging wallpaper *see* wall-papering
hardboard
covering floors 92, 105
hardwood floor 36, 109
equipment 110, 112
finishing 112
laying 110-12
mosaic panels 109, 110
preparation 110
quantities 110
sealing 109, 110, 112
strips 109, 111-12
timber-faced cork tiles 109
wood types 109, 112
high-tech style 35
hot air stripper

I

insulation
cork tiles 109
curtains 114
lining paper 74
sound 28, 51, 105
underlay 105
vinyl papers 73

K

kitchen 37-42
colours 15
flooring 96, *101*
lighting 26, 41
multi-purpose 10
painting 58
planning layout 40
safety 42
units 38-9
ventilation 42
wallpaper 72
window treatments 114, 115
worktops 40
knee kicker 105

L

lacquer 63
ladders 57, 75, 86
stairwell 81
landing 30-2
colours 30
flooring 31-2
furniture 30-1
lighting 32
larder 39
latex paint *see* emulsion

lavatory, understairs 10, 31, 43
lead-free paint 64
levelling compound 92-3
light bulbs 27
lighting 24-7
accent 26-7, 36
background 26, 36, 41
bathroom 45
bedroom 48
ceiling 24
child's room 50
desk 26
dining area 25, 36, 41
downlighters 26
floodlights 26, 36
floor 26
fluorescent 14, 26, 27, 41
general 24-5
hall, stairs & landing 32
kitchen 41
living room 36
pendant 24, 41
task 25-6, 36
uplighters 27, 36
wall 36, 48
lining paper 56, 72, 74
hanging 75
linoleum 96
living room 33-6
arranging furniture 22
flooring 35-6
furniture 35
lighting 36
multipurpose 10
storage 35
styles 34-5
loft conversion 10
loose covers (slipcovers) 20
louvred windows 68

M
maintenance
paintwork 58, 65, 69
sheet flooring 96
tiles 82
wallpaper 72, 73
wood floor 93
making good
floorboards 92
plaster 56
mantelpiece, papering round 80
marble tiles 83, 99
masonry walls 119
metallic papers 44, 57, 73, 79, 87
tiles 83
meters, boxing in 32
minimal style 12, 35, 46
mirrors 12-13, 22, *28*
doors 12, 30, 48
fixing 13
hall 30
lighting 45
tiles 13, 30, 83
mosaic panel floor 109
laying 110
mosaic tiles 83
mould 56
mouldings 28, 34
removing distemper 57
multi-purpose rooms 10
murals 29, 44

N
neutral colours 16, 17, *19*, 103
nicotine stains 54
Novamura 73, 77

O
office 31, 42, 52
orange colours 15

P
pads, painting 59, 66
paint
aerosols 64
emulsion 54, 58, 59
gloss 54, 63, 65-8
lacquer 63
lead-free 64
maintenance 58, 65, 69
quantities 59, 61
stripping 55, 62
textured 18, 55, 58, 60-1
see also painting
paint finishes, decorative 69-70
bag graining 69, *70*, 71
dragging 71
quantities 70
ragging on 38, 46, 69, 71
spattering 51, 71
sponging 38, 46, 69, 70, 91
stencilling 51, 71, 90, 91
stippling 71
paint kettle 81
paint stripper 55
hot air 62
paint tray 58
painting 54-71
brushes 58
concrete floor 93, 94
doors 67
emulsion 58-60
equipment 58-9
gloss 65-8
pads 59
preparation 54-7
radiators 66
rollers 58
skirtings 66
textured paint 58
windows 68
see also paint; paint finishes
paperhanging *see* wallpapering
paperhanging brush 75
parquet floor 109
particleboard *see* chipboard
partition walls 120
pasting wallpaper 72, 75, 76
paste-the-wall coverings 77
patio doors 68
pattern 20-1, 38, 103
pelmet lights 26
pendant lights 24-5
picture rail 16
pictures
displaying 32
lighting 26, 27
pipes, working round 80, 85, 102
plants 23, 26
bathroom 15, *28*, 45
kitchen 42
landing 32
living room 36
plaster
making good 56
new 56
sealing 56
plasterboard walls 120
plumb line 75
plywood shelving 118
preparation
decorative paint finishes 70
floors 92-3, 94
hardwood floor 110
tiling 84
walls & ceilings 54-7
wallpapering 74
woodwork 62
primer
non-toxic 64
on distemper 57
on new plaster 56
on wood 63, 66, 67

Q
quantities
border 91
carpet 106
coving 88
decorative paint finishes 70
emulsion 59
floor tiles 100
gloss 65
hardwood flooring 110
sheet vinyl 97
textured paint 61
wall tiles 83
wallpaper 74
quarry tiles 83, 93, 99
quilting 20

R
radiator
below window 29, 116
painting 66
wallpapering behind 80
ragging on 38, 46, 69, 71
red colours 14, 15
roller blind 12, 39, 46, 115
rollers 58, 59
cleaning 66
emulsion paint 60
patterned sleeves 61
textured paint 61
Roman blind 29, 116
rubber sheet flooring 96
rubber tiles 99-102
rubber underlay 105
rugs 18, 21, 32, 36
runner *see* body carpet

S
safety
decorating stairwell 81
electrical outlets 57, 79, 87
kitchen 42
lead-free paint 64
sanding floorboards 94
stairs 32
samples board 18, 33-4
sander, heavy-duty 94, 112
sanding
floorboards 93, 94
hardwood floor 112
woodwork 62
sash window, painting 68
scaffolding, stairwell 81
scissors, wallpapering 75
screwing into walls 119-20
sculptured vinyl 73
sealer *see* primer
sealing
cork tiles 99
distemper 57
hardwood floor 109, 110, 112
plaster 56
stripped wood 64
seam roller 75
seating arrangements 22, 33, 35
security 32, 68

shades *see* blinds
sheet flooring 96-8
laying 97-8
linoleum 96
rubber 96
vinyl 50, 93, 96, 97-8
shelving 117-21
adjustable 117, 120
battened 117, 121
child's room 49
display 28-9, 32
equipment 120, 121
fixed 117, 121
glass 118
kitchen 39
materials 118
putting up 119-21
sagging 118
slung 117, 121
storage 31, *32*, 35
supports 117
shower area 10, 31
tiling *82*
sitting room *see* living room
sizing 74
skirting (baseboard)
as dado 28
colour 12
painting 65, 66
removing 110
slate tiles 99
slipcovers *see* loose covers
sofa bed 47, *52*
soft modern style 35
space, creating 12-13, *15*, 16, 22-3, *77*, *103*
spare room 52
spattering (paint) 51, 71
sponging 38, 46, 69, 70
border 91
spotlight 26
stain, wood 64
staircase 30-2
carpeting 106
colours 30
dado 28, 30
decorating 81
flooring 31-2
lighting 32
painting 65
stepladders 81
wallpaper 72
steam stripper 55
stencilling 51, 71, 90, 91
stepladders *see* ladders
stippling 60, 71
storage 12
bathroom 12, 44-5
bedroom 12, 48
cellar 10
hall & landing 31, *32*
kitchen 39
living room 33, 35
loft 10
understairs 10
see also shelving
stripping
furniture & doors 62
paintwork 62
textured paint 55
textured paper 72
vinyl wallpaper 55, 56, 72
wallpaper 55, 72
stud wall 120
study 10, 31, 35, 52
sugar soap 54
Supaglypta 72

T

tables 12, 35
task lighting 25-6, 36
teenager's room 51
texture 15, 17, 18-19
textured paint 18, 28, 58, 60-1
patterns 60-1
preparation 54-7
quantity 61
stripping 55
using 61
textured wallpaper 72
cleaning 72
hanging 72
pasting 72
stripping 72
threshold strip
carpet 105, 108
hardwood floor 110, 112
tile cutter 85
tiles 72
carpet 104
ceiling, polystyrene 88
ceramic floor 99
ceramic wall 18, *82*, 83
cork 83, 93, 99-102
drilling into 39
floor 93, 99-102
marble 83, 99
metallic 83
mirror 13, 30, 83
mosiac 83
quarry 83, 93, 99
rubber 99-102
slate 99
vinyl 83, 93, 99-102
worktops 40
see also tiling floors; tiling walls
tiling floors 99-102
equipment 100
quantities 100
see also tiles
tiling walls 82-5
adhesive 82
caulking 85
cutting tiles 85
equipment 83
grout 82
preparation 84
quantities 83
see also tiles
timber-faced cork tiles 109
tool tray 81
traditional style 34
tucking tool 105
tufted carpet 104

U

undercoat (primer) 63, 66, 67
underlay 105
understairs cupboard 10, 31

V

valance lights 26
varnish 64, 95
ventilation 42
vinyl, sheet 50, 96
laying 97-8
quantities 97
removing 93
vinyl silk paint *see* emulsion
vinyl tiles 83, 99, *101*
laying 99-102
removing 93
vinyl wallpaper 72-3
stripping 55, 56, 72

W

wall
knocking down 10
masonry 119
preparation 54-7
revealing brick 28
stud 120
textures 18, 28
wall coverings
cork 18
fabric 18-19, 29, 73
patterns 21
see also tiles; wallpaper
wallpaper 72
Anaglypta 18, 72
borders 21, 28, 30
embossed 18, 72, 86
flock 73
lining paper 56, 72, 74, 75
metallic 44, 57, 73, 79, 87
Novamura 73, 77
painting over 55
patterns 20, 21
quantities 74
ready-pasted 76
stripping 55-6, 72
Supaglypta 72
textured 72, 86
vinyl 55, 56, 72
woodchip 72, 86
see also wallpapering
wallpapering 72, 76, 77-80
ceilings 86-7
corners 79
cutting to length 76
doors 79
electric outlets 79
equipment 75, 87
lining papers 74, 75
mantelpieces 80
pasting 72, 76
pattern matching 73
pipes 80
preparation 74
quantities 74
radiators 80
ready-pasted paper 76
stairwell 81
where to start 77
windows 80
wallplugs (anchors) 119
warm colours 15
wash basin 98, 102
white 14
Wilton carpet 104
windows
adding character 29
children 49, 68
display shelves 32
double glazing 48
painting 68
papering round 80
pivoting 68
shapes 68
see also blinds; curtains
wood
bleaching 64
gloss painting 65-8
paints 63-4
preparation 62
shelving 118
staining 64
varnishing 64
see also hardwood floor
wood floor *see* floorboards; hardwood floor
wood stopping 62, 123
woodworm 62
work station 57
papering ceiling 86
stairwell 81
worktops, kitchen 40

Y

yellow colours 14, 15, 16